GLOBAL ETHICS AND MORAL RESPONSIBILITY

Global Ethics and Moral Responsibility

Hans Jonas and his Critics

Edited by

JOHN-STEWART GORDON
Cologne University, Germany and
Vytautas Magnus University, Kaunas, Lithuania

HOLGER BURCKHART
University of Siegen, Germany

Routledge
Taylor & Francis Group
LONDON AND NEW YORK

First published 2014 by Ashgate Publishing

2 Park Square, Milton Park, Abingdon, Oxfordshire OX14 4RN
52 Vanderbilt Avenue, New York, NY 10017

Routledge is an imprint of the Taylor & Francis Group, an informa business

First issued in paperback 2020

British Library Cataloguing in Publication Data
A catalogue record for this book is available from the British Library

The Library of Congress has cataloged the printed edition as follows:
LoC data has been applied for

ISBN: 978-1-4094-5230-0 (hbk)
ISBN: 978-0-367-60085-3 (pbk)

Contents

List of Tables *vii*
List of Contributors *ix*
Acknowledgements *xiii*

Introduction 1
John-Stewart Gordon, Holger Burckhart and Paula Segler

PART 1: THE PHILOSOPHY OF HANS JONAS

1 Responsibility Today: The Ethics of an Endangered Future 9
Hans Jonas

2 Moral Responsibility for the Preservation of Humankind 23
Walter A. Weisskopf

3 Ethics of Responsibility: Discourse-ethical Perspective of the Justification Problem 41
Holger Burckhart

PART 2: HUMAN NATURE AND THE IMPERATIVE OF RESPONSIBILITY

4 Is Ageing a Gift? Bioconservatism and the Ethics of Gratitude 55
Lawrence Vogel

5 Some Paradoxes Linked to Risk Moderation 73
Nathalie Frogneux

6 Inclusion – A Moral Imperative, but Also Socially Desired? An Essay in the Ethics of Responsibility 93
Holger Burckhart and John-Stewart Gordon

PART 3: ON RELIGION, ETHICS AND NATURAL PHILOSOPHY

7 God in the World of Man: Hans Jonas' Philosophy of Religion 105
Michael Bongardt

PART 4: THE ETHICS OF TECHNOLOGY AND MORAL RESPONSIBILITY

8 What Is Natural about Natural Functioning? Examining an Indirect Argument in Favour of Teleological Naturalism 129
Micha H. Werner

9 Ethics for the Technoscientific Age: On Hans Jonas' Argumentation and His Public Philosophy Beyond Disciplinary Boundaries 147
Jan C. Schmidt

10 Ethics and Responsibility in a Technological Age 171
David J. Levy

11 Refined Marxism and Moral Enhancement 185
John-Stewart Gordon

Bibliography of Hans Jonas' Works *209*
Index *211*

List of Tables

11.1 Jonas' comparison of capitalism and Marxism 192
11.2 Methods of moral and cognitive enhancement 203

List of Contributors

Michael Bongardt studied Catholic Theology in Bonn and Munich from 1978 to 1983. In 1994 he received his doctoral degree after which he prepared his habilitation, completed in 1998. From 1998 to 2000 he lived in Israel and directed an international ecumenical programme for students of theology at Dormition Abbey, Jerusalem. Since December 2000 he has held a professorship at the Freie Universität Berlin, initially teaching Catholic Theology and, since January 2006, Comparative Ethics. He has held various positions in academic administration (Dean of Studies and Dean at the Department for History and Cultural Studies (2003–2007), and, since 2010, Vice President). His special interest lies in the periphery of philosophy, theology and social science, while the focal points of his philosophical studies are the works of Søren Kierkegaard, Ernst Cassirer, Hans Jonas and Jürgen Habermas. The concept of freedom, interreligious and intercultural issues, and the ethical foundations of pluralist, secularized societies lie at the heart of his research.

Holger Burckhart received his doctoral degree at the University of Cologne in 1985. He finished his habilitation in 1997 with his work on *Diskursethik – Diskursanthropologie – Diskurspädagogik*. Since October 2009 he has been rector of the University of Siegen. Since 2007 he has been a board member, and since May 2008 chairman, of the accreditation agency AQAS. His special interest of research in practical philosophy lies in general philosophy of science, transcendental philosophy, philosophy of language and the philosophical basis of educational theory concerning special educational issues. Holger Burckhart is a board member of the Hans Jonas-Zentrum in Berlin and co-editor of the *Kritische Hans Jonas Werkausgabe.* As a guest lecturer, he has visited the University of Bergen in Norway, as well as various Japanese (Tokyo, Sapporo, Osaka) and Chinese (Beijing, Jinan, Shanghai, Hong Kong) universities.

Nathalie Frogneux received her Ph.D. on Jonas at the Institut catholique de Paris (ICP) and Paris IV-Sorbonne in 1998. In 1989–90, she was fellow for a specialization at the University of Milan. From 1991 to 1999 she was Assistant Professor, and from 1998 to 2002 Visiting Professor, at the Department of Philosophy, Faculté de Philosophie et Lettres, Namur, FUNDP. Since 1999 she has been Professor of Philosophy (Anthropology) at the University of Louvain (ISP/UCL). In 2003 for a semester she was a researcher at the Institute for Human Sciences (IWM/ Vienna). She is a researcher at Europè (Centre of Practical Philosophy/UCL) and

LAAP (Centre of Prospective Anthropology/UCL) and a member of LANPRA (Anthropology and Practical Philosophy ICParis).

John-Stewart Gordon has an MA and BA in Philosophy and History from Konstanz University (2001) and a Ph.D. in Philosophy from Göttingen University (2005) in Germany. He was both Adjunct Assistant Professor in Philosophy (2009) and Visiting Professor in Philosophy at Queen's University, Kingston, Canada (2009–10). Since 2010 he has been W1-Professor of Anthropology and Ethics in Rehabilitation Sciences and co-director of the Hans Jonas Research Centre at Cologne University, Germany, as well as permanent Visiting Professor in Philosophy at Vytautas Magnus-University in Kaunas, Lithuania (2012). Furthermore, he is member of the board of *Bioethics* as well as area-editor and board member of the *Internet Encyclopedia of Philosophy*. He has published several books in practical philosophy as single author and editor as well as peer-reviewed articles in international leading journals and encyclopedias including *Bioethics*, *Ethical Theory and Moral Practice*, *Kennedy Institute of Ethics Journal*, *Internet Encyclopedia of Philosophy* and *Oxford Bibliographies Online Philosophy*. He has taught philosophy at Tübingen University (Germany), Ruhr-University Bochum (Germany), Duisburg-Essen University (Germany), Queen's University, Kingston (Canada), Vytautas Magnus-University Kaunas (Lithuania) and Cologne University (Germany).

Hans Jonas studied Philosophy and Jewish Studies in Berlin, Freiburg and Heidelberg and achieved his Ph.D. at Marburg University where he studied under Edmund Husserl and Martin Heidegger. He left Germany in 1933. Hans Jonas taught briefly at the Hebrew University of Jerusalem before moving to North America. In 1950 he moved to Canada in order to teach at Carleton University. From 1955 to 1976 he was Alvin Johnson Professor of Philosophy at the New School for Social Research in New York City. His most influential books, including *The Gnostic Religion* and *The Imperative of Responsibility*, focus on natural philosophy and ethical and social problems created by technology. He died in 1993.

David J. Levy was Visiting Professor of Social Theory and Philosophy at Middlesex University in London. He was the author of several books, including *The Measure of Man: Incursions in Philosophical and Political Anthropology* and *Hans Jonas: The Integrity of Thinking*. He died in 2002.

Jan C. Schmidt is a physicist and a philosopher. He received a Ph.D. in Theoretical Physics (nonlinear dynamics, chaos theory, complex systems theory) and a habilitation in Philosophy (philosophy of science and technology, natural philosophy, history of science). He was a professor's assistant at the Institute of Physics, University of Mainz (1996–99), as well as at the Institute of Philosophy and at the Centre for Interdisciplinary Studies of Technology, Darmstadt University of Technology (1999–2006). He was Associate Professor for Philosophy of Science and Technology at Georgia Tech, School of Public Policy (2006–2008), and since 2008 he has been Professor of Philosophy of Science and Technology at Darmstadt University of Applied Sciences and Visiting Professor for Natural Philosophy at the University of Jena (2011–12). Currently, Schmidt serves as a Vice Dean of the Department of Social Sciences. Additionally, he has worked on policy-related projects at the Wuppertal Institute for Climate, Energy and Environment and as a scientific-technical consultant on projects in the automotive industry and other innovative technology fields. His areas of interest cover ethics, practical philosophy, philosophy of nature, philosophy and history of sciences, philosophy of technology, philosophy of interdisciplinarity and science and technology studies (STS).

Paula Segler studies Philosophy and Educational Sciences at Cologne University and is a student assistant at the professorship of Anthropology and Ethics in Rehabilitation Sciences and at the Hans Jonas Research Centre. Additionally, since 2013 she has worked on the interdisciplinary project 'Global Bioethics'.

Lawrence Vogel received his BA from Vassar and his Ph.D. in Philosophy from Yale. He is Professor of Philosophy at Connecticut College, where he has taught since 1989. Lawrence Vogel is the author of *The Fragile 'We': Ethical Implications of Heidegger's 'Being and Time'* and the editor of a volume of Hans Jonas' later essays, *Mortality and Morality: A Search for the Good after Auschwitz*. His most recent publications, including *Natural-Law Judaism: The Genesis of Bioethics in Hans Jonas, Leo Strauss and Leon Kass*, reflect his special interest in Heidegger's Jewish students – especially Jonas, Strauss, Hannah Arendt and Emmanuel Lévinas – and their responses to the legacy of their teacher.

Walter A. Weisskopf studied at the University of Vienna, Cambridge University and the University of Geneva. He is the author of *The Psychology of Economics* (1955), a classic of psycho-cultural analysis of economics and economic theory, and *Alienation and Economics* (1971). He was the first Chair of the Department of Economics at Roosevelt University (Chicago). He died in 1991 (California).

Micha H. Werner studied philosophy, sociology and literature in Munich, Berlin and Tübingen. After receiving his philosophical doctorate (summa cum laude) at the Freie Universität Berlin in 2001, he worked as an assistant professor and researcher at the Chair for Ethics in Medicine at Tübingen University and from 2002 to 2007 as head of an interfacultary institute for basic studies in philosophy and ethics at the University of Freiburg. Since 2007 he has held the position of a research lecturer for Practical Philosophy at Utrecht University. His research covers questions of normative ethics, meta-ethics and action theory; more specific topics include the ascription of responsibility, modern Kantian ethics, the concept of disease and the ethics of advertising.

Acknowledgements

The present volume, *Global Ethics and Moral Responsibility*, contains 11 outstanding and challenging articles on the philosophy of Hans Jonas, both original and already published, by well-known philosophers and Hans Jonas experts. The contributors are: Michael Bongardt, Holger Burckhart, Natalie Frogneux, John-Stewart Gordon, Hans Jonas, David J. Levy, Jan C. Schmidt, Paula Segler, Lawrence Vogel, Walter A. Weisskopf and Micha H. Werner. We are very thankful to all of them for their great work and their willingness to contribute an article to this fine volume. The journal *Social Research* and the University of Missouri Press granted us permission to use already published articles written by Jonas and Weisskopf, as well as a book chapter by Levy. Their support is greatly appreciated. We would also like to thank Ashgate Publishing for their interest and willingness to publish the book and, in particular, Alison Kirk for her excellent support from the early to the final stages of this volume. Last, but not least, we would like to thank our research assistant Paula Segler for her great help. She not only wrote the introduction with us, but also provided outstanding support with regard to all the editorial work on the book; without her help we certainly would have been lost in the details of the project.

John-Stewart Gordon,
Cologne University, Germany and
Vytautas Magnus University, Kaunas, Lithuania

Holger Burckhart,
University of Siegen, Germany

Introduction

John-Stewart Gordon, Holger Burckhart and Paula Segler

Why Hans Jonas?

In 1979 Hans Jonas, one of the most important German-Jewish philosophers of the last century, published his impressive work *Das Prinzip Verantwortung – Prinzip einer Ethik für eine technologische Zivilisation.*[1] This work deeply influenced the philosophical debate of the 1980s and 1990s, and was the first major philosophical work on the dangers of the ever-increasing technological progress and its (possible) negative consequences for humanity and nature. In particular, Jonas was very concerned about the fast developments in the field of biotechnology, the use of nuclear power (and its contaminated waste products), the global plundering of natural resources and the problem of population explosion, as well as the clearing of the rainforests. Even though the philosophy of Hans Jonas was without doubt widely highly influential, one must nowadays acknowledge the fact that his influence is in decline. The reasons are manifold: some might argue that his way of doing philosophy has become outdated; others, for example contemporary philosophers who are trained in analytical philosophy, are simply unfamiliar with Jonas' rather archaic and complex language (almost comparable to Hegel and Heidegger) and are unwilling to put any serious effort into closely reading Jonas' work.

The goal of this book is to treasure Jonas' memory, as well as to revive his significant oeuvre and philosophical importance for current debate. In this regard, this collection of original papers is fighting against seeing Hans Jonas' philosophy fall into oblivion. The authors not only examine thoroughly the different and important aspects of Hans Jonas' philosophy, they also go beyond Jonas and use him to discuss important contemporary problems and to arrive at original and promising solutions.

The Importance of Hans Jonas' Ethics of Responsibility for Current Debate

In former times, basic human needs were in balance with supply and demand, while in modern times – by virtue of the advantages of industrialization and the fruits of

1 The English translation of the German book, *The Imperative of Responsibility: In Search of an Ethics for the Technological World* was published in 1984 by the University of Chicago Press.

the ever-increasing development of modern technology – a broad range of different and luxurious needs have been created. These have eventually led to an imbalance of supply and demand. Hans Jonas acknowledges this dangerous paradox of modern technology, whereby we produce more than we need by jeopardizing nature and eventually humanity itself. This apparently indefinite process of modern technology causes a number of important global problems such as:

1. **Global exploitation of natural resources:** This includes, for example, the reckless exploitation of non-renewable natural resources (e.g. deep mining), which not only destroys the landscape but also endangers the natural habitats of wild fauna and flora. Only in rare cases does renaturalization take place so that animals and plants can resettle.
2. **Clearing of the rainforests:** This contributes to climate change by damaging the so-called 'green lungs' of the earth. Natural habitats of wild fauna and flora become endangered.
3. **Nuclear power:** The most notable problems here are those of contaminated waste and the occurrence of critical accidents (e.g. Chernobyl 1986 and Japan 2011).
4. **Energy consumption:** Fast-developing countries and industrial countries massively exploit non-renewable resources (e.g. coal, oil) in order either to begin the process of industrialization or to retain high standards of living. This in turn leads to environmental problems such as pollution and global warming.
5. **Global warming:** Human-induced climate change endangers not only the habitats of animals but also the living space of human beings.
6. **Biotechnology:** In the instance of genetic enhancement – to take one example – Jonas believes that this should not be performed since it is impossible to foresee all the consequences it might have for humanity. Furthermore, prenatal diagnostic testing is problematic as well, since it might eventually be used to select only healthy individuals, thereby reducing numbers of disabled individuals, and this might be seen as an act of discrimination (as proclaimed by many people with disabilities and proponents of disability rights).
7. **Population explosion and ageing:** Important advances in medical technology, for example, have led to a global decline in mortality (particularly, at the beginning and end of life), which, in turn, has inevitably led to a society with more elderly people. An ageing population, however, can pose problems: in respect of, for example, the fair allocation of health care resources and the increasing financial burdens placed on health care systems and nursing homes. In addition, food and water supplies become more and more difficult to maintain depending on the progression of overpopulation.
8. **The decline of biodiversity:** Biodiversity is in decline – a fact that is commonly seen to be intrinsically bad – by virtue of the negative consequences of climate change, the clearing of the rainforests, and

environmental catastrophes (e.g. the oil spill caused by BP's *Deepwater Horizon*, Gulf of Mexico, 2010).

In general, Jonas teaches us to think more deeply about the possible negative consequences of our actions against the background of modern technology and its great dangers for humanity and nature. One might rightly claim that Jonas' notion of responsibility is his fundamental expression of universal care for all living beings and the future of humanity in an intact environment.

Hans Jonas' General Account of Responsibility

Jonas' general account of responsibility is best understood against the background of his philosophy of nature and anthropology. His ethical approach is naturalistic in nature, but it does not fall into bare materialism. Jonas' starting point is the decisive question of the existence of humankind as such. By appealing to metaphysics, Jonas attempts to establish an objective justification of morality that is independent of human beings. In particular, he deduces the (categorical) moral duty (i.e. the imperative of responsibility) from nature itself, by appealing to a teleological account of nature in which the preservation of one's existence is seen as an immanent end that is good as such. Thereby Jonas counters the popular opinion that nature is a mere object which can be controlled by human beings at their discretion. Nature itself provides the justification for its continuing existence as the foundation of life. It follows, then, that the most general task of responsibility concerns the protection of the existence of humankind and nature (including animals). Jonas' notion of responsibility is characterized by two main features: non-reciprocity and the heuristic of fear, which are dealt with in the order that follows:

1. **Non-reciprocity:** Jonas refers to responsibility in the context of asymmetric power relationships. The increasing power of human beings corresponds with more opportunities for action, and this amounts to an increased responsibility. According to Jonas, responsibility concerns not only present humanity but requires us also to consider future generations and animals as well. That means that moral actions do not only occur between human beings, but also between human beings and non-rational beings – as well as nature – as part of a 'universal' care. Thus Jonas' ethics can be seen as a valuable attempt to overcome the anthropocentric perspective.
2. **Heuristic of fear:** Generally speaking, the heuristic of fear is a conservative precautionary principle. Jonas famously proclaims priority of the bad over the good prognosis because the far-reaching effects of the technological, economic and social development are unpredictable. His ethics – anti-utopian by nature – is rather based on 'pragmatic' considerations of urgent global problems.

Jonas' ethics is necessarily future-facing and focuses upon the determination of the negative impacts stemming from rapid technological progress on humanity, animals and nature, in order to prevent global problems such as climate change or the exploitation of non-renewable natural resources. Ethical reasoning and decision-making must precede the application of technology; otherwise, one simply assigns ethics the role of a mere tool that has only a corrective and compensatory function. However, according to Jonas, the task of ethics should also be 'prognostic' and attempt to avoid terrible future consequences. Furthermore, Jonas stands in the tradition of deontological theories that rely on categorical duties, though he successfully refines the deontological form of reasoning by putting animals (or, at least, the moral status of animals) and nature (that is, the protection of the environment to avoid global warming and other environmental damage) on the agenda.

Contributions

This book is formed of four main parts, which are tied together by Jonas' notion of responsibility as applied to different contexts. The introductory section, 'The Philosophy of Hans Jonas', offers a critical overview of the important features of Hans Jonas' ethics of responsibility and additionally points out the strengths and weaknesses of his approach. The second part, 'Human Nature and the Imperative of Responsibility', deals with topics concerning human nature against the background of moral responsibility, and examines some highly important contemporary problems such as inclusion and disability, ageing, and the vulnerability of future generations. The third part, 'On Religion, Ethics and Natural Philosophy', provides a discussion of Hans Jonas' philosophy of religion, and critically examines the complex relation between ethics and nature in his philosophy. The final part, 'The Ethics of Technology and Moral Responsibility', concerns the important theme of ethics and responsibility in the (bio-)technological age by appealing to Hans Jonas' general approach and the idea of moral enhancement. The following brief overview will, we hope, facilitate access to the chapters.

The first part *The Philosophy of Hans Jonas* contains two previously published and one original article. Chapter 1, 'Responsibility Today: The Ethics of an Endangered Future' (1976), is a paper by Jonas himself, where he offers a brief and clear exposition of his subsequent ethical masterpiece of 1979. In 'Moral Responsibility for the Preservation of Humankind' (1983), Walter A. Weisskopf thoroughly examines Jonas' ethical approach by appealing to three main problems: the dichotomy of fact and value, the biological roots of responsibility for others and future generations, and Jonas' critique of the so-called 'Marxist utopia'. The first original chapter of this collection is Holger Burckhart's substantial contribution 'Ethics of Responsibility: Discourse-ethical Perspective of the Justification Problem', in which he discusses Jonas' ethics against the background of discourse-ethical considerations and examines its importance for moral competency.

The second part, 'Human Nature and the Imperative of Responsibility', contains three original chapters. Following Jonas, Lawrence Vogel – in 'Is Ageing a Gift? Bioconservatism and the Ethics of Gratitude', vividly defends the idea that one should not enhance human beings in order to prolong the natural human lifespan. Chapter 5, 'Some Paradoxes Linked to Risk Moderation', by Nathalie Frogneux, examines the way Jonas' philosophy deals with the important problem of the vulnerability of future generations in the context of ethical and political decisions. In the last chapter, 'Inclusion – A Moral Imperative, but Also Socially Desired?', Holger Burckhart and John-Stewart Gordon wholeheartedly reject the exclusionary approach to persons with disability. By following Jonas – who supports the idea of equally respecting each human life – Burckhart and Gordon convincingly argue that one should adhere to the inclusionary approach, and this is justified by their particular discourse-ethical approach.

The third part, 'On Religion, Ethics and Natural Philosophy', is similarly formed of three original chapters. Chapter 7, 'God in the World of Man: Hans Jonas' Philosophy of Religion', by Michael Bongardt, examines Jonas' multifaceted thoughts on religious and metaphysical traditions by paying close attention to his critics. Micha H. Werner analyses Jonas' so-called 'teleological naturalism' in his contribution, 'What Is Natural about Natural Functioning? Examining an Indirect Argument in Favour of Teleological Naturalism', by using the prima facie reasonable example of medical practice. He comes to the conclusion that – despite the prima facie reasonableness – the use of the example of medical practice, in order to show that Jonas' teleological naturalism is convincing, eventually fails. In the last chapter in this section, 'Ethics for the Technoscientific Age: On Hans Jonas' Argumentation and His Public Philosophy Beyond Disciplinary Boundaries', Jan C. Schmidt deals with Jonas' view that ethics and nature are closely related. He offers a thorough and systematic critique of Jonas' critics, and convincingly defends Jonas' approach from an analytical perspective.

The last part, 'The Ethics of Technology and Moral Responsibility', contains one previously published and one original article. From a bird's-eye view, David J. Levy discusses a broad range of topics related to Hans Jonas' ethics of responsibility in his even-handed contribution 'Ethics and Responsibility in a Technological Age' (2002), by pointing out the great significance of Hans Jonas' philosophy. The last chapter, 'Refined Marxism and Moral Enhancement', by John-Stewart Gordon, examines the issue of whether a sophisticated form of Marxism is better equipped to deal with the possible dangers of modern technology in a more responsible and sustainable way by additionally proposing the idea of morally enhancing human beings.

We hope that this collection of intriguing contributions will do justice to the importance of Hans Jonas' philosophy, and will revive interest in both his ethical reasoning and his notion of responsibility. With great technological power comes great moral responsibility – towards both humanity and nature.

PART 1
The Philosophy of Hans Jonas

Chapter 1
Responsibility Today: The Ethics of an Endangered Future[1]

Hans Jonas

Care for the future of mankind is the overruling duty of collective human action in the age of a technical civilization that has become 'almighty', if not in its productive then at least in its destructive potential. This care must obviously include care for the future of all nature on this planet as a necessary condition of man's own. Even if it were less than necessary in this instrumental sense – even if (science-fiction style) a human life worthy of its name were imaginable in a depleted nature mostly replaced by art – it might still hold that the plenitude of life, evolved in aeons of creative toil and now delivered into our hands, has a claim to our care in its own right. A kind of metaphysical responsibility beyond self-interest has devolved on us with the magnitude of our powers relative to this tenuous film of life, that is, since man has become dangerous not only to himself but to the whole biosphere.

There is no need, however, to debate the relative claims of nature and man when it comes to the survival of either, for in this ultimate issue their causes converge from the human angle itself. Since, in fact, the two cannot be separated without making a caricature of the human likeness – since, rather, in the matter of preservation or destruction the interest of man coincides, beyond all material needs, with that of life as his worldly home in the most sublime sense of the word – we can subsume both duties as one under the heading 'responsibility toward man' without falling into a narrow anthropocentric view. Such narrowness in the name of man, which is ready to sacrifice the rest of nature to his purported needs, can only result in the dehumanization of man, the atrophy of his essence even in the lucky case of biological preservation. It therefore contradicts its professed goal, the very preservation of himself as sanctioned by the dignity of his essence. In the truly human aspect, nature retains her dignity, which confronts the arbitrariness of our might. As one of her products, we owe allegiance to the kindred total of her creations, of which the allegiance to our own existence is only the highest summit.

---

1 This paper was presented to the Wunsch International Symposium on 'Ethics in an Age of Pervasive Technology' held at Technion City, Haifa, and at the Residence of the President of the State of Israel, Jerusalem, 22–5 December 1974, to mark the fiftieth anniversary of the Technion – Israel Institute of Technology. Reprinted with permission from *Social Research* 43:1 (1976), 77–97.

This summit, rightly understood, comprises all the rest under its obligation. In other words, the duty toward nature is part of our humanist duty, well beyond the calculable material necessities that point in the same direction.

The Common Destiny of Man and Nature

This is not to take a harmonistic or idyllic view of the relationship. In the choice between man and nature, as the struggle for existence poses it time and again, man of course comes first, and nature, even when allowing for her own rights, must give way to his superior right. Or, should the idea of anything intrinsically 'superior' be questioned here, the simple rule holds that egoism of the species – each species – takes precedence anyway by the order of life in general, and the particular exercise of man's might vis-à-vis the rest of the living world is a natural right based on the faculty alone. In other words, the mere fact of superior power legitimates its use. This has in practice and without reflection been the attitude of all times, when for long the odds were by no means so clear, when often man felt more on the defensive than the offensive, and when nature as a whole appeared invulnerable, thus in all particulars free for his untrammeled use.

Western religion and metaphysics added their sanction of transcendental uniqueness to this natural anthropocentric bent. But even if the prerogative of man were still insisted upon as absolute, it would now have to include a duty toward nature as both a condition of his own survival and an integral complement of his unstunted being. We have intimated that one may go further and say that the common destiny of man and nature, newly discovered in the common danger, makes us rediscover nature's own dignity and commands us to care for her integrity over and above the utilitarian aspect. A sentimental interpretation of this command is ruled out by the law of life itself, which is obviously part of the 'integrity' to be preserved. For encroaching on other life is *eo ipso* given with belonging to the kingdom of life, as each kind lives on others or codetermines their environment, and therefore bare, natural self-preservation of each means perpetual interference with the rest of life's balance. In simple words: To eat and to be eaten is the principle of existence of just that manifoldness which the command bids us to honor. The sum total of these mutually limiting interferences, always involving destruction in the particulars, is on the whole symbiotic but not static, with those comings, goings, and stayings known to us from the dynamics of prehuman evolution. The hard order of ecology (first seen by Malthus) prevented any excessive predation by a single life form on the whole, any monopoly of a 'strongest', and the coexistence of the whole was assured in the change of its parts. Even the increasingly one-sided interference of man was no decisive exception to this rule until quite recently.

Only with the superiority of thought and with the power of technical civilization made possible by it, one form of life, man, has been enabled to endanger all others (and therewith also himself). Nature could not have incurred a greater hazard than to produce man. As long as practical intelligence and theoretical intellect went their separate ways, his impact on the balance of things remained tolerable. But unlike the contemplative intellect of old, the aggressive intellect bred by modern science and discharged into the administration of things confronts nature not merely with its thought but with actions of a scope no longer compatible with the unconscious functioning of the whole. In man, nature has disturbed herself and has only in his moral endowment left herself an unsure substitute for the shattered sureness of her self-regulation. It is a terrifying thought that on this fickle ground her cause should now rest – or let us say more modestly: so much of what man can see of her cause. By the timescale of evolution and even the much shorter scale of human history, this is an almost sudden turn in the fate of nature. Its possibility lay hidden in the initial fact of free-roaming knowledge and will that with man had burst into the world, but its reality matured slowly and then suddenly appeared. In this century the long-prepared point has been reached where the danger becomes manifest and critical. Power conjoined with reason carries responsibility with it. This was always self-understood in regard to the intrahuman sphere. What is not yet fully understood is the novel expansion of responsibility to the condition of the biosphere and the future survival of mankind, which follows simply from the extension of power over these things – and from its being eminently a power of destruction. Power and peril reveal a duty which, through the commanding solidarity with the rest, extends from our being to that of the whole, regardless of our consent.

Let me repeat: The duty we talk about has become apparent only with the threat to the subject concerned. Previously it would have been senseless to talk about such things. What is in jeopardy raises its voice. That which had always been the most elementary of the givens, taken for granted as the background of all acting and never requiring action itself – that there are men, that there is life, that there is a world for both – this suddenly stands forth, as lit up by lightning, in its stark peril through human deed. In this very light the new responsibility appears. Born of danger, its first urging is necessarily an ethics of preservation and prevention, not of progress and perfection. In spite of this modesty of aim, its commandments may be rather difficult to obey and perhaps demand more sacrifices than any asked so far for the betterment of the human lot. It is a consequence of freedom's negative power in its present ascendancy that the 'permitted and not permitted' has priority over the positive 'ought'. This is only the beginning of morals and, of course, insufficient for a positive doctrine of duties. Fortunately for our theoretical task, and unfortunately for our situation today, we need not go into the theory of the human good and the 'best life', which would have to be derived from a conception of man's 'essence'. For the moment, all work on the 'true' man must stand back behind the bare saving of its precondition, namely, the *existence* of mankind in a sufficient natural environment. In the total danger of the world-historical Now we find ourselves thrown back from the ever-open question, *what* man ought to be, to the first commandment, hitherto never in need of enunciation: *that* he should be – indeed, as a human being. This 'as' brings the essence, as much as we know or divine of it, into the imperative of 'that' as the ultimate reason for its absoluteness and must prevent its observance from devouring the ontological sanction itself; that is, the policy of survival must beware lest the existence finally saved will have ceased to be human. Considering the severity of the sacrifices that could be necessary, this may well become the most precarious aspect of the ethics of survival that is being imposed on us now: a ridge between two abysses, where means can destroy the end. This ridge must be walked in the uncertain light of our knowledge and in honoring that which man has made of himself in millennia of cultural endeavor. But what now matters most is not to perpetuate or bring about a particular image of man, but first of all to keep open the horizon of *possibilities* which in the case of man is given with the existence of the species as such and – as we must hope from the promise of the *imago Dei* – will always offer a new chance to human essence. This means that the 'No to Not-Being' – and first to that of man – is at this moment and for some time to come the primal mode in which an emergency ethics of the endangered future must translate into collective action the 'Yes to Being' demanded of man by the totality of things.

The Apocalyptic Situation

All this holds on the assumption here made that we live in an apocalyptic situation, that is, under the threat of a universal catastrophe if we let things take their present course. On this subject I now have to say a few things, well known though they be. The danger derives from the excessive dimensions of the scientific-technological-industrial civilization. What we call the Baconian programme – namely, to aim knowledge at power over nature, and to utilize power over nature for the improvement of the human lot – lacked indeed in its capitalist execution from the outset the rationality as well as the justice with which it could have been conjoined. But its intrinsic and self-reinforcing dynamics, necessarily propelling into extravagance of production and consumption, would probably have overwhelmed any society, considering the short range of human targets and the truly unforeseeable magnitude of its success.

Thus the danger of disaster attending the Baconian ideal of power over nature through scientific technology arises not so much from any shortcomings of its performance as from the magnitude of its success. This success is in the main of two kinds: economic and biological. Their necessarily crisis-bound mutual relation is by now becoming manifest. The economic success, long considered alone, meant increased per capita production of goods, both in their quantity and variety, together with reduction of human work, thus heightened prosperity of many and even involuntarily heightened consumption of all within the system – *ergo*, enormously increased metabolism of the social body as a whole with the natural environment. This itself had its dangers of overstraining finite natural resources. But these dangers are raised to a higher power and accelerated by the – at first less visible – biological success: the numerical swelling of this metabolizing collective body, that is, the exponential population growth within the geographical reach of the health benefits of technological civilization, which far exceeds the reach of its economic benefits and by now covers the globe. This not only adds a new quantitative dimension to the first process, increasing its tempo and multiplying its effects on the balance of global metabolism; it also very nearly deprives it of whatever freedom it may otherwise have to call a halt to itself. A static population could say at a certain point: enough, but a growing one has to say: more! Today it becomes frighteningly clear that the biological success not only may nullify the economical by leading back from the short feast of affluence to the chronic weekday of poverty, but that it also threatens mankind and nature with an acute catastrophe of enormous proportions. The population explosion, seen as a problem of planetary metabolism, takes the helm away from the welfare aspiration and may increasingly compel an impoverishing mankind to do just for the sake of immediate survival what for the sake of happiness it was free to do or leave: the ever more reckless plundering of the planet. Inevitably the latter will have the last word when eventually it denies itself to the overdemand. Imagination recoils from the prospect of mass dying and mass killing that will accompany such a situation of *sauve qui peut*. The equilibrium laws of ecology, for so long held off by art, which in their natural state prevent the overgrowth of any one species, will assert their right all the more terribly the more they have been bullied to the extreme of their tolerance. How after this a remnant of mankind will start afresh on a ravaged earth defies all speculation.

This is the apocalyptic perspective calculably built into the structure of the present course of humanity. It must be understood that we are here confronted with a dialectic of power which can only be overcome by a further degree of power itself, not by a quietist renunciation of power. Bacon's formula says that knowledge is power. Now the Baconian programme by itself, that is, under its own management, has at the height of its triumph revealed its insufficiency in the lack of control over itself, thus the impotence of its power to save not only man from himself but also nature from man. Both need protection now because of the very magnitude of the power man has reached in the pursuit of technical progress, where the growing power engendered the concurrently growing necessity of its use and thus the strange impotence to stop the ever-continued and foreseeably self-destructive progress of itself. Bacon did not anticipate this profound paradox of the power derived from knowledge: that it leads indeed to some sort of domination over nature (that is, her intensified utilization), but at the same time to the most complete subjugation under itself. The power has become self-acting, while its promise has turned into threat, its prospect of salvation into apocalypse. Power over the power is required now before the halt is called by catastrophe itself – the power to overcome that impotence over against the self-feeding compulsion of power to its progressive exercise. After the first-degree power, directed at a seemingly inexhaustible nature, has changed into a second-degree power which wrested control of the first from the user's hands, it is now up to a third-degree power to enforce the self-limitation of the rule that carries along the ruler, before it shatters on the barriers of nature. This third degree means power over the second-degree power, which was no longer man's but power's itself to dictate its use to its supposed owner, to make of him the compulsive executor of his capacity, thus enslaving man instead of liberating him.

Marxism and the Apocalypse

From which direction can this third-degree power be expected which still – in time – reinstates man in the control of his power and breaks its tyrannical self-activity? It must, in the nature of the problem, emanate from society, as no private insight, responsibility, or fear can measure up to its task. And as the 'free' economy of Western industrial societies is the very source of the dynamics which drifts to the mortal danger, we look quite naturally to the alternative of communism. Can this bring the necessary help? Is it tuned to it? Under this point of view alone, Marxist ethics should be examined today – that is, under that of salvation from disaster, not under that of fulfillment of mankind's dreams. One looks at Marxism because its professed concern is with the future of the whole human enterprise (as it talks of 'world revolution'), for the sake of which it dares to ask from the present any sacrifice and, where it rules, can also enforce it. It is at least more difficult to see how the capitalist West could accomplish this. That much is clear that only a maximum of politically imposed social discipline can ensure the subordination of present advantages to the long-term exigencies of the future. But as Marxism is a form of progressivism, and by no means sees itself as an emergency policy but as the road to a higher realization of man, it partakes also of the dangers common to the whole meliorism of modern times.

It is not by chance that socialism appeared with the beginnings of the machine age and that its scientific accreditation by Marx was based on the condition of capitalism created thereby. Expressed with rough simplification: Only this condition made socialization seem worth while, quite apart from the fact that it also made it appear necessary and politically attainable in the light of the crisis theory of capitalism and the pauperization theory of the proletariat. Only modern technology makes possible such an increase of the social product that its just (equal) distribution does not result in general poverty – whereby the feeling of injustice would be remedied but little else. In an economy of want, the just distribution of the insufficient makes only a slight difference in favor of the many, and it even has to be said that under such circumstances the injustice of concentration of riches and liberties in the few can at least benefit culture, for which in times of primitive technology a terrible price had always to be paid. (What would classical civilization, the fruits of which we would hardly like to miss, have been without the slave economy?) Equal poverty of all, guaranteed by the state, may be morally less revolting than the riches of a few vis-à-vis the poverty of the many, but this gain alone would not have lent wings to the socialist ideal to make history. Stated brutally: Only the magnitude of the prize awaiting the proletariat made the revolution worth while. This is entirely legitimate. It seems somewhat at odds with this reasoning that just where the prize already in existence was the highest – that is, in the advanced industrial countries – the masses so far have not chosen this way, and that today, contrariwise, just in the poorest countries socialism recommends itself as a means of creating that very prize after the capitalist model. But the prize is at least in sight through that model, and the anomaly of Marxism winning in backward rather than advanced societies does not alter the fact that the proof of material surplus already furnished by modern technology, if not at home then elsewhere, is an important factor in the modern socialist ideal.

Indeed, wherever socialism came to power, industrialization was the hallmark of its actual and resolute politics. It is therefore still true today that Marxism, progressivist as it was from the beginning, born under the sign of the 'Principle of Hope' and not the 'Principle of Fear', is no less dedicated to the Baconian idea than its capitalist rival, with which it competes here: To equal and finally surpass it in the fruits to be earned from technology was everywhere the law of its will. In short, Marxism is by origin heir to the Baconian revolution and in its own view its rightful executor, a better one (meaning: more efficient) than capitalism has been. It remains to be examined whether it can also better become its master. Our anticipated answer is that it can be so only if it reinterprets its role from bringer of consummation to preventer of disaster, that is, by renouncing its breath of life – Utopia. This would be a much changed Marxism, almost unrecognizable except for the external principle of organization. The inspiring ideal would be gone (we don't know whether the pain would be salutary or not). The classless society would then appear no longer as fulfillment of mankind's dream but very soberly as the condition for mankind's survival in the approaching area of crisis.

It is a task for political science, with the help of psychology, to examine the chances presented here by Marxism – in its reality, not merely by its doctrine – and to compare them to the chances offered by other sociopolitical systems. No more should here be said, except the truism that our problem is an eminently political one, as seen by John Herz with great clarity. To him and to his colleagues of the same discipline, there falls an important task in our context, for which I wish them first of all courage for the unpopular and, if need be, even for the highly unpalatable. I am going to apply myself now to some preliminary questions of ethical theory which may be of service in the search for a political way.

The Heuristics of Fear

I contend that we need today an imaginative-anticipatory *heuristics of fear* to lead us to the discovery of the duties, even the ethical principles, with which to meet the challenge of coming events. Just as we should not know about the sanctity of life without knowing about killing and without the commandment 'Thou shalt not kill' having brought this sanctity into focus; and just as we should not know the value of truth without being aware of lies, nor of freedom without the lack of it, and so forth – just so in our search after an ethics of responsibility for distant contingencies can an anticipated *distortion* of man help us to detect that in the conception of man which is to be preserved from it. And we need the *threat* to the image of man – and rather specific kinds of threat – to assure ourselves of his true image by the very recoil from these threats. As long as the danger is unknown, we do not know what to preserve and why. Knowledge of this comes, against all logic and method, from the 'where from'. This is perceived first and teaches us, by the revulsion of feeling which acts ahead of knowledge, to see the value whose antithesis so affects us. *We know what is at stake only when we know that it is at stake.*

Because this is the way we are made: The perception of the *malum* is infinitely easier to us than the perception of the *bonum*; it is more direct, more compelling, less given to differences of opinion, and most of all not looked for. It is forced upon us by the mere presence of the evil, whereas the beneficial can be there inconspicuously and remain unperceived without reflection (to which we must have special cause). We are not unsure about evil when it comes our way, but of the good we become sure only via the experience of its opposite. It is doubtful whether anybody would ever have praised health without at least the sight of sickness, praised sincerity without the experience of trickery, and praised peace without knowing of war's misery. We know much sooner what we do not want than what we want. Therefore moral philosophy must consult our fears prior to our wishes to learn what we really cherish. And although the heuristics of fear is not the last word in the search for goodness, it is at least an extremely useful first word and should be used to the full of its ability in a sphere where so few unlooked-for words are vouchsafed us.

Now, where this word is not vouchsafed us on its own – that is, by evil already present – it becomes our duty to look for it, because there too the guidance of fear is indispensable. That is the case with the 'ethics of the future' which we are looking for, where that which is to be feared has not yet been experienced and has perhaps no analogies yet in past or present experience. Then the creatively imagined *malum* has to take over the role of the experienced *malum*, and this imagination does not appear on its own but must be intentionally induced. Therefore the anticipatory conjuring up of this imagination becomes itself the first, quasi-introductory duty of the ethics we are speaking about.

Thus the heuristics of which we talk is a prognostic which extrapolates from presently recognizable trends in the technologic industrial process. Such extrapolations are of course uncertain. Each can be arguably opposed by others without a conclusive estimation of the relative probabilities. And, as we demand a considerable certainty of prognosis when asked to forgo a desired and certain near effect in favor of a distant effect which will anyway no longer affect us, it could easily come about that the theoretical weakness of all predictions causes us to choose the one best suited to the interest of the day and for the rest trust our luck (or rather that of posterity). But in this way all the gains of our hypothetical heuristics are kept from timely application by the uncertainty of the prognostics, and the finest principles stay fallow until, perhaps, it will be too late.

But just this uncertainty, which threatens to make the ethical insight ineffectual for the responsibility toward the future – an uncertainty not confined, of course, to the prophecy of doom – has itself to be included in the ethical theory and become the cause of a new principle, which on its part can yield a not uncertain rule for decision-making. It is the rule, stated primitively, that *the prophecy of doom is to be given greater heed than the prophecy of bliss*. The reasons for this shall be briefly pointed out.

First, the mere probability relation between lucky and unlucky results of unknown experiments is generally like that between either hitting or missing a target. The hit is only one of innumerable alternatives which otherwise are more or less wide misses. And although in small matters we may allow many such misses in order to benefit from the rarer chances of success, we may allow but few where greater things are concerned. And in the really great, irreversible ones, which go to the roots of the whole human enterprise, we really must allow none. Natural evolution works with small things, never plays for the whole stake, and therefore can afford innumerable 'mistakes', in its single moves, from which its patient, slow process chooses the few, equally small 'hits'. The big enterprise of modern technology, neither patient nor slow, compresses – as a whole and in many of its single projects – the many infinitesimal steps of natural evolution into few colossal ones and forgoes by that procedure the vital advantages of nature's 'playing safe'.

To the causal *extent* is thus added the causal *tempo* of technological interference with life's system. It is therefore far from true that 'taking his own evolution in hand' – that is, replacing blind and slow-working chance with conscious and fast-working planning – would give man a surer prospect of evolutionary success. On the contrary, it would inject entirely new elements of insecurity and hazard, which rise in proportion as the stakes are raised and the times are shortened in which the unavoidable (and no longer small) mistakes can be corrected. If we add to this the anyhow existing disproportion of probabilities shown above, we must accept the command to allow, in matters of such capital eventualities, more weight to threat than to promise and to avoid apocalyptic prospects even at the price of thereby perhaps missing eschatological fulfillments. It is the command of caution in the face of the revolutionary style which the evolutionary 'either-or' technique assumes under the aegis of technology with its inherent playing for the whole stake – so foreign to natural evolution.

To this general consideration has to be added the fact that there is something peculiar about the 'en route' to which one might wish to leave the necessary corrections. Experience has taught us that developments set in motion by technological acts with short-term aims tend to make themselves independent, that is, to attain their own compulsive dynamics, an automotive momentum, by which they become not only, as stated, irreversible but also forward-pushing and thus overtake the wishes and plans of the initiators. The once-begun takes the law of action out of our hands, and the accomplished facts, created by the beginning, become cumulatively the law of its continuation. Granted then that we can 'take our own evolution in hand', it will slip from that hand by the very impulse it has received from it; and here more than anywhere else applies the adage that we are free at the first step but slaves at the second and all further ones. So we have to add to the first observation – that the speed of technologically fed developments does not leave itself the time for self-correction – the further observation that in whatever time is left the corrections will become more and more difficult and the freedom to make them more and more restricted. This heightens the duty to that vigilance over the beginnings which grants priority to well-grounded fears over against hopes, even if no less well grounded.

A Certain Principle of Ethics

So much for the reasons for the 'prophecy rule'. Let us formulate now the ethical principle behind it. We started out with the observation that the *uncertainty* of all long-term projections, which in the balance of its alternatives seems to paralyze the application of principles to the sphere of facts, is in its turn to be taken as a fact, for the right treatment of which ethics has to find a principle which itself is no longer an uncertain one. So far I have already discussed the practical rule in which that principle issues, namely, to give in matters of a certain magnitude – those with apocalyptic potential – greater weight to the prognosis of doom than to that of bliss. The premise of the whole argument was that today and further on we do have to deal with actions of just that magnitude, which is itself a *novum* in human affairs. This *novum* renders obsolete the tacit standpoint of all earlier ethics that, given the impossibility of long-term calculation, one should consider what is close at hand only and let the distant future take care of itself. This still goes for the private sphere of action where enticing as well as threatening distant perspectives are nothing more than idle fantasies. But in the new actionsphere of planetary technological planning, the fantasies are not idle: projection into the distance belongs to its nature and duty, and *its* uncertainty must therefore be met by another rule.

We know its contents. Its principle we shall learn when we reflect on the element of *game* or *bet* contained in all human action concerning its issue and side effects, and ask ourselves for what stake it is ethically permissible to gamble. To compress our discourse, let us take only the extreme case of the permissible.

One would not deny the statesman the right to risk his nation's existence for its future if really ultimate issues are at stake. In this manner the awesome but morally defensible decisions about war and peace come about when, for the future's sake, the stake is the future itself. It has to be added that this should never happen because of the enticement of a wonderful future but only under the threat of a terrible future; not to gain a supreme good (an immodesty in any case) but only to prevent a supreme evil.

The latter consideration has always priority and alone the excuse of dire necessity, for one can live without the supreme good but not with the supreme evil. There never is a good reason for the alternative of win all or lose all.

Add to this now that the sum total of the interests at stake in the 'bet' of technological progress has an incomparably wider compass than anything which normally is at stake in human decisions. Even when in the fateful hour the political leader hazards the whole existence of his tribe, his city, his nation, he yet knows that, even should they be destroyed, mankind and a living world on earth will go on. Only in the framework of this overarching supposition is the single hazard, in certain extreme cases, morally defensible. But not even for saving his nation's life must the statesman use means that can destroy mankind. Now, my point is that among the possible works of technology there are some which cumulatively have just that global extent and depth, namely, the possibility to endanger the whole existence or whole being of man in the future.

But there exists (as I can here only postulate axiomatically) an *unconditional duty* of mankind to exist, which must not be confounded with the conditional duty of each and every man to exist. The right of the individual to commit suicide is arguable; under no circumstances has mankind that right.

Herewith we have found a principle that forbids certain technologically feasible 'experiments' and the pragmatic expression of which is just that rule for decision-making to give the bad prognosis precedence over the good one. The ethical axiom which validates the rule is therefore as follows: Never must the existence or the essence of man as a whole be made a stake in the hazards of action. It follows directly that bare *possibilities* of the designated order are to be regarded as unacceptable risks which no opposing possibilities can render more acceptable. The rule that even imperfect palliatives are to be preferred to a promising radical cure from which the patient may die is valid for the life of mankind though not always for the individual patient.

We have here an inversion of Descartes' principle of doubt. In order to ascertain the indubitable truth we should, according to Descartes, equate everything doubtful with the demonstrably false. Here on the contrary we are told to treat, for the purposes of decision, the doubtful but possible as if it were certain, when it is of a certain kind. In short, the principle forbids any *va-banque* game with the cause of mankind.

This principle for the treatment of uncertainty is itself not uncertain at all, and it bids us unconditionally – that is, not just as an advice of moral prudence but as an unqualified command – if we accept responsibility for what will be. Under such responsibility, caution, otherwise a subsidiary matter of our discretion, becomes the core of moral action. The first rule is, therefore, that no condition of future descendants of humankind should be permitted to arise which contradicts the reason why the existence of mankind is mandatory at all. The imperative that there be a mankind is the first one, as far as man alone is concerned.

An Ontological Imperative

With this imperative we are, strictly speaking, not responsible to the future human individuals but to the *idea* of Man, which is such that it demands the presence of its embodiment in the world. It is, in other words, an ontological idea, which does not, however, as the 'ontological proof', alleges concerning the concept of God, guarantee the existence of its subject already with the essence – far from it! – but says that such a presence *ought* to be and to be watched over, thus making it a duty to us who can endanger it. It is this ontological imperative, emanating from the idea of Man, that stands behind the prohibition of a *va-banque* gamble with mankind. Only the idea of Man, by telling us *why* there should be men, tells us also *how* they should be.

Kant's differentiation between hypothetical and categorical imperative applies here, too. The hypothetical (of which there are many) says: *If* there are human beings in the future – which depends on our procreation – then such and such duties are to be observed by us toward them in advance. But the categorical commands only *that* there be *human beings*, with the accent equally on the *that* and the *what* of the obligatory existence. For me, I admit, this imperative is the only one which really fits the Kantian sense of the categorical, that is, the unconditional.

Let us return once again to the 'heuristics of fear' I am suggesting. For many, the apocalyptic potential of our technology is concentrated in the atom bomb. I am sure that they do not exaggerate the peril. But it has one consolation: It lies in the realm of arbitrary choice. Certain acts of certain actors can bring about the catastrophe – but they can also remain undone. Nuclear weapons can even be abolished, without this requiring all of modern existence to change. (The prospect is admittedly small.) Anyway, decisions still play a role – and in these: fear. Not that this can be trusted; but we can, in principle, be *lucky* because the use is not *necessary* in principle, that is, not impelled by the production of the thing as such (which rather aims at obviating the necessity of its use).

My main fear rather relates to the apocalypse threatening from the nature of the unintended dynamics of technical civilization as such, inherent in its structure, whereto it drifts willy-nilly and with exponential acceleration: the apocalypse of the 'too much' with exhaustion, pollution, desolation of the planet. Here the credible extrapolations are frightening and the calculable timespans shrink at a frenzied pace. Here averting the disaster asks for a revocation of the whole lifestyle, even of the very principle of the advanced industrial societies, and will hurt an endless number of interests (the habit interests of all!). It thus will be much more difficult than the prevention of nuclear destruction, which after all is possible without decisive interference with the general conditions of our technological existence. Most of all, the one apocalypse is almost bound to come by the logic of present trends that positively forge ahead toward it; the other is only a terrible contingency which may or may not happen.

Therefore, with all respect for the threat of sudden destruction by the atom bomb, I put the threat of the slow incremental opposite, overpopulation and all the other 'too much', in the forefront of my fears. That time bomb, whose ticking so far cannot be checked, competes in destructive power, alas, with any amount of hydrogen bombs. The apocalypse which threatens here from a total *development* (not just a single act) seems to me not smaller than the sudden one of an atomic holocaust, its consequences possibly as irreversible, and to its coming everyone of us contributes by mere membership in modern society. This apocalypse waits for our grandchildren, if we are lucky enough till then to have avoided the nuclear peril.

Darkest of all is, of course, the possibility that one will lead to the other; that in the global mass misery of a failing biosphere where 'to have or have not' turns into 'to be or not to be' for whole populations and 'everyone for himself' becomes the common parole, one or the other desperate side will, in the fight for dwindling resources, resort to the *ultima ratio* of atomic war – that is, will be driven to it. Probably the bomb (in a 'primitive' form) will become widely enough available so that not only poor nations but even small terror groups will be able to operate with it. The apocalypse 'with a whimper' can be preceded by several small 'bangs', even if we will be spared the 'big bang'.[2] *Both* must be prevented. Where the greater cause for pessimism is may be moot. For me personally only the overall drift with its entirely non-diabolic automatism has the traits of an almost inevitable *fatum*, which the sudden murder of mankind has not. But over that point there need be no quarrel.

The purpose of all predictions is in any case that they be translated into practical politics, namely, in the sense that the actions induced by them will promote or prevent their coming true. Prevention ranks foremost of the two, as the prediction in the sense of warning is naturally and rightly a stronger motive for the exertions of statecraft, surely a more compelling command to responsibility than the call of promise. At any rate, we have reached this point today. In that sense we have to understand, for example, the function of the population estimates for the next decades and into the coming millennium. Those results of the forecast which, by virtue of the quantities already in the running, are unalterable (except through mass extinction) call for early preparations to meet the food requirements, etc., without havoc to the environment. What beyond that fixed part is still open to influence calls for a policy of timely deflection of the curve away from the direction to disaster. The prophecy of doom is made to prevent its coming, and it would be the height of injustice later to deride the 'alarmists' because 'it did not turn out so bad after all'. To have been wrong may be their merit.

In this vein I call on all the Jeremiahs of our time – those I mean, who are this *because of their expert knowledge* – to do their best with their unmitigated visions that in the end they will be proven wrong.

2 This is one of Robert Heilbroner's somber visions in An Inquiry into the Human Prospect.

Chapter 2

Moral Responsibility for the Preservation of Humankind[1]

Walter A. Weisskopf

Hans Jonas' book *The Principle Responsibility*[2] (1979) is a reaction to what could be described as the abandonment of any belief in a transcendent dimension, in a realm of the unknown, the mysterious, the holy, and the divine; and to the apocalyptic eschatological mood that permeates the Western world. Much of what was previously considered positive in the West – progress, natural science, technology, democracy, and the market economy – is now in doubt, and the beliefs in these institutions are disintegrating.

Professor Jonas, who combines in his background the best of the German and American traditions, deals with almost everything that relates to this condition, but foremost with these questions: What kind of changes have to take place in our ethos in order to create an atmosphere of responsibility for the future of humankind? Is ontology, that most encompassing of philosophical enquiries, still capable of grounding a theory of ethical responsibility?

Jonas has written a magnificent book which enlarges our moral horizon beyond the pursuit of short-run material self-interest so prevalent today in the United States. However, one may have doubts about the very possibility of deriving 'ought' from 'is', a task at which philosophy has failed for centuries. As an appeal to intuitive, self-evident moral truths, the book is uplifting and prophetic; it should generate the kind of enthusiasm that has moved and changed history. The moral principle of total responsibility for the preservation of humankind seems to be self-evidently valid. However, the scientific and philosophical justification of such

---

1 Reprinted with permission from *Social Research* 50: 1 (1983), 98–125.

2 The all-encompassing breadth of this book makes it difficult to do justice to its multitude of ideas. Another difficulty is its language, which Jonas himself calls 'archaic'. Its style reminds one of Hegel, Max Weber, and Heidegger. This author, who was born to the German language, found it difficult to translate quoted passages. I have also tried to keep apart what Jonas said and what I thought he said, mainly by putting the page numbers of the book in parentheses. It is to be hoped that the book will soon be translated into English. Readers of this review who read German should not feel relieved of the task to go back to the original. I want to express my thanks to Professor Reiner Schürmann, Chairman of the Philosophy Department of the Graduate Faculty of the New School for Social Research, for valuable help in revising and editing this review.

a principle, which Jonas attempts, is not. In our present impasse, 'rational' and 'scientific' arguments alone cannot help. Nevertheless, it is much more important in the present world crisis to accept Jonas' faith in philosophy and his prophetic vision than to dwell on the deficiencies in his reasoning.

The 'solution' lies in the generation of a 'faith' in the future of humankind. Since philosophers have not been convincing when they have tried to construct a philosophy of *praxis* upon a philosophy of being, an ethics for our technological age is a task for prophets and not for intellectuals. What intellectuals can do is to remove the mental rubble that has been amassed during the last four centuries of Western history and that bars access to the doors of holistic and transcendental perception. Although Professor Jonas tries to perform this task, he may not have succeeded, since he deliberately avoids religious argumentation. But his book represents a step in the right direction. Because we believe that Jonas is 'emotionally right' but 'rationally wrong', this critique has been written with a 'bleeding heart'; if some readers feel it should not have been written under these circumstances, this reviewer may silently agree.

In what follows, I will be using terms such as 'religion' and 'the transcendental dimension' that will antagonize some readers. They are not Hans Jonas' terms. The aversion to that aspect of human experience to which they refer is, however, at the very bottom of our predicament. We will have occasion to elucidate this line of thought; but it should be stressed that when talking about 'religion' we mean a general human experience of the sacred and the holy (Otto 1958). We do not refer to either the established churches and denominations nor to the many corrupted forms of faith flourishing today in the United States, such as fundamentalism, 'moral majority', transcendental meditation, or the American perception of Eastern religions; neither do we refer to the many cults and gurus which populate the suburbs and exurbs of California. What is at stake – and what Jonas does not take into account – is the recognition that there is a realm of the unknown, a depth-dimension of being, a realm of mystery, of faith in things unseen, an experience of the *tremendum et fascinosum* that is manifest in human history but that has been repressed by formalistic rationalism, natural science, and technology but also by denominational dogmatism. This realm has been buried under a tombstone with the inscription 'God is dead'. Intellectuals can, at least, uncover the psychological reality of such experiences. Mythologists like Joseph Campbell, Mircea Eliade, Gerhardt Scholem, and, last but not least, Carl Georg Jung and the Eranos group have pointed the way to follow. Jonas undertakes a trip in this direction; but he hesitates to cross the threshold. Intellectuals look into the promised land like Moses, but they can never enter it.

We have chosen for discussion three groups of problems Jonas deals with: the dichotomy of fact and value; the biological roots of responsibility for others and for the future of humankind, especially the parent–child relationship; and Jonas' critique of what he calls the Marxist utopia.

The Dichotomy of Fact and Value

Jonas' main argument runs like this: Humankind has acquired, through science and technology, the power to influence nature and to change radically the conditions of human existence. Technology and industrialization have been enormously successful; but their very success has brought us to the brink of an abyss: the possible destruction of humankind. Our excessive power to change and to destroy creates an ethical responsibility to prevent such destruction. The basic principles of the new ethics are: humankind has no right to suicide; humankind must be preserved; human beings have a duty toward their progeny to enable them to live on this earth; the primary ethical imperative is that there should be a human species; the pursuit of national and individual interests does not justify endangering the existence of others.

These axiological postulates are derived by linking the ideas of the good and of value with purpose in human *and nonhuman* nature. It is argued that the higher purposes and end of humans must also be present, at least as a seed, in non-purposive human organs such as the digestive apparatus and in prehuman living entities. Purpose then is universal in nature although unconsciously and unintentionally. But purpose implies evaluation and thus value, that is, the idea of a norm, of a 'should be'. A norm, however, implies the idea of the good. Purpose, value, and the good in nature are the creation and the maintenance of life, including the life of humankind. Because today its existence is threatened, we have the moral duty to prevent this result.

The Kantian and neo-Kantian tradition made a sharp logical distinction between statements of fact and statements of value; between *Sein* and *Sollen*, is-ness and ought-ness, being and norm. This dualism, which Jonas helps to perpetuate, is a symptom of degeneration. In all premodern cultures moral values were derived from religious beliefs, from ideas and perceptions which were experienced as facts. The dichotomy of 'is' and 'ought to', of fact and value, although logically valid, is ontologically false. This is another way of saying that human beings have always derived their moral norms from something believed to be a fact of experience. The clearest example is the Ten Commandments; they are felt to be valid and binding because they originated in a command of God, a God who defined himself as: 'I am who I am' (Exod. 3:14), that is, as being itself. Thus the Ten Commandments were held to establish moral obligations because they originated in being. This is true of all moral codes with a religious origin.

The emergence of modernity (the last four hundred years in Western history) did not really bring about a change in the derivation of moral norms. Since the Enlightenment, such norms have been derived from nature and reason. That means that, in line with the cultural trends in the West, the derivation of values was secularized; instead of deriving the good from a religious and sacred dimension, men derived it from a natural and profane sphere, *but still from a realm of facts.* That realm of facts was demoted from the transcendent to the immanent, but facts were – and are – still considered a ground of value. Thus the 'ought to' was still derived from what 'is'. And Jonas remains within this tradition.

Jonas, however, fights a gigantic battle on two fronts: on the one hand, against the argument that one cannot derive an 'ought to' from an 'is' by pure logic; on the other hand, against what would be our own argument that the 'is' from which values are derived must be of a 'religious'/transcendental character. He tries to avoid this predicament by making a distinction between the 'religious' and the 'metaphysical'. He assumes the necessity and rationality of metaphysics as broader than pure logic and as independent of religious foundation. However, he admits that religious belief has an answer which philosophy must search for with only uncertain possibility of success (Jonas 1979, 91). He considers his basic imperative 'that man should be' as a metaphysical verity and rejects the denial of metaphysical truth by natural science. Jonas considers this denial as tautological; science deals only with physical objects and thus arrives at the nullification of all metaphysics (Jonas 1979, 91). However, Jonas himself derives his first moral principle 'that humankind should be' from observations about nature.

He starts with the wider imperative that there should be something and not nothing (Jonas 1979, 90). The 'should be' in this imperative represents a statement of value and not a statement of fact. This imperative that there should be something and not nothing is rooted in the Hebrew–Christian tradition, in the idea of the goodness of creation, which again is derived from the 'fact' that God said: 'Let there be light' (Gen. 1:3). Without this religious belief, it is not easy to justify the postulate that being is more valuable than nonbeing. Jonas argues that being is a necessary prerequisite of value; but this seems to be circular reasoning. If the positive evaluation of being is derived from value, and values are derived from facts, what is the ground for the positive evaluation for both? Only God could be the source and the ground for the goodness of both being and value; and the acknowledgement of this source is made impossible by the modern rejection of religion. Even Jonas, an ontologist and a metaphysician, is shying away from religious argumentation.

Jonas derives value from purpose and argues that purpose is universal in nature. This implies that there is no essential difference between 'subjective' (intentional) and 'objective' (unintentional) purpose. Jonas refers to human actions such as walking which have a conscious, intentional, subjective purpose; and to the workings of the digestive organs which fulfil a purpose of an objective nature without any conscious deliberate intention. Jonas asserts that will, aim, and purpose are *objectively* present in such reflexive phenomena of life. This assumption rests on a monistic theory of continuity in emergent evolution, from the atomic to the crystallic to the organic to the highest form of life in human consciousness. Because of this evolutionary continuity, the highest levels teach us something about the lower levels (Jonas 1979, 135). Jonas criticizes what he calls 'the abstinence of natural science' when it reduces the higher levels to the lower ones – eliminating final causes and recognizing only efficient causes in nature. He concludes that the conception of purpose without subjectivity – that is, purpose without conscious intent – is compatible with a scientific view of nature. Subjective conscious purpose must have emerged out of objective purpose in prehuman nature.

It is difficult to see the cogency of this argument unless it were based on intuitive faith and, more concretely, on religious belief. Natural science as we know it has not been able to 'explain' the great leaps in being: from nothingness to being; from inorganic being to life; and from nonhuman to human life with consciousness, will, purpose, and finite freedom in action. Science has *described* these stages and enlarged greatly our knowledge of *how* this evolution took place; but it has not been able – and probably never will be – to tell us *why*. There are questions which cannot be answered by science and logic; therefore, scientific positivism has established the postulate that they should be covered with silence (Wittgenstein 1963).

This, however, is only another way to state that ontological, metaphysical questions – the most pressing ones for humankind – require a nonscientific religious treatment. Jonas' argument is a magnificent rationalization of what human beings want to believe: that there is a plan and purpose in the universe and that it is good. There is no reason to reject such a belief because science cannot justify it unless one postulates that only science can give answers and that everything can be dealt with by the methods of science. This is the hubris and the superbia of the scientific establishment; it inflates the competence and jurisdiction of natural science and elevates a part into the whole: partial scientific knowledge is identified with all knowledge. And last but not least, this prohibition of metaphysics is not in itself a scientific judgment but a normative one: the scientific imperative that excludes all other sources of knowledge but 'scientific' ones is a normative postulate and not a logical conclusion from facts.

Jonas assumes that purpose implies value and that value implies the good. This chain of reasoning is again doubtful if based on purely logical and scientific grounds. That human beings can pursue good or bad purposes is obvious. If that is so, there must be another standard than purpose from which the idea of the good is derived. The universe, nature, and humankind, if purposive, may have good or bad purposes. Even if one rejects the idea of an accidental, haphazard, and purposeless universe, it could be the plaything of a malicious demon and could serve bad purposes. Even the belief in a purposeful deity does not necessarily imply a benevolent deity. Jonas' conviction about the connection between purpose, value, and the good requires, whether he admits this or not, faith in the goodness of creation. Thus Jonas, like all modern thinkers, is involved in a struggle with religion and in a futile attempt to arrive at a faith with the help of science and logic which could only be reached with a religious basis.

The Biological Roots of Responsibility for Humankind's Future

We turn now to Jonas' derivation of our moral responsibility toward others and toward the future of humankind from the parent–child relationship. His line of thought runs as follows: responsibility requires power; one is not responsible for an event one has not brought about. Responsibility rests on the causal imputation of past deeds (Jonas 1979, 172). There is, however, also a responsibility of power in respect to deeds to be done in the future: a responsibility for doing things because one has the power to do them. Thus the holding of power, the ability to do something, involves an obligation to do it. The holder of the power *should* exercise this power. This situation generates responsibility. 'If love is added, it lends wings to the responsibility through the dedication of the person who has learned to tremble for the fate of what is worth to be and what is loved' (Jonas 1979, 178). This is the kind of responsibility for the future of mankind that is needed today; and it will help in the understanding of the quoted passages to think of the statesmen and politicians who are and will be responsible for the future existence or nonexistence of mankind. Responsibility exists for the welfare of others whose welfare one has the power to affect. The careless driver acts irresponsibly not because he endangers himself but because he endangers others (Jonas 1979, 176). Such responsibility is not reciprocal: one is responsible to help those who are wanting and in need of help without compensation of any kind. The foremost example of this is the responsibility of parents for their helpless infant children. Jonas arrives finally at the categorical statement: '*the ultimate object of our responsibility for others is the preservation of the mutual loyalty on which the common We, society and community rests*' (Jonas 1979, 179). This responsibility for the needful other is 'substantial, a good in itself, imposing an absolute obligation, like any obligation imposed by nature', an 'irrevocable and unconditional obligation' (Jonas 1979, 179).

It is not possible to present here all of Jonas' complex and erudite arguments for the parallels between the responsibilities of the parents toward their infants and of the statesmen toward their fellow beings, toward society, and toward the future of mankind. In both cases he detects a primary responsibility of man for man. His argument about the chain of causation from purpose to value to the good, and his arguments about the responsibility to preserve humankind in the future, are interconnected: the preservation of humankind is a 'first command' 'because the possibility of goodness and greatness has to be kept open' (Jonas 1979, 186). The two responsibilities (of the parents and of the statesmen) have also in common the orientation toward the future. The aim of parental responsibility is nurture and education for the future life of the infant; the aim of the statesman is to protect the historical future of mankind.

Jonas derives his postulate of responsibility from evolution and from the innate love of parents for their offspring. The facts on which this derivation rests are doubtful. The idea of universal objective purpose, value, and goodness is a projection of ideals into nature. Jonas considers ambiguity as the essence of human nature (Jonas 1979, 381). Ambiguity is also the essence of the universe, of nature which produced humans. Without faith in a transcendental dimension, it is hard to maintain the belief in a continuous universe and a continuous evolution; without such faith a meaningless universe with everything human as an exception and aberration from the nonhuman world is much more plausible. This is why natural science cannot find a place for values in a world of facts.

The parent–child relationship is, like everything human, equally ambiguous. The facts about child murder, neglect, abandonment, abuse, mistreatment, and torture make this obvious. Some sociologists may interpret this as corruptions of the noble savage by society; but Jonas, who recognizes the ambiguity of human life, cannot use this escape. The nobility and validity of Jonas' ethos of responsibility are impaired by his attempts to derive ideals from nature and not from faith.

The Critique of Marxist Utopia

In his last two chapters, Jonas tries to connect his moral philosophy with some of today's political trends. He finds two ideologies which are dangerous to humankind: (a) the ideas of progress, which he relates to the Baconian ideal of power over nature through knowledge; and (b) the idea of liberation from physical necessity through material abundance and leisure, which he identifies with the 'Marxian utopia'. The two are so closely related in Jonas' view that he calls Marxism 'the executor of the Baconian ideal' (Jonas 1979, 256). The critique of Marxist utopia, it seems, is meant to be the underlying intent of the entire undertaking; indeed, it is hinted at in the very title of the book. *The Principle of Responsibility* is an explicit rejoinder to Ernst Bloch's *The Principle of Hope* (1959).

The striving for the ideals of progress and liberation requires the ever-increasing use of science, technology, and industrialization; these endeavors, however, endanger humankind because they have severed the solidarity between the human and the nonhuman organic world (Jonas 1979, 245–6). The ineluctable laws of ecology prevented any excessive power of any one species so that no one species could endanger the whole (Jonas 1979, 347). However, modern technology has invalidated this law and is endangering the globe. Jonas talks about these dangers only in the last chapters of his book. However, already in his first chapter he mentions as forms of excessive human power over nature prolongation of life, behaviour control, and genetic manipulation (Jonas 1979, 47 ff.). Later he mentions some of the widely discussed ecological dangers caused by 'the technical reconstruction of the earth by unchained technology' (Jonas 1979, 327).

Both capitalism and communism encounter the problem of food shortages. The attempts to overcome these shortages by new technologies and chemical methods are already today leading to chemical poisoning of inland and coastal waters (much of it caused by industry) and spread through the organic chain; salinization of the soil through continuous irrigation; erosion of the soil through overcultivation of grasslands; detrimental climatic effects through deforestation (with atmospheric reduction of oxygen). The ecological literature abounds with such examples. Jonas also warns that synthetic fertilizers will not solve the problem of scarcity of foodstuffs because they are forms of energy and, therefore, their shortage is part of the scarcity of energy. Similarly, the scarcity of mineral raw materials is connected with the ever-increasing amounts of energy necessary for the mining of deeper-lying sources of minerals, and thus ultimately caused by the shortage of energy. Jonas points to the shortage of non-renewable energy sources and the insufficient technologies to exploit the renewable ones, such as solar energy, and to the limits in the use of hydroelectricity. Finally, Jonas points to the ultimate thermal problem of the loss of energy in heat and the problem of entropy.

It may be significant for Jonas' 'optimism' that he mentions the danger of nuclear destruction, which for many is the greatest danger to the future of humankind, only in connection with nuclear fusion as a possible solution for the energy problem. In case fusion should become technically possible, he recommends its wise use and mentions likelihood of its abuse in the hands of the powerful (Jonas 1979, 337).

In view of the present political mood in the United States and the almost totally militarized situation in the world, such pious exhortations seem to be rather futile. It may be that Jonas assumes that the dangers to the existence of humankind are so well known and have been so deeply internalized in the minds of people as to make it unnecessary to point them out again. However, in view of the (perhaps subconscious) attitude of social sadism that permeates our present policies, this does not seem to be the case at all. There is a deep nihilistic mood of hate against humankind lurking behind the cuts in spending for social purposes, the resumption of chemical and biological warfare preparations, and the callous disregard for the health of children in the Third World in the vote against guidelines for artificial bottle feeding of infants – to say nothing about the irrational increase in spending for armaments and for ever-deadlier weapons such as cruise missiles, neutron bombs, and laser beams.

Jonas considers the prolongation of life as one of the questionable extensions of human power over nature (Jonas 1979, 47 ff.). However, he does not discuss one of the greatest dangers to the future of humanity: the population explosion. There is little doubt among experts that, with present technology and present economic and political institutions, the world as a whole will face hunger, malnutrition, and starvation. All these evils will, under present circumstances, be very unevenly distributed. There is much hue and cry about the increasing reality of genocide, war, politically manipulated starvation, terrorism, and violence. Some may be inclined to see in these trends a 'cunning of history' or of nature to bring about a decrease in population. The same could be said about the threat of nuclear war, which would certainly 'solve' the population problem but in an inhuman and unacceptable way, creating at the same time innumerable other insoluble problems. That these are not desirable solutions is obvious; but they raise questions for Jonas' new ethos of responsibility.

If we assume, for the sake of argument, that a reduction of population or at least a decline in its growth rate could be brought about by political means, does this mean 'preservation of mankind' in the sense Jonas uses this term throughout his book? He certainly means that we are responsible for the survival of human beings and everything that human existence includes; but how many human beings would fulfill this postulate? Could one not argue that war, even nuclear war, with its killing of millions of people, that genocide, starvation, even all the ecological ills caused by modern technology, would still be compatible with the 'preservation' of human beings as a species? Jonas' grand idea that there should be something rather than nothing, that there should be human beings and not merely nonhuman life and inorganic nature – could it still be fulfilled by a minimum number of people surviving? It is clear from the high moral tone of Jonas' book that this is not at all what he means. His basic paradigm, the care of the parents for their children, shows clearly that he is imbued with the spirit of charity, compassion, and love. His grand concept of 'responsibility' implies responsibility of each of us for each of us, for the caring for and sharing with all humankind. Jonas talks about the *total* responsibility of the parents for their children and of the statesmen for all of the subjects (Jonas 1979, 189–90). 'The statesman has to take care of everything' (Jonas 1979, 192); one can assume that this means also: of everybody.

This raises, of course, such questions as the legitimacy of abortion and of the 'right to life', where life and our responsibility begin, from what point in time we are responsible for its existence. Jonas touches on this problem, for whose existence are we responsible, when he deals with the prolongation of life by modern medicine (Jonas 1979, 47 ff.). He points out that this apparent 'escape from the curse of mortality' may 'result in a detriment for humankind' (Jonas 1979, 50). If this is so, then what are the limits of our responsibility? Does it include the obligation to promote medical research into longevity even if this longevity is detrimental for humankind as a species? Such questions raise the ultimate one: Do we have the right to prevent overpopulation by even quite 'humane' means, if this brings shortening of the lifespan to many individuals? Is this what is meant by 'responsibility for the preservation of humankind'?

Jonas sees in the environmental dangers and limits 'a veto of nature' against the utopia of material progress and abundance' (Jonas 1979, 332). He sees clearly that they are not caused merely by errors in the technological and economic exploitation of nature but that they are essential characteristics of modern science, technology, and economy. The dangers lie in the *over-dimensionality* of these endeavors (Jonas 1979, 251). Our civilization suffers from the compulsion to exercise its power over nature without restraints and thus has brought about the dangers of destruction of humankind. To say 'no' to nonbeing, to resist the technological temptations, has become a primary moral obligation (Jonas 1979, 249).

Marxism vs. Capitalism: A Simplistic Opposition

Jonas then turns to the question whether Marxism or capitalism is better equipped to meet these dangers. He sees Marxism as the executor of the Baconian ideal of material progress. Marxism tries to integrate Baconian domination of nature with a reconstruction of society and the expectation of a new superior human being; and only Marxism can today be considered seriously as the source of a new ethos (Jonas 1979, 250). However, Marxism builds on the technological successes of capitalism. Without that technology, equality and fairness of income distribution would not be attainable goals. Without the technical possibility of material abundance, the socialist ideal could not even be conceived (Jonas 1979, 258). Jonas considers abundance under capitalism as an 'irrational' goal and, in its capitalist form, to be '*without justice*' (Jonas 1979, 251; italics mine). Hence, the attractiveness of Marxist ideals in spite of the fact that both systems require the same technology.

A comment on Jonas' terminology. He uses the term 'Marxism' to mean every system that is not capitalist, without defining these terms. The economies existing today are all mixtures of 'command' and 'free market' economies. There are great differences in the degrees and proportions of these mixtures, ranging from the overwhelming command character of the Russian and Chinese economies to the predominance of private enterprise in the United States. However, the term Marxism for those command economies is misleading because the ideas of Marx do not really apply to present-day communism or socialism. 'Statist' would be a better term; 'state capitalism' would also be appropriate but clumsy. Also, the term 'capitalism' is by no means unequivocal. England, France, West Germany, and Japan, although considered capitalist, contain many more statist elements than the United States. There are, of course, enormous political and cultural differences between Marxism and capitalism as Jonas uses these terms; but *economically* the differences are of degree, not of kind. Even the United States has a mixed economy to which terms like oligopoly, monopoly, managerial, and corporate capitalism would apply much more than the term free-enterprise system. 'Marxism' and 'capitalism' have become rather invectives and ideological insults on the present political scene in the United States. However, we shall follow Jonas' terminology, keeping these qualifications in mind.

In order to provide protection against future destruction, Marxism, according to Jonas, would have to change from a utopia of abundance to a 'modest' non-eschatological orientation. Jonas is ambivalent about this possibility. At first, he gives Marxism a plus but finally he arrives at a negative answer (Jonas 1979, 271–86). His initial positive answer (Jonas 1979, 256–70) is based on the commonly used argument that production for use is more rational than production for profit. Central planning to satisfy collective needs might avoid the waste of the competitive market and production for extravagant consumerism (Jonas 1979, 260). However, there are, on the other side of the scale, the defects of a centralized bureaucracy; the greater flexibility of a competitive market may be preferable. Profitability is essentially an irrational factor which generates cost-benefit rationality (measured in money) in production but irrationality in consumption (Jonas 1979, 261; Weisskopf 1971, 109). Whether 'production for `use' is preferable to 'production for profit' depends on the definition of the needs to be satisfied, basically a psychological question. From the purely economic point of view, the relative merits of a competitive free market versus a centrally led bureaucratic economy are difficult to determine.

There is, however, a definite advantage of centralized power in preventing the destruction of humankind (Jonas 1979, 262). A 'rational,' benevolent, well-informed tyranny could prevent the dangers of destruction (Jonas 1979, 262). Here Jonas raises the most vital question of his book: How can an intellectual, ethical, and political elite which would take on responsibility for the future of humankind be created and with what powers should such an elite be invested (Jonas 1979, 263)? Jonas cannot, of course, provide a recipe for such an elite; but he sees in Marxism some traits which would facilitate this process. He attributes to Marxism a 'moralism' – to live and to sacrifice for the whole – and he also attributes to Marxism a spirit of frugality (Jonas 1979, 263). However, the Puritan–Protestant worldly asceticism, described by Max Weber as one of the decisive factors in early capitalism, has been lost in the development from an economy of scarcity to one of relative affluence; and this trend has also influenced all kinds of Marxist economies, to which Jonas himself ascribes the ideals of abundance and leisure. Jonas raises the question whether in spite of the ascetic element in communism it can be turned away from the goal of abundance to the goal of preventing extreme poverty over the entire globe and the destruction of humankind (Jonas 1979, 275). Can the enthusiasm for the utopia of abundance and freedom from necessity be rechanneled into enthusiasm for 'modesty' and restraint in material opulence? This is not only a domestic question in the Western countries but a central point in the global class struggle for which there are *theoretical* Marxist answers but no answers in communist praxis (Jonas 1979, 265). Here Jonas points again to hope rooted in faith as the only ground for such an expectation.

Socialism, according to Jonas, may have advantages over capitalist democracy in promoting sacrifice for the sake of preservation of humanity because it embraces 'equality'. A turn toward economic sacrifice and asceticism would require the general conviction that the distribution of sacrifice is based on 'justice' and that justice requires some sort of 'equality'. But even a Marxist society, with the same organization of production and technology as prevalent today, would not be classless and would have difficulties convincing the 'less equal' to sacrifice for the 'more equal'.

Jonas struggles with the problems of the 'noble lie' and of 'false consciousness.' He does not reject a policy of introducing the 'principle of fear' under the mask of the principle of 'hope' (Jonas 1979, 266) – raising the hope of future abundance in order to induce present sacrifices, although the hope would be disappointed because the sacrifices are intended to prevent disaster, not to establish opulence. He ascribes correctly to such fictions as the ideals of abundance and equality an important role: they are a factor in the events of history (Jonas 1979, 270). Such fictions are what Plato called *doxai* (opinions, not truths); sometimes a useful *doxa* has to be false because the truth might be intolerable. This is perhaps an important truth of our present situation: we do not have an elite which would lead us in the right direction (preserving humanity); anyway, no leadership which would get the masses to sacrifice personal benefits for the sake of others; they may have to be deceived about the goals by a 'rosy' utopia.

After these preliminary credits to Marxism, Jonas reverses his conclusions on the basis of what he calls a 'concrete examination of Marxist reality'

(Jonas 1979, 271 ff.). Communist countries have not eliminated the profit motive and the maximization drive; they have only collectivized it and directed it against other countries (Jonas 1979, 271). Competition with other countries and the alleged necessity for armaments induce every industrial economy, capitalist and communist alike, to destroy the environment. World communism would not be a protection against regional and national egoism (Jonas 1979, 273). Marxism embraces, as said before, the same cult of technics as capitalist societies, even more so; communism is imbued with an almost religious faith in technology (Jonas 1979, 276). Marxism, like capitalism, is obsessed with technological 'progress' and accepts the Baconian ideal of power over and exploitation of nature. Like capitalism, it generates technological alienation and uses technology as an 'opium for the masses'. That the division of labor and the subjection of workers to the machine is a source of alienation – an idea expressed in Marx's early writings and more and more spreading in the counterculture in the West – is not accepted by Marxian doctrine in Russia (Jonas 1979, 275 f.). Communists do not accept any doctrine of limits to growth, and they hold an engineering view of humans and of society. 'Behavior control' through political oppression was rampant in Russia long before it became fashionable in Western and other societies, although the instruments may have been modernized (Jonas 1979, 271–9).

Jonas also rejects – and rightly so – the utopia of a new human being that would emerge in a classless society. He is highly doubtful of the assumptions about this society: its cultural superiority, the moral superiority of its citizens, and the creation of material abundance, a precondition of the first two assumptions (Jonas 1979, 280–85). However, he does not stress sufficiently that such assumptions are also made by capitalist ideologists and admirers of the free-market system. All three assumptions are made and applied by today's conservative spokesmen in the United States. Thus when Jonas finally rejects Marxism as a way to preserve humanity, he does so with arguments which apply also to capitalism and Western societies. Actually, without making this quite clear, he feels correctly that the worldwide trends in communist, socialist, and capitalist countries are alike and are diametrically opposed to his principle of responsibility for the future of humanity. Although he is attracted at first by certain traits of Marxism which might be favorable to the realization of his principle of responsibility, he then takes back this 'plus' and rejects Marxism with arguments that apply equally to capitalism.

Utopia East and West

In his last chapter, Jonas presents his anti-utopian answer to Marxism; but again his answer contains also an implicit critique of capitalism. He discusses at first what he should have discussed earlier – the external limits to abundance: the problems of food shortages, raw-material shortages, energy limits, and thermal overheating of the atmosphere. His insufficient attention to the dangers of nuclear destruction and of the population explosion has been mentioned. In any case, all these dangers and obstacles to abundance are not merely Marxist but equally capitalist problems. Seemingly concerned mainly with the 'Marxist utopia', Jonas criticizes the 'civilization of always more' (Bertrand de Jouvenel), communist and capitalist alike.

To Jonas, the utopia of abundance stands in the way of meliorism. The utopian, fascinated by his vision of the ideal future, 'hates everything that is' (but so does the nihilist) and opposes all attempts to improve it, short of complete revolution. This was the point of view of the early socialists who rejected social reform, social legislation, even unionism; they believed that capitalism could not be improved and was doomed in any case. If Jonas is fighting this kind of Marxism, he is fighting with the past (or with some insignificant splinter groups among Marxists). The entire trend of Western labor parties and unionism in the twentieth century has been toward melioristic revisionism and, in the United States, toward business unionism (Perlman 1949) to improve the position of workers within the existing system. This led to the 'deproletarianization' of large parts of the laboring class in the West. In a way, even Russian communism could be interpreted as a revisionist accommodation and as a turning away from the utopia of a classless and stateless society. The idea of the 'withering away' of the state was given up and turned into its opposite, an all-powerful state ruled by a 'third-class' bureaucracy.

Although Jonas is right that utopia is antagonistic to melioristic reform, the present despair about 'liberal' reform in the United States may be caused more by the *absence* of any utopian beliefs than by their presence. There is a movement away from social change and reform, from what, with a sneering bias, is called 'liberalism'; there is an attempt to dismantle all the institutions of what is known as New Deal, Fair Deal, Great Society, and War against Poverty. All this, however, is a far cry from a turn toward responsibility for the preservation of humankind. Rather it represents a revival of the class struggle in reverse: it is a struggle of the haves to push the have-nots back into the position of the laboring classes in early capitalism. For those who share Jonas' concern with caring and responsibility for the helpless, this trend is a source of despair – and not the despair about the impossibility of a classless society. Despair about reform, the throwing in of the towel on social betterment, is a Western capitalist phenomenon and not a Marxist or communist attitude.

Jonas devotes considerable space to the content and substance of the Marxist ideal of a classless society. He does so in spite of the paucity of material on this subject (recognized by him, Jonas 1979, 112–43). He relies almost exclusively on Marx's writings on this subject and, for modern ideas, on the writings of Ernst Bloch. This is a dead-end street; the idea of a classless society does not play an important part in today's Marxist praxis. Jonas reminds us that the classless society represents to Marx the famous leap from the realm of necessity into the realm of freedom. This leap is expected to bring about liberation from 'necessary' labour and a life of 'leisure', a concept stressed especially by Ernst Bloch. Such a classless society would realize the principle: 'From each according to his abilities, to each according to his needs' (Jonas 1979, 344; Marx 1978). It is stressed by Jonas that Marx and most modern Marxists consider a highly developed technology as a prerequisite of a classless society. However, Marx always, especially in his early writings, considered the division of labor, an inevitable by-product of technology, as a cause of alienation. But modern technology, even in a classless society, will require more and more mechanization, automation, cybernation, and robots and, therefore, more and more division of labor. It will need a growing class of mechanics, engineers, and scientists (Jonas 1979, 146). Thus there is an inner contradiction in the theory of classlessness. Marxists, being obsessed with the idea of the class struggle and with the capitalist class as the archenemy, overlooked the dangers of technology for liberation and freedom. This may be excusable in the case of Marx, who shared the technical optimism of the nineteenth century, but is not so easily explained in the writings of modern Marxists.[3]

If the Marxist (and incidentally the capitalist) optimism in respect to technology were justified and the majority of people would be freed from necessary utilitarian labor, the problem of redefining 'leisure' would arise. Ernst Bloch views the classless society as 'the earthly paradise of leisure' (Jonas 1979, 348 ff.). This is not a new and not an exclusively Marxist ideal. In the 1950s and 1960s, when there was a general belief in infinite economic growth, affluence, and abundance in the United States, it was predicted that we would soon reach such a situation in which only a minority would find employment in the traditional sense (Weisskopf 1966; Michael 1962; Perk 1966; Galbraith 1958). Ernst Bloch talks about the happy marriage of body and mind (*Geist*); he predicts the elimination of the difference between manual and intellectual labour in the classless society; he extols the possibility that human beings, freed from necessary labour by technics, will seek their happiness in pursuing a 'hobby'. Jonas criticizes all this cogently: with the body the mind will also become unemployed. One cannot meaningfully fill one's day with leisure by pursuing a hobby. Bloch criticizes capitalism because its alienated form of labour makes necessary outlets for certain human 'needs': athletics and sports for kinetic-muscular need; crossword puzzles and chess problems for intellectual needs; nourishment with visual images on TV for perceptual-sensory needs (Jonas 1979, 352). But to build a fulfilling life on these pursuits seems impossible.

One could, without the help of Marxism or free-market libertarianism, envisage a society in which work is separated from income and income is separated from the pursuit of profit and gain. Such a society would require a redefinition of needs, of work, and of leisure. That was the attitude among various social groups in the past. When the civil service was built up in England in the nineteenth century, a class of people emerged whose goal was the rendering of public service. Income had little to do with the substance of their work. The same was true in the monastic orders of the Middle Ages, especially among the Benedictines: their work and their 'income' had nothing to do with each other. After tilling the soil, their 'leisure pursuits' were pastoral and religious activity for the glory of God. One could

3 For example, Marcuse (1955) expects from technology the liberation from unnecessary alienated labor.

imagine that in the future people might fill their nonworking time by producing cultural goods and rendering important services not destined to be sold for gain.

Our present concept of leisure means not producing for sale. But the term 'leisure' could be replaced by the term 'play' in the sense of Huizinga's *Homo Ludens*: he considers all cultural activity as 'play on a high level'. Bertrand de Jouvenel has defined play as 'the activity which procures satisfaction in such a way that the goal is merely the final point of such an activity; labour is the activity which is only justified by the end' (de Jouvenel 1959, 15). In a 'utopian' society work could assume more of the characteristics of play thus defined; the sharp distinction between work and play would be obliterated because it serves only the purposes of a profit-oriented economy. People would then live their lives joyfully, even in suffering, until the end, with modest demands on the material level and with unchained creativity in all other dimensions.

Be this as it may, Jonas rejects the utopia of abundance (at least in its Marxist form) because of the external limits and the internal contradictions we have discussed. He emphasizes also what he calls 'the anthropological error of utopia' (Jonas 1979, 383). His starting point is Ernst Bloch's doctrine of the 'not yet', the non-essentiality of all previous humanity, coupled with the eschatological expectation of a future new human person. That this is one of the deepest roots of all utopian thinking and feeling, and not dependent on any specific vision of any ideal future, is recognized but insufficiently stressed by Jonas; he does not see – and he cannot rightly admit – that his call for a new morality of responsibility for the future also requires such an eschatological expectation and that such an expectation cannot be pushed aside as crude belief in miracles (Jonas 1979, 374). Bloch grounds his utopia in an ontology of the 'not-yet-being' (*Noch-Nicht-Sein*) condensed in the formula: 'The subject is not yet its predicate, S is not yet P' (Jonas 1979, 376). The subject has a longing for self-actualization; innate is a hidden teleology: the utopian dream says yes to the telos. The capitalist human being longs to become the socialist Adam.

Jonas distinguishes this utopia from previous similar ones because it assumes, not a complete universe with a tendency toward actualization, but a universe which is – in principle – incomplete. Bloch rejects everything in the past that seems to most of us very positive: great art and all great science, which, for him, is mere *Vor-schein*, a prelude to future socialist glory. Jonas is at his greatest in refuting this negativism vis-à-vis the past when he describes his experience of perfection and fulfilment in contemplating Bellini's *Madonna* in the sacristy of St Zacharia in Venice: 'where in a balance of gigantic forces the universe seems to hold still for one heartbeat to allow the highest reconciliation of contradictions in a work of human hands' (Jonas 1979, 381). This is not a prelude but timeless glory. It is 'utopia' beyond any 'not-yet', 'dispersed moments of eternity in the flux of time' (Jonas 1979, 381).

Here Jonas reveals his 'faith' and his 'religion'. 'The real human being was always there … in his heights and lows, in his greatness and wretchedness, his happiness and his misery, his exculpation and his guilt – briefly in his essential *ambiguity*' (Jonas 1979, 382; italics mine). Trying to remove this ambiguity means eliminating the human being and its inexhaustible and inexplicable freedom. Human beings are never unequivocally good or bad, saints or monsters. 'To believe in the possibility of one without the other … is an illusionary secularistic conception of nature and of happiness.' It is contradicted even by 'the most naive religious knowledge about sin and temptation but also by profane knowledge of indolence and caprice of heart' (Jonas 1979, 382). The great danger today lies in the utopian belief of futurology and social engineering, in the possibility of constructing an unambiguous future human being and society. The hope lies not in robotization but in free human beings with their inner conflicts and contradictions.

The ideal of an unambiguous and completely 'rational' and 'efficient' human being is attributed by Jonas to Bloch and to Marxism; but it is also the ideal of modern capitalism, of the 'new utopians' among the computer experts and organization men in the West. The almost complete automation and cybernation of work and production, administration, and research aims at eliminating 'human error' when the machine and the robot triumphs (Anders 1961; Boguslaw 1965; Scorer 1977).

Jonas reduces the error of utopia to a mistaken idea of the essence of the human being (Jonas 1979, 383), which is his essential 'questionability' (*Fragwürdigkeit*). 'Man is a marginal phenomenon' (*Grenzphänomen*) of nature, with his innate transcendence, his open either-or which can never escape the 'as well as'; his unanswerable 'why' and 'what for'. 'These margins cannot be transgressed into a future of light without shadows; nor backwards into the unequivocal animal nature' (Jonas 1979, 383). There is no existence without 'alienation' except in moments of mystical elevation. It is the basic error of utopia 'to try to translate the mystical here and now into a continuous objective public existence' (Jonas 1979, 383), into a classless society or the immanent kingdom of God in the here and now.

We have translated some of the most crucial and moving statements of Jonas from his answer to the utopia of both East and West; it is a negation of utopia, which is incompatible with the human essence. The desire for a utopia is in contradiction to the 'truth of man' (Jonas 1979, 384), This truth implies 'that there is no such thing as the nature of man; he is neither good nor bad; but he has the ability for goodness and badness – yes, to be both at the same time – and this is part of his essence' (Jonas 1979, 385). The human condition is not that there is a wealth of goodness and virtue buried in man which has only to be liberated in order to become actual. There are merely predispositions to various forms of self-actualization; but there is a 'duty to improve the chances for the *bonum humanum*' (Jonas 1979, 385), the moral obligations toward justice, goodness, and reason (which I would translate 'common sense'). But Jonas wants to free these moral demands from what he calls 'the bait of utopia' (Jonas 1979, 385–6). Unmerciful optimism has to be replaced by compassionate skepticism (Jonas 1979, 386). It is not sufficient to identify and remedy 'bad' conditions such as slavery and misery. Any actions to remove such conditions raise 'the riddle of freedom' with its hidden errors such as indolence and sloth on the one hand and arrogance and superbia on the other hand; both are dangers to any movement toward the *bonum humanum* (justice, goodness, and common sense). At the end, Jonas talks about preserving 'God's image'. We have to learn awe and trembling, which unveil to us something 'sacred, something that cannot be violated under any circumstances, a sacredness which can be envisioned without religion' (Jonas 1979, 393). The ultimate aim is the flourishing of human beings in their unstinted (*unverkümmerte*) reality.

As said before: A critique, or even an evaluation of Jonas' book is such an awesome task because of its high idealistic moral standards, which one has to admire and to accept, and the difficulties of agreeing with his philosophical derivations of these moral precepts. Jonas presents a prophetic exhortatory tract to save humanity from self-destruction. In this attempt he keeps within the limits of the intellectual academic tradition. He is critical of this tradition and rejects many of the tenets of deterministic, positivistic, naturalistic science; but he still derives his ideal of responsibility from a 'scientific, rational' world outlook. He rests his appeal for preserving humanity on what some might consider an anthropomorphistic interpretation of nature, with purpose, value, and goodness as part of it; and his critique of utopia is based on what he calls an anthropological error of utopia, essentially a scientific procedure. It could be interpreted as a desperate outcry of an intellectual who wants to find a way out of a predicament which is insoluble with purely intellectual and scientific means. This is perhaps an unfair evaluation coming from another intellectual who finds himself in the same position; but who knows a brother better than a brother?

However, Jonas does not build us a bridge from what is to what he wants the future to be. *His ideal of responsibility itself is a utopia* and may be unrealizable for reasons similar to those he advances against the utopia of progress and against the Marxist utopia. The world is ruled today by destructive forces, by individual and social greed, aggression and destruction in alliance with dread, fear, and anxiety about the future. Human reaction to the threat of nonbeing has always been a mixture of dread and courage, and the courage was almost always supported by a utopia (Tillich 1956–75, 157 ff.). Today, dread has more and more replaced courage.

American psychology has rejected Freud's concept of the death instinct. It should have recognized that there is, in our present world, an overwhelming death *drive*; we are driven, internally and externally, toward growing violence and destruction. How can, out of this witches' brew, a general feeling of responsibility and caring arise? Where are the groups, the nations, the leaders who would form the avant-garde of a movement toward this responsibility? Everything that is done today consists in fighting destruction with means of destruction: poverty with spending cuts, arms with more arms, crime with more prisons, guns with more guns, and so forth. There is no philosophy that could make sense of all this. Only the simplest kind of religious belief in a divine providence that has, for the punishment of our sins, surrendered – perhaps temporarily – the world to demonic and satanic forces could explain the present trends – a belief which is hardly acceptable to academic intellectuals, including this author.

There are today two possible world views: One can believe that humanity is different from the rest of nature; that humans are cursed with consciousness, finite freedom, ambiguity, and openness to temptation and self-destruction; that humanity is an aberration in the universe, a dead-end street, possibly a divine experiment that failed and has to be brought to an end. In this case – compatible with the present conditions of the globe – Jonas' principle that humankind has to be preserved would be invalid.

One can also believe in the goodness of creation and in the human person being an *imago dei*. This is Jonas' conviction. It raises, in view of the present apocalyptic situation, the age-old question of the theodicy: How did evil come into this world so that human beings are exposed to temptation and evil? If we are *imagines dei*, there may be hope. After reviewing Jonas' magnificent book, one does not dare to call such hope a utopia.

References

Anders, Günther. 1961. *Die Antiquiertheit des Menschen*. Munich: Beck.

Bloch, Ernst. 1959. *Das Prinzip Hoffnung*. Frankfurt: Suhrkamp.

Boguslaw, Robert. 1965. *The New Utopians*. Englewood Cliffs: Prentice Hall.

Galbraith, John Kenneth. 1958. *The Affluent Society*. Boston: Houghton Mifflin.

Jonas, Hans. 1979. *Das Prinzip Verantwortung: Versuch einer Ethik für die technologische Zivilisation*. Frankfurt: Insel Verlag.

Jouvenel, Bertrand de. 1959. 'Organisation du travail et l'aménagement de l'existence'. *Free University Quarterly* 7(2).

Marcuse, Herbert. 1955. *Eros and Civilization*. Boston: Beacon.

Marx, Karl. 1978. 'Critique of the Gotha Program'. In *The Marx-Engels Reader*, edited by Robert C. Tucker, 525–41. New York: W.W. Norton.

Michael, Donald N. 1962. *Cybernation: The Silent Conquest*. Santa Barbara: Center for the Study of Democratic Institutions.

Otto, Rudolph. 1958. *The Idea of the Holy*. New York: Oxford University Press.

Perk, William. 1966. 'The Great Transformation'. *American Scholar* 35(2): 358–69.

Perlman, Selig. 1949. *The Theory of the Labor Movement*. New York: Augustus M. Kelley.

Scorer, Richard Segar. 1977. *The Clever Moron*. London: Routledge & Kegan Paul.

Tillich, Paul. 1956–75. 'Die politische Bedeutung der Utopie im Leben der Völker'. In *Gesammelte Werke*, edited by Paul Tillich. Stuttgart: Evangelisches Verlagswerk.

Weisskopf, Walter A. 1966. 'The Psychology of Abundance'. In *Looking Forward: The Abundant Society*, edited by Walter A. Weisskopf and Raghavan N. Iyer. Santa Barbara: Center for the Study of Democratic Institutions.

———. 1971. *Alienation and Economics*. New York: Dutton.

Wittgenstein, Ludwig. 1963. *Logisch-philosophische Abhandlung, Tractatus logico-philosophicus*. Frankfurt am Main: Suhrkamp.

Chapter 3
Ethics of Responsibility: Discourse-ethical Perspective of the Justification Problem

Holger Burckhart

Dedicated to Gunnar Skirbekk, Bergen (Norway)

Initial Considerations on Responsibility as a Topic of Practical Philosophy/Ethics

In ethics responsibility is traditionally determined by causally effected human activity, which is attributed to different individuals. Irrespective of whether we are referring to co-subjects, circumstances or objects,[1] when ascribing responsibility we claim that an agent (an acting subject), whose wilful autonomic action is presupposed, is able to stand towards himself and towards others for his action and, if necessary, for its impact. This means that he is able to account for the motivational and/or relevant reasons for his action.

This expectation is drawn from the freedom to act that we attribute to ourselves and, as logical subjects, imply reciprocally – at least since Kant. Without such an imputation, discourse about responsibility would be senseless, at least in the moral sense, and limited to morally neutral causality (see also Gewirth 1978, Steigleder 1999, Düwell 2000). According to this first instance, responsibility seems to simply be an aspect of our moral competence and of its development or formation, and not something that results from our onto- and phylogenetic development or something that is quasi-biologically natural and characteristic of humans. Initially, and as a result of Kant's idea of liberty, responsibility implies a reciprocal expectation. It means that we *expect* ourselves, and any other logical subject, to be able to justify our actions and thoughts – including, and in particular, the resulting consequences of those actions and thoughts. This, in turn, means that we can reasonably represent our actions and thoughts. Here, we attribute a *first moral quality* to responsibility, as we insinuate that it includes freedom of action as well as the ability to substantiate. In other words, we expect an individual – that is, a person who is aware of his or her own existence, or an eccentric positional living being – not only to make its actions and thoughts the subject of a theoretic-formalistic discussion, but also to take responsibility for them. Thus we start

1 In natural law it was to both non-human and non-living ecospherical elements (such as meteorological conditions, which were personified and to which sacrifices were made) that 'responsibility' was attributed in the sense of legal responsibility.

attributing responsibility by simply stating something, and in so far as we engage ourselves through the act of stating we commit ourselves to substantiating such statements and our motives for implementing it.

Making something the subject of a discussion (that is, talking about something) is the first stage of the principal obligation to state reasons.[2] In this case, responsibility is determined by the individual attribution of causality of freedom; that is, by implying the existence of somebody else, and reclaiming for oneself the idea that acts or thoughts are 'originated', so that there would have been alternative actions or thoughts. This would make it possible to give reasons for acting or thinking in one way rather than another. In this way responsibility primarily refers to a personal-individual responsibility for some decision, and a subsequent responsibility derived from – or at least caused by – the first responsibility (see also Burckhart 2000).[3] Herewith a *second level of moral quality* is given.

Let us look at this problem even more radically. We bear responsibility, but how is it *possible* for us to do so? What are the sensuous requirements we imply and redeem anticipatively?[4]

According to the above, a reasonable discourse about responsibility can be excluded if we subsume it as a part of the human biological constitution. But we cannot reduce responsibility to a specific moral framework like 'welfare' or 'fairness'. And it is also problematic to consider responsibility normatively, in relation to the human being or to human dignity (see also Böhler 1998, as well as Burckhart 2000). This – at least if we use a metaphysical-ontological version of the concept – would result in the unpleasant consequence of making impossible any reason why there should be an obligation to act – that is, an obligation to assume responsibility. In any case, such an obligation cannot be substantiated without the allegation that responsibility is a part of being *human*. This would only be possible at the expense of a petitio principii (Apel 2000, especially 27–38). The only way out seems to be the arguable (or at least dialogic) statement that responsibility is an indispensable moment of the reasonable implementation of reference to humans. In this case, a human is seen as a sample of the species,

2 An interesting circle arises on one hand from the situation of the responsibility of 'responsibility' (can we take responsibility for making 'responsibility' responsible or for claiming it to be such?) or on the other hand from the modes of justifying (feelings next to arguments, speech next to pictures and imagery) with which we present at the same time ourselves and possibly also our idea of 'responsibility', or of 'taking responsibility' (pictures claiming co-responsibility [*Guernica*]), and also explain ourselves for the mode we choose to express how we 'assume responsibility'. In other words, the responsibility mode is identical with the explanation medium of the choice of the responsibility medium.

3 Within the framework of scientific responsibility this leads to a dilemma – about which scientists have expressed their concern and which has been rejected by ethics – between utilization of knowledge and research as allegedly 'socially neutral'. Here, subsequent responsibility is removed from the research process.

4 I see these issues as analogous to Kant's introductory question in his theoretical philosophy. They are targeted at transcendentality.

which is claimed to be rational and able to refer back to others as well as to itself, and to reflect the same – that is, to be able to return to this reference. I will return to this possibility below. Herewith a third stage of the moral aspect of responsibility has been attained. To gain additional insight into dimensions of the term 'responsibility', further differentiations are necessary.

In accordance with Kurt Bayertz, I strictly distinguish – both synchronously and diachronously – the imputation insight of responsibility from the causality insight and the principal insight (Bayertz 1995). *Responsibility as imputation* represents the first stage of the history of responsibility in Western ethics. According to Bayertz, this results from the relationship between humans and nature or the embeddedness of the human in nature. The cause of something – perhaps a natural phenomenon or human or animal action – is 'guilty'. In this form, liability is given to nature and any complaint is made against nature.[5] This corresponds to a sociomorphic or anthromorphic interpretation of nature (Bayertz 1995, 6–7).

The consolidation of the reflection of causality, an event that occurred in the history of philosophy, led to the emancipation of a 'rule of logic'. *Causality* gains its own dignity and is not simply the explanation of a plan of vengeance, impregnated with morality, any longer.

One consequence of this change was the separation of nature and society, of standard and natural law. Responsibility was limited to the autonomous person, who was able to act and to cause. Kant's third antinomy is an excellent example of this; it addresses the problem of 'causality out of necessity' versus 'causality out of freedom'. First we see human emancipation from a stance dominated by nature, through which responsibility was *transcendentally*, *anthropologically* 'turned', which made the idea of responsibility possible.

The third stage urbanizes and radicalizes the transcendental idea of autonomy. The reasoned object *per se* is not the subject of guilt or the subject of responsibility, but the individual as acting subject becomes the holder of responsibility. Responsibility is thus the *principle* of human action, and we reach the above-mentioned *third stage of the moral aspect* of responsibility.

Accordingly, in the early stages of moral development responsibility can be understood as a collective responsibility, independent from individual autonomy. In the second stage the human is identified as an individual actor and as transcendental – philosophically, and qua autonomy, it will be possible for him to take responsibility or to be guilty. This requires the categorical imperative and the commission of the act, on one hand, and on the other the categorical imperative requires exactly this individual responsibility with respect to the moral law. Only at the third stage does the individual person become a social, intentionally acting subject.

5 See also the mentioned proceedings against animals. Here the idea of causality has to be understood as an explanation model and not as a thinking category (see Bayertz 1995, 6–7).

The individual is no longer just one component of a prestabilized cosmos, as an autonomous, categorically composed subject, but is a part of a social community that must be able to take responsibility for her, and for which she must also be able to take responsibility.

This definition of responsibility is used metaphorically nowadays. The current stage of development started with the Aristotelian–Christian standardized ethics that pursued a superordinated cosmos, which led to a Judeo-Christian commitment ethics, according to which God ceded us the world, and subsequently to Kant's duty-based ethics, which appropriated an exploitation of our freedom.

First, the qualitatively new sense of collective responsibility – not towards the clan, but towards the survival and existence of the world – altered the focus on responsibility. Hans Jonas, who saw responsibility as a principle of being a human, provided a new quality of responsibility.[6]

Hans Jonas binds responsibility to our 'authority' (or competency) to act. This also means, for him, our 'authority' to take responsibility through acting, to feel and show (in the sense of justifying) responsibility for the consequences of one's actions. This in turn includes responsibility for the evaluation of our actions and their consequences. Höffe defines this trilamination as responsibility for liability, for accountability, and for action (Höffe 1993).

As it is within our power to take action, it is in our power to take responsibility – according to Jonas. We have to do so: it is given to us to take responsibility; therefore it is an integral part of ourselves. Such a metaphysical-ontological concept takes us back to Aristotle. Even Jonas has to recognize this. Although his way of reasoning about theology, biology, and moral psychology contrasts Aristotle's determination of responsibility, metaphysical teleology and human entelechy remain, for him, reductionist, personalized terms of responsibility. The latter becomes the archetypical responsibility relationship in Jonas' notes about the relationship between parent and child or between politicians.

Correspondingly, Jonas cannot overcome the personalized, concrete sense of responsibility (Böhler 1998). Through the metaphysical-ontological foundation on one hand, and the reduction of responsibility to a double-digit relation and even to a hierarchical relation on the other, Jonas closes his mind to the view that responsibility always involves a 'co'. I am responsible for my action, for example with respect to the family, state, society, or nature. I must take into account their perspectives and must adapt my actions correspondingly. I am therefore 'co-responsible' (Apel and Burckhart 2001). To put it more precisely, I – as an individual – must realize that my responsibility, as co-responsibility, has to exceed the individual attribution of those who are responsible or concerned, and has to be orientated towards the world, or towards the whole. This does not

6 It is only on empirical evidence that, concerning this development, and *after* the question of Auschwitz, the question of individual and collective guilt of a nation followed; a philosophically new idea is focused on the change from an individual and its autonomy to inter-subjectivity, which enables the individual as such to 'appear' in the first place.

mean a collective responsibility but a contextual responsibility for the world as the sphere in which I can set out claims of acceptance and validity *and* which enables me to do this reasonably. What I refer to is the so-called discourse universe, which not only includes the interests of non-humans and the non-living existence of the ecosphere, but also requires these to be considered.

Embedded in these I keep my personal responsibility, which only now gains, through enforceability, a moral sense. In this sense, co-responsibility is – according to Karl-Otto Apel – primordial (Apel and Burckhart 2001).

With regard to a responsible ethical tenor, we can be assured that ethics is by no means at its end, but at the end – at least near the actual 'bad ending' (Jonas) – ethics demonstrates once more *that* it works and *how* it works, and how it can effect something. It works through applying validity and purpose before applying the factual.

Surmounting the Metaphysical-Heuristic Fundamentals of Hans Jonas' Ethics of Responsibility through a Dialogical-Discursive Future Ethics of Co-responsibility

Jonas' ethics is limited in the dimensions of its theoretical basis. Implications such as basic metaphysical assumptions – e.g. the concept of God, nature or freedom – or of empirical kinds involving theories of objects – e.g. a 'given' responsibility, or a given metabolism as a form of freedom – can easily be deciphered by means of motivational theory.

In the following, some critical points about, as well as possibilities of, Jonas' concept of responsibility will be presented in two steps. First, an ethically motivated criticism of Jonas' concept of motivation is given, so as to present *the possibilities of a transformation.* I would then like to conclude with Jonas himself, who claims that *fatality would be a capital sin.*

Let me quote Jonas first, in order to make the background of my criticism more visible:

> The alternative, still open for us, is involved in our action of the present – in it, against it, for it. It is a moral examination of the state of our civilization as a single person and as a group, repeated at all times; in fact it is an examination of the maturity of our humaneness, whether we act well or badly in dealing with that stress, which will not disappear. [...] A new solidarity of mankind begins to dawn on us. We are connected through a common guilt, a common responsibility invokes us. In the dazzling light of this new opening horizon racial conflicts fade and their screaming should become silent. I know, it will not become silent, but from now on we can silence it with a new appeal to the authoritative community which was never obvious before. (Jonas 1994a, 24–5)

The extension of the dimension of human responsibility with regard to the future, in which life should still exist, is pithy. Despite defending theodicy, 'the power to end the course of this world ... still stays in the hands of humans ...'. At the core of his philosophy is the status of a human in the Being, 'about the interpretation of the relationship between the nature, the life and the mind ...' (Jonas 1994a, 19–29).

This is the point where some central problems of Jonas' ethics manifest directly. First, his theory of ethics is established reflexively in an ontological teleology of values, immanently entitled to realization, which, at the same time, implies a problematic naturalistic coincidence of Being and Having to Be. Secondly, it is established in a metaphysical-biological understanding of freedom, which leads to his special sense of responsibility. In this connection the problem is that Jonas reifies the term 'responsibility', insofar as he obviously proceeds from the assumption that we *can* take (over) responsibility as something 'being laid out ready'.

Overlapping these two points, third, there is a relationship of responsibility between the human and nature, because one is embedded in the other. Human life is unshakeably linked to the existence of nature; it is a part of the latter, so that the survival of human beings is tied to the protection of nature. Due to his evolutionary characteristic, the human has a special responsibility for nature. It is an explicit duty, which, according to Jonas, results strictly from nature itself, but also from the creation and the self-determination of the human. To drop this responsibility for nature – or to evade this responsibility – is a sin against humans themselves.

Jonas' thought revolves around the 'first imperative', namely 'that mankind is!' (Jonas 1979, 64)[7]. But it is not one or another real society or a social formation under examination here, but rather the idea of a human being. Yet even here it is possible to make further critical points: already in the basic approach responsibility is not reciprocal, and nor is fairness substantiated. Caring – archetypical for the child or for the state – is a non-rational explanatory moment, the execution mode is only being demanded humanitarian. Decisions about action, especially at a practical level, may not and cannot be motivated or decided by the principle of care. Accordingly, Irrgang[8] calls for a discursive – or institutional – interdisciplinary definition of responsibility. In this definition, both the conceptual mistakes of an ontological-metaphysical view of nature, as well as the methodical mistakes of the naturalistic fallacy, must be overcome. An end in itself and the worth of

---

7 Also in Böhler 1994, unpublished manuscript, at the place indicated, 17–18. In another form, as is generally known, these ideas follow the modern natural philosophical approach, as taken by *inter alios* Meyer-Abich or Spaemann in his ethics of emotion (see lso Heiland 1992.)

8 Irrgang, '"Hans Jonas Prinzip Zukunftsverantwortung" within the context of the philosophical ethics and in dialogue with it.' Lecture held on the occasion of the Jonas conference in Meissen in 1996. Irrgang also set off Jonas' ethics against utilitarianism and the philosophy of nature. In contrast to this, he proposes a scientific, pragmatically established and interdisciplinarily organized discourse-ethics of action.

nature cannot be reasonably consolidated in terms of ontology, and nor can they be applied impetuously to practical-ethical action or used criteriologically. This fades out the limits of culture, time, and individualism totally, as well as their interests.

The closest thing to the transcendentally pragmatic two-stage discourse ethics of responsibility inaugurated by Karl-Otto Apel is a reflexion on the historical dimension of the ethics of responsibility. This closeness, however, will prove untenable in the explanatory-reflexive point of view, as Wolfgang Kuhlmann convincingly shows in his article 'Prinzip Verantwortung versus Diskursethik' (The concept of responsibility versus discourse-ethics). Kuhlmann's view centres around the principle of fairness – which is not caught up with Jonas' idea of a principle of sympathy and responsibility – as well as around a rationally substantiated obligation to preserve the idea of being a human. This is instead of a focus on the metaphysical-ontological idea of the principle of fairness, with all its deficits, in statements and commitments. Kuhlmann asks for a ethical-moral explanation of responsibility and questions the validity of Jonas' target phrases. This kind of discourse ethics offers the opportunity to consolidate Jonas' ideas about nature and humans reasonably and reflexively, without rejecting his thoughts on content.

> This solution [the transcendental-discourse-ethical solution] can cover especially the responsibility to take an effect on the option for continuing existence of the endangered species of humans, and, for their sake, the responsibility to save the conditions for human existence in the nature. These are unquestionably the central responsibilities according to Jonas' ethics. (Kuhlmann 1994)[9]

Kuhlmann refers to deficits in Jonas' statements that are difficult to deny. His points are echoed by Dietrich Böhler and Horst Gronke. Böhler refers to the one-sidedness of Jonas' definition of responsibility. With respect to fixation of the definition of responsibility to the item of responsibility – for example, to nature, or to a productive imbalance, as can be found in Jonas' *The Principle of Responsibility* – it is important to consider the relation – which dialogically refers to possible validity – of being justifiable to others (as possible discourse-partners in a boundless discourse-universe, which, counterfactually, must always be anticipated as already realized) (Böhler 1994, 260; see also 264 ff., 270 ff.). Jonas ignores this dialogicity, both as an ethical and a reason-reflexive moment of foundation.

Consequently, with regard to the rigorous, reason-reflexively oriented legitimation and verification of the liability of the responsibility-principle itself, this discourse with Jonas shows an obvious deficit, to which, according to my mind, the only reasonable alternative is the transcendental-discourse-ethical form of explanation. But, to use Böhler's words, the motivating force of Jonas' ethics

9 Also in this sense see articles by Apel and Gronke (in Böhler 1994), and also Böhler 1994 (esp. 257–62 and 273) and Werner 2003.

remains beyond controversy. Jonas undoubtedly indicates the trend for finding solutions for the long-term care of the future in the micro, meso and macro sector of the ecosphere, which is, of course, shared by humans.

In that sense Jonas' reasoning is centred on the urgent problem of 'our' nature: its term, its biological, physical, chemical status, and its cultural and religious evolution, as well as its confrontation and its 'being touched' (in two senses) by its own humanity. This is the human's special responsibility towards himself and his species in view of his integration in nature, the care of which is his primary duty.

For Jonas, the boundary of responsibility remains a 'question' (see also Jonas 1994b): a question of how nature will continue, how it will be continued, how it can or should continue. And the question, to which Jonas addresses himself several times, is – in our protected, democratic everyday life, which consists of responsibility for the future but is still pervaded by possible catastrophes in the relationship between human and nature – what can be expected of us? Would we be justified in taking even a dispensation of democracy into consideration – a cancellation of fundamental freedoms – to save nature and to prove the 'moral idea of humankind' (Böhler 1994) or to draw nearer to this idea?

The discourse with and about Jonas answers many of these questions. But the answers are partly questions themselves.[10] The possible, perhaps existential, ethical imperative, or the dispensation of democracy, should be provided with 'management' systems from an abrogated democratic discourse. 'Provided' in the sense of Jonas' 'heuristic of fear' as a quasi-catharsis, which also guides the extra-democratic situation in its deficit of rationality. In this dialogue with Jonas it becomes clear that Jonas wrangles over the primacy of saving nature and how the dispensation of democracy would (or could) be the price of its salvation.

If Jonas had used another concept for nature or the human rather than his favoured ontologically-metaphysically based conception, if he had utilized a specified teleology and anthropology (a heuristic of fear and responsibility) as well as another term for responsibility, he could have developed a moral-ethical explanatory statement like Böhler in his article, 'In dubio contra projectum'. The procedural problems of the principle of responsibility could have been solved more appropriately in the sense of explanatory theory, and far more efficiently in practice.[11]

Thus far, the dialogue with Jonas cannot solve the explanation and application problems related to an ontologically and metaphysically based concept of responsibility, but it has illuminated some problems and proved the strength of Jonas' approach. Jonas opens up aspects of responsibility from the internal-scientific or election-cyclic political perspective of the nature-human situation. This makes the dialogue with Jonas highly important. While Jonas' general thesis – of 'in dubio pro humanitate' (specified by) 'et pro natura' – reasonably and

10 See also Böhler 1994, 37 ff., 47, 210 ff., 265 ff., 273 ff., 403 ff.

11 Like Böhler, for example, who refers to short-term solution strategies with long-term relevance for stressed decisions in the politics, economics, medicine, etc. (Böhler 1994).

necessarily results in 'in dubio contra projectum', without interpreting 'in dubio pro malo' in a pessimistic way, it always takes into account the possibly calamitous result of one's action and considers the possible collective results of one's action. This does not mean causing panic, discarding technology, or fatalism, but rather it means the duty of a steady readiness to take responsibility.[12] So 'Fatalism would be a capital sin' is Jonas' point (see also Böhler 1994, 66).[13]

Co-responsibility as a Principle of a Dialogical-Discursive Future Ethics[14]

In referring to Böhler, Kuhlmann, Apel and Gronke in the previous section, I suggested possibilities for transforming the general idea of Jonas' ethics of responsibility. The essence of this idea is an intersubjective, universal, reciprocal responsibility for the future of humankind. It is based on an idea about the human being, which sees the human as a creature who can behave reciprocally and reflexively towards himself and towards the others, and who can presuppose counterfactually in order to anticipate others as equal claimants. First the other enables the 'me'; he is the 'other' of my own demands, or even the possibility of placing my demands.

Hence if we think of ourselves as creatures that lay claim to reason and value (and this is what we do while speaking), then we must have been taking the co-subjects (and their world), as well as ourselves and our world, for granted. All the same, we must anticipate the possibility that we refer to them – in speech, in pictures, in (social) texts, etc. (To show this, see also Burckhart 1999.) This reflexion on this basic structure of human relations manifests the dialogue as a centrepiece of human performance (see also Braun 2000), and shows the dialogicity to be an excellent feature of human rationality (see also Burckhart 1999). More explicitly, the conditions that allow discourse to reach its possibilities, and its possible realization, if seen explanation-reflexively, are the nadir of a universal-reciprocal future ethics of responsibility. We are not (only) responsible because we can, but because otherwise we deprive ourselves of the reasoned basis of ourselves.

12 Therefore, especially with regard to responsibility for the consequences, Jonas' ethic of responsibility makes it possible to explain that the scientist or the representative of applied sciences must justify himself for the results of his action, even if he cannot (fore) see them in specie.

13 See also W.C. Zimmerli and others in a discussion with Hans Jonas: 'Vom Profit zur Ethik und zurück.' In Böhler 1994, 224 ff. There, Jonas gives his view of the status of 'in dubio pro malo' as a restriction and a veto with respect to decisions, which risk 'the whole interests of other persons' (see Böhler, 'In dubio …', at the place indicated).

14 See also currently Kettner 2000, as well as Apel and Burckhart 2001. A project by Jürgen Sikora on this topic, 'Zukunftsverantwortliche Bildung', terminated at the end of 2001.

In contrast with one-sided reciprocal theories of ethics – e.g. Christian charity, Kant's 'deontology', Lévinas' 'countenance ethics', Buber's 'Me-You-It ethics' – the approach here is universal-reciprocal. This means that the interests of all who are taking part in life, and thus all who influence claims to reason and worth that are feasible now, must be considered.[15] This includes the unborn, as well as mentally deficient and sleeping, those participating in physical, chemical, biological, or technological projects, and also those who are affected and participating.

We are constantly co-responsible for this dimension of the current and future biological, socio-ecological and economical environment. Consequently, responsibility will not jade by being born on behalf of another, a determined X (for example, the welfare of a child) or a determined Y (for example, our parents), but also in all cases 'in view of' and 'with respect to' the idea of a better world for humankind, or, more explicitly, with respect to the discourse universe per se. The personal responsibility for X and towards Y is unaffected, but will be, in view of the idea of a better world or of the discourse-universe respectively, overwritten by co-responsibility in which we as humans can constitute reasonably in the first place. Those who cannot represent their own interests by themselves must be represented by lawyers. The consequences that are not apparently calculable are, like all empirical insights, under fallibilism-reserve (clause reserving errors: *in dubio pro malo*) and all restrictions of the freedom of choice are to be justified as reciprocally-universal themselves.

Jonas can motivate us towards this procedure of discourse-ethics and sensitize us to difficulties in rationality with ourselves. From the perspective of discourse ethics, four imperatives can be formulated for a dialogical, universally reciprocal future ethics of co-responsibility:

1. Save the status that enables a dialogue;
2. Encourage situations that enable dialogue;
3. Prevent circumstances that restrain dialogue;
4. Ensure the option for a permanently accomplished and worthy life with regard to its sense and validity.

Closing Words with Hans Jonas

Fatalism would be a capital sin, or about a realistic modesty.

> It is [...] no coquetry of modesty but an always delicate balance of accomplishing and failure, which I can reach after a long track of fairly honest self-examination. [...]
>
> Next to the mentioned subjective the embarrassment has also another, more serious objective reason. And the reason is the apprehension or the suspicion of

15 This would also be the point of origin for ecological as well as Internet ethics.

> a futility of the word, even of the true word, if this comes into conflict with the constraints, the needs, the interests, and the authorities of the moment, reaching too far into the future so that it becomes powerless in the present. [...]
>
> With my improvised speech I wanted to express the idea that fatalism would be a capital sin of the moment. The approaching, impending fortune which is caused by ourselves through our current bad management of the Earth, this disaster will be more certain if we glance at it as inevitable. Therefore, I warn against the inner danger of fatalism, which is almost as big as the outer danger, which for its part only exists due to our guilt anyway. Fatalism – viz. thinking of fortune as something inevitable, not changeable – is self-fulfilling and will effect exactly in this, what our despair sees as irrevocable.
>
> As an old man who has often experienced the unconsciousness of the word I want to tell you following: Oh, don't believe, don't accept the claim that things are inescapable. Don't let yourself be seduced by the advice of the alleged objective necessity, which you seem to confront. Stick to the way you are thinking, what you are thinking, what you are saying and how you are spreading ideas in the reciprocal communication, how you are spotting the difference in the course of things: in other words – participate, intervene! (Jonas 2005, 53f.)

There is no guarantee of success; but we can be sure that refraining from effort, surrendering our endeavour, will bring disaster; the disaster that we can foresee and the foreseeing of which is exactly what should be prevented, so that after all it is valid: *in dubio pro malo* in the sense of a consequentialistic ethics. It is not pessimistic (*rien ne va plus*) but *in dubio contra projectum et pro vita*! To turn it into the language of discourse ethics is to save, support, claim for *Logon didonai, sic*. It is an explanation through the power of arguments in the medium of all together – all against each other, and of the discourse – as this is the only way to save, support, and claim for the real permanence of life![16]

Mankind is not running empty, is not in need of ethics immediately, and neither is ethics running empty and the human arising as *homo lupus*. Instead, Jonas elucidates moral courage and engagement, but also heuristics as a sign of practical and practised moral competency.

References

Apel, Karl-Otto. 2000. 'First Things First. Der Begriff primordialer Mit-Verantwortung'. In *Angewandte Ethik als Politikum*, edited by Matthias Kettner, 21–50. Frankfurt a. Main: Suhrkamp.

16 Rightly, Jürgen Sikora (1999) calls the attention to the fact that *pro malo* and *pro vita* should actually be hierarchically proportional. *Pro malo* should be subsumed under *pro vita*, as the first results from the second. If there were no longer *pro vita*, then *pro malo* would also become absurd and incongruous.

Apel, Karl-Otto and Holger Burckhart, eds. 2001. *Prinzip 'Mitverantwortung'.* Würzburg: Königshausen & Neumann.

Bayertz, Kurt. 1995. *Verantwortung. Prinzip oder Problem?* Darmstadt: Wissenschaftliche Buchgesellschaft.

Böhler, Dietrich. 1994. *Ethik für die Zukunft. Im Dialog mit Hans Jonas*. Munich: C.H. Beck.

———. 1998. 'Verantwortung, Dialog und Menschenwürde'. In *Erlanger Studien zur Ethik in der Medizin,* edited by Andreas Frewer. Erlangen and Jena: Palm & Enke.

Braun, Edmund. 2000. 'Zur Grundlegung einer transzendentalpragmatischen Anthropologie'. In *Die Idee des Diskurses*, edited by Holger Burckhart, Horst Gronke and Jens Peter Brune. Markt Schwaben: Eusl-Verlagsgesellschaft.

Burckhart, Holger. 1999. *Diskursethik. Diskursanthropologie. Diskurspädgogik.* Würzburg: Königshausen & Neumann.

———. 2000. *Erfahrung des Moralischen.* Hamburg: Verlag Dr. Kovač.

Düwell, Marcus. 2000. 'Die Bedeutung ethischer Diskurse in einer wertpluralen Welt'. In *Angewandte Ethik als Politikum*, edited by Matthias Kettner. Frankfurt a. Main: Suhrkamp.

Gewirth, Alan. 1978. *Reason and Morality*. Chicago: University of Chicago Press.

Heiland, Stefan. 1992. *Naturverständnis. Dimensionen des menschlichen Naturbezugs*. Darmstadt: Wissenschaftliche Buchgesellschaft.

Höffe, Otfried. 1993. *Moral als Preis der Moderne*. Frankfurt a. Main: Suhrkamp.

Jonas, Hans. 1994a. 'Rassismus im Lichte der Menschheitsbedrohung'. In *Ethik für die Zukunft. Im Dialog mit Hans Jonas*, edited by Dietrich Böhler, 19–29. Munich: C.H. Beck.

Jonas, Hans. 1994b. 'Naturwissenschaft versus Natur-Verantwortung? Hans Jonas im Gespräch mit Eike Gebhard'. In *Ethik für die Zukunft. Im Dialog mit Hans Jonas*, edited by Dietrich Böhler, 197–212. Munich: C.H. Beck.

———. *Das Prinzip Verantwortung: Versuch einer Ethik für die technologische Zivilisation*. Frankfurt a. Main: Insel Verlag, 1979.

Kettner, Matthias, ed. 2000. *Angewandte Ethik als Politikum*. Frankfurt a. Main: Suhrkamp.

Kuhlmann, Wolfgang. 1994. "Prinzip der Verantwortung' versus Diskursethik'. In *Ethik für die Zukunft. Im Dialog mit Hans Jonas*, edited by Dietrich Böhler, 277–302. Munich: C.H. Beck.

Steigleder, Klaus. 1999. *Grundlegung der normativen Ethik.* Freiburg: Alber.

PART 2
Human Nature and the Imperative of Responsibility

Chapter 4
Is Ageing a Gift? Bioconservatism and the Ethics of Gratitude[1]

Lawrence Vogel

Authenticity: Gratitude versus Creativity

In an essay playfully called 'Thank Who Very Much', Ronald Aronson holds that the core of 'spirituality' is 'the experience of gratitude for the natural and social *gifts* on which we depend to make something of our lives': gifts that are evident when we take a good hike or enjoy a family celebration together. As Aronson puts it, 'one's map of dependence … sketches the paths for one's gratitude. It tells, after all, the story of our connections with the world and the universe, and it gives us a core of obligations and a core of meaning' (Aronson 2007). The spirit of 'thanks-giving' need not be sustained by faith in a Creator or belief in a transcendent purpose we help to actualize on earth, much less in cosmic history as a whole. I agree with Aronson that life may be received as a gift even if there's no Giver, and there can be plenty of purpose and meaning in life even if there's no purpose and meaning of life.

In the context of debates over technologies like sex selection and the enhancement of muscles, height, mood and memory, Michael Sandel has focused our attention on the importance of gratitude for 'the giftedness of life' (Sandel 2007, 26–9). The danger that lurks within the charms of enhancing our progeny, Sandel warns, is not so much that these techniques may violate our children's autonomy, or prove unsafe, or not be equally available to all, but rather that they express a stance of 'hyperagency': the Promethean aspiration to remake nature, including human nature, to gratify our desires or serve whatever purposes we will. The problem here is an overzealous drive to mastery that jeopardizes our appreciation of 'the gifted character of human powers and achievements', for a) our own talents and powers are not wholly our own doing, despite our efforts to

1 Thank you to my fellow symposiasts Jack Caputo and Trish Glazebrook for zesty conversation during a winter storm at the Duquesne conference on 'posthumanism', and also to attendees, most especially Sarah MacMillen (Sociology) and Dan Burston (Psychology). I benefited in preparing the paper from a trial run with students at Connecticut College and especially from comments by my generous colleague Melvyn Woody. I wrote this paper in the wake of the death of my parents, Naomi and Walter Vogel. I dedicate this essay to their memory.

develop and exercise them, and b) not everything in the world is open to whatever we may desire or devise.

Sandel enumerates two larger stakes involved. First, enhancements threaten crucial human goods embodied in social practices that bring us together. We choose our spouse, but not our children. Parenting – with its norms of unconditional love and 'openness to the unbidden' – ceases to be a school for humility when it is replaced by 'hyperparenting' where mothers and fathers enlist their children in an arms race, using every pharmaceutical and genetic means available to ensure their kids a competitive edge. In athletic and artistic endeavours, the use of performance-enhancing drugs erodes our admiration for natural talents and gifts. And institutions of social solidarity require humility in the face of privilege and the willingness to share the fruits of good fortune.

Second, Sandel contends, changing our nature to fit the world is actually disempowering, not an exercise in freedom. It distracts us from reflecting critically on the world and deadens the impulse to work for social and political improvements. We should try to change the world to fit our nature: creating arrangements more hospitable to the gifts and limitations of imperfect human beings. To focus so much on the individual body, not the body politic, betrays resentment about the need for the hard, collaborative work of politics.

Sandel does not imply that everything given is good. We are better off, he admits, for having conquered polio and smallpox. Much progress has resulted from pushing back 'the given' for the sake of a better world. But, in some domains, this can be 'an overdeveloped reflex' – a mania for control – that does damage to the goods of humility and solidarity. Consistent with his communitarian political philosophy, Sandel calls on us to cherish unchosen aspects of our identity that are otherwise derogated as mere 'encumbrances'.

Critics of enhancement technologies, like Sandel, alert us to the pitfall of letting ourselves become, in the later Heidegger's formulation, 'standing reserve': raw material to be remoulded at our will. They stress, as Eric Parens puts it, that 'if we forget that life is a gift, we will fail to honor our responsibility for the mysterious whole which we have not made'. Parens argues, however, proponents of enhancement technologies share with critics the ideal of authenticity, but interpret it differently (Parens 2005, 37). While critics express gratitude for what's given, proponents stress the importance of summoning the courage, as Nietzsche put it, to 'create ourselves' or 'become who we are'. The tension between gratitude and creativity as interpretations of authenticity cuts across simple dichotomies between political conservatives and liberals or between faithful and secular people.

The Question: Is Ageing a Gift?

I want to turn our attention from moulding children to reshaping old age, and ask: How does ambivalence between authenticity as gratitude and as creativity bear on the question of whether we should, if we could, radically extend the 'natural human lifespan' through techniques such as tissue reengineering and the genetic modification of telomeres responsible for the ageing of our cells?

'Posthumanists' look forward to a day when biotechnology enables us to transcend limits – like ageing and even mortality – that have long been regarded as essential to human nature. In 'Why I Want to be a Posthuman When I Grow Up', Nick Bostrom states that the majority of humankind already desires a 'greatly enhanced healthspan capacity implicitly', by virtue of our ordinary desire to stay alive and healthy (Bostrom 2006, 6). Bostrom's argument is straightforward: if life is good, then more life is prima facie better. Decline in subjective well-being isn't due to ageing *per se*, Bostrom insists, but to health constraints. The rare, but expanding, cohort of 90-year-olds with mind and body intact occupy a privileged position for judging whether a longer life is worth the trouble, and most agree that it is. And if this is true at currently realized ages, Bostrom concludes, then it would be good for many to become 'posthuman' by radically extending their healthspan. But a line of philosophers – most notably, Hans Jonas, Leon Kass and Daniel Callahan, whom I shall label 'bioconservatives' – reject 'posthumanism' on the grounds that our natural lifespan is a gift for which we should be grateful, not an arbitrary limit we should seek to creatively overcome.

Having witnessed the steady, sometimes agonizing decline and eventual death of both my parents in the past decade, I'm sympathetic with those who, upon hearing my topic – 'Is ageing a gift?' – abruptly answer, 'Not for most people I know!' Another typical response is: 'Ageing is all right, so long as you're healthy.' The force of the response is, of course, 'so long as you're not really ageing'. The upshot being, as many confess: 'I hope I live a long, robust life, and then die in my sleep.' And the posthumanists' wish that biotechnology may help us radically extend our lives reflects this same attitude: 'We don't want to be older longer,' they say. 'We want to be younger longer!'

Following Heidegger, it's a commonplace of existentialism that mortality is at the core of our being, not a condition our souls enable us to transcend. Embracing our finitude opens up the possibility of living authentically: of discerning what really matters and making the most of our time. This cliché, however, abstracts from the fact that our relationship to death changes as we grow older in an ageing body. Mid-life crises are made of the thought: 'All of a sudden it's as if the roller-coaster has left the peak and is speeding down the tracks.' Death accelerates towards us as we approach the limit of our natural lifespan, and our bones and sinews remind us of their winding down. If we live long enough, our friends, and even our children, start dying off and the younger generation comes into their own, reminding us of what we are no longer – and where we are going.

So the question must surface: If we accept mortality as a blessing that grants urgency to life, does this require receiving ageing as a gift, too? Should ageing be understood as part of the natural course of life for which we should be grateful, or is it more akin to a disease we ought to combat? Wouldn't it be better to die without having aged, or having aged at a much slower pace, if we could? Should our natural lifespan be regarded as a moral norm that limits what we ought to do in the name of improving our condition? What could it mean to speak of the ageing process as 'a gift': an inextricable part of the blessing of mortality?

Sherwin Nuland's *How We Die*: The Case of Bubbeh

Sherwin Nuland, a medical doctor, gives us a clue in his book *How We Die*. Its hero is his grandmother Bubbeh. Nuland's mother died when he was 11, and he became Bubbeh's boy, unaware that she was already 89. Only after Bubbeh took on the role in their Bronx shtetl of 'Yiddishe mater et_magistra to an extended group of struggling young immigrants' did Nuland become conscious of 'just how ancient Bubbeh was' (Nuland 1994, 46). It gradually dawned on him that she was in decline: not from disease (she rarely needed a doctor) but from old age. Her walk became an increasingly unsteady shuffle, her vision began to fail, she visited the bathroom more often at night, and eventually lost the strength to eat. Her spirit withered, too, as her old combativeness dissipated, she stopped attending synagogue and even ceased praying at home. Finally, Bubbeh died at 96 after a series of strokes.

Nuland takes solace in the words Thomas Jefferson offered to the 78-year-old John Adams: 'But our machines have now been running seventy or eighty years, and we must expect that, worn as they are, here a pivot, there a wheel, now a pinion, next a spring, will be giving way; and however we may tinker them up for a while, all will at length surcease motion' (Nuland 1994, 46). Though a certificate announced the cause of Bubbeh's death as 'cerebrovascular accident' (or CVA), Nuland refuses to accept that 'the process [he] had been watching for 18 years had ended in a named acute disease'. Nuland prefers 'a worldview that recognizes the inexorable tide of natural history' over one 'that believes it is within the province of science to wrestle against those forces that stabilize our environment and our very civilization'. Denying he is a Luddite, for he 'glor[ies] in the magnificent benisons of modern scientific achievement', Nuland observes nonetheless that:

> For plants and animals, renewal requires that death precede it so that the weary may be replaced by the vigorous. This is what is meant by the cycles of nature. There is nothing pathological or sick about the sequence – in fact, it is the antithesis of sick. To call a natural process by the name of a disease is the first step in the attempt to cure it and thereby thwart it. To thwart it is the first step toward thwarting the continuation of exactly that which we try to preserve, which is, after all, the order and system of our universe. (Nuland 1994, 58)

Our natural lifespan, with its inherent limits, frames our natural life cycle, and, in this regard at least, we ought to respect the wisdom of nature and embrace with gratitude the gift not only of mortality, but of the ageing process itself. Nuland endorses the classical prescription, 'Felix opportunitae mortis!' ('Be happy for the opportunity of dying'), but also, beyond that, the imperative, 'Felix opportunitae senescens!' ('Be happy for the opportunity of ageing'). He concedes:

> There will always be those who persist in seeking the Fountain of Youth, or at least delaying what is irrevocably ordained. But there is a vanity in all this, and it demeans us. At the very least, it brings us no honor. Far from being irreplaceable, we should be replaced. Fantasies of staying the hand of mortality are incompatible with the best interests of our species and the continuity of humankind's progress. More directly, they are incompatible with the best interests of our very own children. Tennyson says it clearly: 'Old men must die; or the world would grow moldy, would only breed the past again'. (Nuland 1994, 86)

Ageing and dying are good not only for society, Nuland assures us, but for the individual as well:

> Those who would live beyond their nature-given span lose their framework, and with it lose a proper sense of relationship to those who are younger, gaining only the resentment of youth for encroaching on its careers and resources. The Fact there is a limited right time to do the rewarding things in our lives is what creates the urgency to do them. Otherwise, we might stagnate in procrastination. The very fact that at our backs, as the poet cautions his coy mistress, we 'always hear / Time's winged chariot hurrying near' enhances the world and makes the time priceless. (Nuland 1994, 86)

To be sure, making a virtue of necessity is better than railing against it. But what if what we have come to know as the natural lifespan is not a necessity after all, but a limit we can radically extend? We know how much harm has been done by presuming that what's natural is also morally right and what's unnatural morally wrong. To vilify a human tendency or practice as 'unnatural' has been a long-standing way of rationalizing prejudices against racial intermarriage, homosexuality and same-sex marriage, contraception, abortion, cloning, and even, in days of yore, wearing glasses. The naturalistic fallacy – that we can't derive an 'ought' from the way nature happens to be – is an axiom for beginners in philosophy. Just because it is 'unnatural' to imagine human beings living for hundreds of years, doesn't entail that it would be a bad thing. So perhaps Nuland's Stoic concession to 'the wisdom of nature' is old-fashioned: a consolation prize we need no longer accept.

The Posthumanist Critique of 'the Pro-Aging Trance'

'Posthumanists' would hear in Dr Nuland's words not the voice of wisdom, but a lament of resignation to the status quo. Once upon a time, average human life expectancy was between 20 and 34 years, though it stretched to 54 for those lucky enough to make it to the age of 15. Due to social and medical advances, but without any evolutionary changes in human biology, we have seen a tripling of life expectancy at an exponential rate in the past few thousand years. To make large gains in the future, it would be necessary to slow or reverse the ageing process itself. Preventing and curing specific diseases can have only a limited impact. Even if we were able to eliminate heart disease and cancer, life expectancy would increase by only eight or nine years, for ageing weakens the body for predators such as stroke and pneumonia.

Arthur Caplan thinks ageing should be defined as the ultimate disease. He asks why deterioration associated with ageing is considered 'natural', while similar processes in the young like progeria are regarded as diseases (Caplan 2005). Ageing, he notes, produces the same consequences as life-threatening illnesses. Viral infections are just as ubiquitous as ageing.

And because any morbid process in the body counts as a disease, there is a prima facie reason for labelling ageing as a disease, too. Caplan describes how awkward it is for teaching physicians to feel obligated to label obviously disease-like infirmities of old age as 'natural' in order to discourage students' inclination to treat the elderly. He suggests that ageing should be called abnormal and unnatural if this opens the door for reclassifying it as a disease.

It is tempting to label ageing as 'natural', Caplan tells us, by saying that it serves an evolutionary purpose or function. As Nuland says, nature favours clearing away the old for the sake of the young. But given that selection acts on individuals and genotypes, not on the species, it's nonsense from an evolutionary view, Caplan argues, to say that ageing works in order to benefit the species. It's more plausible that ageing is an inadvertent by-product of an increased metabolic rate early in life that maximizes reproductive advantage, but then subverts organic functioning later on. In so far as it parallels other disease processes, Caplan concludes, it's reasonable to label it a disease. As a stochastic or chance phenomenon, it's plausible to call it 'unnatural' rather than an intrinsic part of human nature.

Biogerontologist Aubrey de Grey prophesies that someone currently alive will survive to be a milligenerian, based on developments now in the making, such as tissue regeneration and genetic engineering aimed at repairing telomeres whose deterioration makes the body more vulnerable to all the ailments that bring down the elderly (de Grey 2007). According to posthumanists like Bostrom, de Grey and Ronald Bailey, with the conquest of ageing, one's risk of dying in any given year would be like a 20-year-old's, and life expectancy might increase to 1,000 years.

While no one yearns for 'prolonged senescence' – a longer life at the price of a much longer period of decrepitude – the hoped-for route involves 'compressed morbidity' accompanied by 'decelerated', 'arrested' or even 'reversed' ageing. Although Bostrom doesn't foresee immortality as a realistic possibility, he doesn't oppose it in principle. The more feasible version of a posthuman healthspan, however, is a much longer, more vibrant life capped off by a relatively efficient demise. Do we already want this 'implicitly'? Should we go along with Bostrom in desiring a 'greatly enhanced capacity for health and longevity'?

Ronald Bailey certainly thinks so. In a biotechnologically engineered simulacrum of B.F. Skinner's *Walden Two*, Bailey imagines a year 2100 when a 150-year-old great-great-great grandmother will be playing a competitive game of tennis with her 30-year-old great-great-great granddaughter, and later sits down 'to chat about some academic discipline she studied in the 1980's with as much acuity and memory as her 50-year-old great-grandson, who is studying it now' (Bailey 2006). And, by the way, the grandson is imagined playing a mean game of football while 'sporting new versions of an arm and lung that got damaged in a car wreck'. In addition to being green and clean, Bailey's is 'a remarkably peaceful and pleasant world'. 'Even beyond their health and wealth', its inhabitants are 'better than well'. 'Anti-social tendencies and crippling depression are managed by individual choice through biotech pharmaceuticals'. Bailey predicts that our descendants, armed with techniques to repair telomeres and regenerate tissues, 'will look back and thank us for making their world of longer, healthier lives possible'.

Aubrey de Grey goes even further, claiming that ushering in the era of the posthuman healthspan is a moral imperative. It's obvious to him that the decline associated with ageing is 'both tragic and potentially preventable'. That many, if not most, people accept ageing as part of life is, according to de Grey, just 'sour grapes': a rationalization based on the assumption that there's nothing much we can do about it. De Grey calls such thinking 'the pro-aging trance': a 'rationalization' that's 'stunningly irrational from an objective standpoint'. He contends, furthermore, that 'geronto-apologists' discriminate against people who could benefit from anti-ageing discoveries. He presents the posthumanist agenda as a great 'humanitarian' cause aimed at saving lives, and charges that 'our inaction today costs lots of lives'. Although he agrees with bioconservative Leon Kass that sometimes our repugnance at a possible course of action provides evidence of its immorality, de Grey uses this 'non-cognitivist' point to express his repugnance at 'the pro-aging trance':

> Old people are people, too, so aging must be seen for what it is: a scourge that deprives far more people of far more healthy years than any other ... To persist in defending aging is psychologically excusable – fear of the unknown is a reasonable emotion, in particular – but it is ethically inexcusable. (de Grey 2007, 7)

De Grey's argument that when it comes to longevity we can't have enough of a good thing receives tacit support from an unlikely quarter: Thomas Nagel's classic essay 'Death'. Against Epicurus' claim that death is not an evil to be feared because it is nothing to the dead person, Nagel holds that death can harm the deceased by depriving them of the goods of life, even if they cannot be aware of the loss. Based on his deprivation theory, Nagel argues that we should regard death at *any* age as a misfortune, even 'a tragedy', for 'if there is no limit on the amount of life it would be good to have, then it may be that a bad end is in store for us all' (Nagel 1979, 10).

On Nagel's view, we are ambivalent about the acceptability of death at a ripe, old age because we view it from two conflicting perspectives. Objectively, or 'observed from without', he contends, we have a natural lifespan with a limit of about a century. But subjectively, or 'viewed from within', we find ourselves living towards an open-ended future with indeterminate and not essentially limited possibilities. The objective inevitability of death is subjectively irrelevant, Nagel states, so long as one looks forward to more of a good thing. Consequently, 'the fact that it's worse to die at 24 than at 82 does not imply that it is not a terrible thing at 82 – or even 806' (Nagel 1979, 9).

Whereas Aubrey de Grey defends the posthumanist stance on longevity as 'rational from an objective standpoint', Nagel gives it implicit backing by insisting on the legitimacy of the 'subjective' point of view. For de Grey, an attachment to our current natural lifespan is overly 'subjective' because it's a prejudice rooted in the assumed impossibility of doing better and getting what we really want – and also because it keeps us from being impartial about the requirement of saving humanity from needless suffering. Nagel's claim that it would be a 'tragedy' to die – even at 806 – requires subordinating an 'objective' acknowledgement that we are now lucky to be healthy at 82 to the 'subjective' truth that death at any time robs us of goods we usually want more of.

Because Nagel's work mounts a defence of 'subjectivity' – or first-personal experience – as a valid point of view for gaining insights into consciousness, the meaning of life and ethics, his reflections on 'mortal questions' are often embraced by those who want to build a bridge between analytic and Continental philosophy. And on a reading of existentialism that highlights what Eric Parens calls 'authenticity as creativity', there is an affinity between Nagel and the 'existentialist' view that the ageing body is a dimension of facticity upon which we must project meaning in light of the possibilities available to us. If, with the help of biotechnology, ageing turns out to be a much more malleable condition than it has ever been before, why shouldn't we be creative with it and extend our years well beyond their current, contingent limits?

Consequentialist Worries about Radical Life-Extension

Considering that today most children the world over lack basic vaccine protection, 40 million Americans lack health insurance, our health care system is going bankrupt, and wonder drugs often yield pernicious side-effects that aren't known for decades, it feels indulgent and virtually obscene to even speculate about the 'geron-topia' depicted by Bostrom, Bailey and de Grey. But they do have responses to the most obvious 'consequentialist' objections to their agenda.

Generally speaking, posthumanists share Arthur Caplan's faith that humans are clever and culture is flexible enough to adjust to longer lives. Many in the past might have settled for their shorter healthspan – believing it to be God's plan or nature's way. But few today would prefer returning to the past. Despite overpopulation, environmental pressures and ageism, we live at least as well and happily now as we did in days of yore. And the same, he surmises, will be true of our posthuman future. Granted, we will need to establish social policies that are compatible with longer productive lives: including devoting a fair proportion of resources to the young, not allowing seniority on the job to create stasis in the workplace, and not using medical technology aggressively once life has become a burden or too painful. Also, we will need to rethink career paths, the funding of social welfare programmes, and the definition of extended families. But, Caplan assures us, we can adapt.

To the charge that supporting an ever older population would place an unfair burden on the young, Nick Bostrom replies that an increased healthspan would enable people to contribute financially and otherwise for longer, and there is no reason to expect end-of-life health care to grow more expensive than it already is today.

To concerns about overpopulation, posthumanists reply that reducing poverty is a better way of slowing population growth than shortening lives, and there's no necessary connection between longer lives and more childbearing. John Harris goes so far as to doubt whether we should assume it is necessary or desirable to create future generations at all. 'Is there a moral difference', he asks, 'between 1) a future with a billion people succeeded by another billion different people and 2) x billion people living indefinitely and replacing themselves only when they are killed?' (Harris 2007, 69)

On the face of it, the use of anti-ageing enhancements would be unjust because the rich will gain further advantages over the poor, and this will create 'parallel populations' between the haves and the have-nots both at home and abroad. But, Harris retorts, it is wrong to deny goods to some simply because we cannot make them available to all. We already live in such a world, but hope that over time more people will gain access to opportunities – such as cancer treatments – that are currently available to only a few.

Although I suspect that the posthumanists are cheerful and optimistic to a fault, and fail to elaborate in realistic detail what their imagined future would really look life, the consequentialist debate seems to miss the point: that there is something out of synch with the rhythmic meanings of human life in the wish to have too much of a good thing. The primary issue has to do with whether we ought to receive mortality and ageing as intrinsically valuable 'gifts' of nature: conditions for the possibility of a humanly good life. Even granting the posthumanists their rosy predictions for the sake of argument, would the alteration of 'our natural lifespan', as we have known it for time immemorial and increasingly as a matter of average life expectancy, be devastating for the experience of meaning in our lives?

Bioconservatives, Ageing and the Ethics of Gratitude

I believe that 'bioconservatives' like Hans Jonas, Leon Kass and Daniel Callahan would rise to the defence of Dr Sherwin Nuland in his feeling of gratitude for the gift nature granted by letting his grandmother, Bubbeh, withdraw from life after almost a century of health. They would agree that posthumanists betray hubris, not wisdom, when they call Bubbeh's death a 'tragedy' and wish it could have been prevented. They would deny the posthumanists' accusation that they are guilty of age discrimination for accepting that growing old – not only chronologically, but biologically – is part of what it means to affirm our mortality. And they plead innocent of the charge that they commit 'the naturalistic fallacy' by treating ageing as the way things ought to be just because that's the hand nature happens to have dealt us. I want to track 'bioconservative' responses to the diagnosis that they are, as de Grey puts it, caught in the spell of a 'pro-aging trance.'

Hans Jonas: 'The Burden and Blessing of Mortality'

As Hans Jonas argues, 'the naturalistic fallacy' – that you can't derive an 'ought' from an 'is' – depends upon an ontological assumption: that Being harbours no intrinsic goodness (Jonas 1984; for an abbreviated version see Jonas 1996, 99–114). Our existence as psychosomatic wholes – as organisms in ageing bodies – gives us a privileged perspective on the goodness in Being. Here's the skeleton of Jonas' argument. If the neediness and vulnerability that come with being alive were not somehow essentially good, then an inanimate or dead universe would be just as good as one that contains life. But the presence of life in the universe is ontologically better than its absence because life says 'Yes' to Being and so confirms its goodness. The claim that life is good smacks of theodicy, but Jonas by no means believes that everything happens 'for the best'. His point is that we should feel responsible to future generations and protect the fragile web of life whose goodness we are able to discern. And we should be grateful for our ageing, mortal body as the medium through which we've been given a chance to make the world a better, if imperfect, place (and better for being imperfect).

For Jonas, ironically, the burden of mortality is associated with its ever-present possibility, while the blessing is rooted in its necessity (Jonas 1996, 87–98). The possibility of death is felt inwardly in the organism's concern for its own being and the needful freedom it enacts in staying alive. An organism's being is its own doing. 'Through negated 'not-being', 'to be' turns into a constant 'choosing of itself'. Life is spurred on by the burdensome threat of death.

How can the necessity and certainty of death, then, be a blessing? Civilization is built around protecting people from violent, and so premature, death. Is it right, Jonas asks, to combat not only premature death, but 'death as such'? Echoing Nuland, Jonas defends the ancient injunction 'Felix opportunitae mortis!' on the grounds that death serves both the common and the individual good. As for the common good, civilization requires the ever-repeated turnover of generations. 'Natality', a concept Jonas borrows from Hannah Arendt, is humankind's safeguard against lapsing into boredom and routine as each newcomer is unique and amounts to a fresh beginning.[2] (For this reason Jonas regards human reproductive cloning

2 For her use of 'natality', see Arendt 1958.

as wrongful.) And natality gets its scope from mortality, for the dying of the old makes room for the young. An ever-older population puts pressure on the limits of environmental tolerance, and in this respect, Jonas might say, radical life-extension would lead to much older group who would be, in effect, outstaying their welcome.

Even if mortality serves the common good, the individual, Jonas concedes, might wish to be exempt while feeling 'grateful for the bounty paid by others'. But it's a mistake, he contends, to long for more than the natural lifespan. The Struldbrugs. or 'Immortals', found in *Gulliver's Travels* are miserable, and find each other's company intolerable. They are universally pitied and despised. Still, although spared death, they grow old. What if we had scientific control not only over death but also the ageing process? Would this, Jonas asks, be desirable for the individual subject? There are limits to what our brains can store, and the simple truth of our own finitude, he argues, is that we could go on interminably only at the price of either losing the past (and so sacrificing personal identity) or living only in the past (thereby forgoing a real present). Trying to keep pace with change is 'doomed to inglorious failure', especially as the pace has quickened. Consequently, 'not even the fountains of youth promised by biotechnology can justify extorting from nature more than its original allowance to our species for the length of its days' (Jonas 1996, 98). The private good coincides with the common after all, Jonas concludes, but it must be perceived by thought, for it isn't felt by experience which wants more, more, more.

Still, death is a blessing for the individual 'only after a completed life in the fullness of time'. Because such a life is good, it is the duty of civilization to combat premature death. But awareness of our mortality – a non-negotiable limit – may be necessary as an incentive to number our days and make them count. We should balance being grateful for mortality with loving life. Likewise, we should hope to age well, but not to defeat ageing as such. According to Jonas, we are so used to thinking of the evils posed by our novel technological powers such as nuclear weaponry that we are inclined to overlook the fact that the primary danger of biotechnology lies not in its use for evil purposes, but in 'the bait of utopia'. The perfect may well be the enemy of the good.

Jonas' argument finds a parallel in Bernard Williams' defence of the view that immortality would be a fate worse than death (Williams 1973). Drawing on Karel Čapek's play *The Makropulos Case*, Williams imagines a woman stuck in biological middle age for over 300 years. She either suffers from boredom, having seen it all before and too many times, or else reinvents herself over and over, thus compromising the prolonged sense of personal identity that immortality was supposed to give her. She is, as Jonas puts it, torn between either losing the past to keep up with the present *or* living only in the past and losing a vital present. Either way, the immortality project is doomed to failure.

To this, posthumanist John Harris replies: if immortality is a side-effect of preventing or treating a range of diseases, it would be cruel to say to a sick person, 'You must die sooner because we can only cure you by radically extending your lifespan.' Furthermore, he states, 'only the terminally boring are in danger of being terminally bored, and perhaps they deserve a shorter life' (Harris 2007, 65). Even if personal identity is put under strain, Harris avers, this is all right so long as there is continuity between life stages. Furthermore, 'multiplication of selves in the same body is so ecologically sound, environmentally healthy and population efficient that it might become the preferred method of procreating for all except the most unregenerate eco-wastrels or sex-obsessed chauvinists' (Harris 2007, 67).

I resonate with Williams and Jonas as voices of wisdom against Harris. But the richness of Jonas' philosophy of the organism lets him see an important layer that is missing from Williams' account of why a life can go on for too long. An interpretation of personal development in terms of 'continuity over time' alone fails to reflect a recognizably human process of 'maturing'. Contemporary philosophical debates about 'personal identity' (epitomized by the work of Derek Parfit) are not really about 'persons' because they imagine 'minds' disconnected from the ageing body, lived time, the cycle of generations and the possibility of wisdom that comes with 'growth towards wholeness', not mere chronological ageing with its assimilation of more and more experience. Posthumanists want more 'freedom from constraint' because they believe that will leave them free to reinvent themselves all the time, and so stay 'forever young'. Life gets its density and weight, however, from the pressures of time, lived through the ageing body and our relationship to generations.

Leon Kass: 'L'Chaim – Intimations of Mortality'

Following Jonas' lead, Leon Kass argues that 'health as wholeness' – not the prevention of death or the prolongation of life – is the end of medicine (Kass 2002). On Kass's view, 'health as wholeness' is a natural standard, not a moral norm or a value as opposed to a fact. Health isn't the opposite of death, for one can be unhealthy and alive. If health can be restored, it's not medicine but the patient who is keeping himself alive. And death will come when health cannot be restored. The primary aim of medicine, Kass concludes, is to prevent premature deaths and to relieve suffering.

Still, Kass admits, when the posthumanists ask, 'If life is good, and more is better, then why not regard death as a disease to be cured?', we stumble along, lacking a reasonable standard, and so fall back on whatever people happen to desire. Ethical questions about ends must be raised, Kass reminds us, even if the means are safe, equally available, and non-coercive. But our 'repugnances' to them – based on an attitude of 'proper respect for what is naturally or dignifiedly human' – are difficult to translate into sound moral arguments. If life shouldn't be as long as we can make it, he asks, how many years are 'reasonably few'?

Kass acknowledges Michael Sandel's point that the attitude of mastery over nature implicit in our stance of 'hyperagency' fails to respect 'the giftedness of nature'. But modesty born of gratitude for the world's 'givenness' will not by itself tell us which things should be left inviolate, for nature includes disease and catastrophe, and nature isn't equally generous with her gifts. Only if there is something *precious* in 'the given' – beyond the mere fact of its 'giftedness' – does it serve as a restraint against efforts that would degrade it. We must ask, therefore: What is inherently good about human finitude and the natural life cycle with its rhythm of rise and fall?

The hyperagentic tendency of biotechnology invites us to dream of 'ageless bodies' (Kass 2003). But many of life's most precious goods are inseparable from the body's ageing process. What might an individual's life look like, Kass asks, if everyone made the same choice in favour of stopping the march of ageing at the ripe young age of 30? The same arguments that count against the desire for immortality also condemn the wish for radical life-extension. Living with bodily decline culminating in death is a key condition, Kass claims, for engagement, seriousness, a taste for beauty, the possibility of virtue, ties born of procreation, and the quest for meaning. Even doubling life expectancy – not to mention joining the Methuselah Project's dream of 1,000 years – would deflect us from realizing fully 'the aspirations to which our lives naturally point'. The prize should be living well, not merely living more. And hyper-prolongevity is hostile to children, for it is incompatible with accepting the need for human renewal and procreation. Far from contentment, the quest for a much longer life is likely to fuel anxiety over health and fear of death. Only decline and decay enable us to accept mortality at all; they make the leap into not-being less cruel as our bodies prepare us to let go of life.

Daniel Callahan: The Natural Life Cycle, Generativity and a Tolerable Death

Daniel Callahan worries that Kass offers no foothold for basic questions such as: When should a doctor stop trying to restore health? And when should researchers cease trying to cure processes that destroy wholeness? Though 'health as wholeness' may work well enough for individuals, it provides no guide for the group where the issue is: Should the model of wholeness be average life expectancy, or the vital maximum now attainable, or an increased maximum? The answer to this question, Callahan holds, is a value choice that cannot be read out of 'nature' or deduced from a classical analysis of health. Even granting Kass's point that a good life, defined by 'higher' aspirations, is more important than more life, it's not clear why it wouldn't be better to lead a good life for much longer, if one could.

Biotechnology today is changing what it means 'to live a life'.[3] The modernization of ageing, Callahan claims, is based upon a thin, individualistic theory of health according to which the individual should seek what in her own private judgement will bring her happiness, so long as this doesn't harm others. The problem is that harm to other groups is inevitable in the absence of unlimited resources, and there is harm in the relativism of diversity, which leaves no mean

---

3 For his most complete view on these matters, see Callahan 1987. For a more recent elaboration of his thoughts in the context of a debate with de Grey and other 'posthumanists', see Callahan 2007.

for the aged unless they can supply it for themselves. The desire for the unlimited unfolding of new possibilities and experiences makes death at any time equally unacceptable – or, ironically enough, equally acceptable.

A prevalent early twentieth-century theory of old age, 'disengagement theory', which held that the elderly should gradually disappear, has been properly attacked as an ageist stereotype. But the modern view – and posthumanism is an exacerbated version of it – has swung to the opposite extreme. It treats age as a purely chronological matter, potentially existing without the biological attrition traditionally associated with it. Though the modern view opens up new possibilities of vital involvement by the elderly, it rests on the illusion that the old can remain as socially indispensable as younger people.

Callahan adds two more considerations to Kass's norm of 'health as wholeness' in order to specify the goals of medicine in the face of ageing: 'the wholeness of life' tied to 'the natural life-cycle'. One can fail to enjoy 'the wholeness of a life' in two ways: 1) living in adequate wholeness as a body but beyond the point where the person's life possesses meaning for them and 2) premature death, where a person's body loses wholeness before they've been able to live out a full life. The 'wholeness of a life' is tied to the ideas of (1) 'a natural life-span' and (2) 'a tolerable death', that is, a death relatively acceptable because timely within a fitting lifespan.

Callahan doesn't intend to read correct theories of ageing and death out of nature, but instead proposes a different use of the word 'natural' grounded in 'persistent patterns of judgment in most cultures of what it is to live out a life manifesting wholeness and relative completeness'. The heart of this pattern is the belief that death at the end of a long, full life is fitting and orderly, not an evil. The concept of 'a tolerable death' is biographical, not biological. It involves possibilities accomplished and obligations discharged, and should be experienced by others as sad, but not tragic. 'A natural lifespan' refers to life's possibilities achieved. Though it's impossible to do everything conceivable, by the age of 65, Callahan says, most of us will have had a chance to experience a sufficient range of the opportunities that life affords. Neither ageing nor death is objectionable *per se*. What we object to are unkind ageing and premature or cruel death marked by degrading and unbearable pain. It's telling that we don't look back with bitterness or sharp regret at the death of an elderly person who lived a long, full life 30 or 40 years ago. Sherwin Nuland's Bubbeh is a case in point.

This approach embraces all stages of life, including the period of decline associated with the ageing process. On Callahan's view, the primary form of vital involvement in old age should be helpful leave-taking oriented towards the young. The old are moral conservators who offer a living memory of the past and perspective on the present and future. Furthermore, they should, Callahan says, be proponents of hope for future generations: models of 'grace under adversity', neither bitter – as if decline and death are evils – nor self-preoccupied –as if old age frees them for the self-preoccupation of saying, 'Now, it's my turn.' The most important virtue of old age is 'vigor of spirit': the determination to work to the end for a future one won't be there to share. The premise is that death after a long, full life may be sad, but it is not an evil. Though longer life may bring benefits and delights to many, the failure to have such years is not a self-evident evil. In his most recent writings, Leon Kass concurs with Callahan (Kass 2003).The lived time of our natural lives has 'a trajectory and slope'. Meaning derives in part from the fact that we live as links in a chain of generations. Our flourishing depends upon the goods that accompany 'three multiples of generation in the natural life-cycle: 1) coming of age, 2) flourishing, ruling and the replacing of self, and 3) a time of savoring and understanding, but still intimately linked to one's descendents to care about their future and to play a guiding and supporting role'. Flourishing, therefore, does not require an ageless body and a happy soul, but rather 'a life lived in rhythmed time, mindful of time's limits, appreciative of each season, filled first of all with intimate human relationships' that are ours only because we know of decline and death. The core of happiness, Kass states, is 'fine aspiration acted upon': 'engaged and energetic being-at-work of what nature gave us'.

Conclusion

There is an inexpugnable aspect of contingency and incongruity about the particular forms that embodiment and death take. That's why any particular disease or even organ failure presents only a contingent occasion for mortality: why biotechnologists can always say, 'One needn't die of that!' and set out to cure the disease or replace the organ. The fact that I am a male body, not a female, or in a body that harbours no allergies, is contingent, even though I could not exist or act without a particular body. By the same token, although I know that death is always pending and I have to die somehow, I needn't die in any particular way or at any particular time. This feeds the cause of posthumanists who rely upon the contingency of any particular duration or cause of death in order to press the medical profession to defeat this contingency – and ultimately the 'disease' of ageing itself.[4]

By appealing to 'the naturalness' of the ageing body, bioconservatives do not commit themselves to classical essences, but to the exigencies of 'the human condition'. Among these exigencies is embodiment, which renders us needy and vulnerable, and engages us in nature at large. What's at stake in the debate about radically extending the human healthspan are the 'organic' roots of time and meaning in life. Bioconservatives (Kass 2003) ground the meaning of existence in 'the organism' – against the dualistic tendency of post-Cartesian philosophical modernity. The 'posthumanist' dream of living for 1,000 years in 'ageless bodies' would have us neutralize, as much as possible, the organic basis of the natural life cycle (with its rise and decline) and the relationship we now feel between our own 'maturing' as individuals and our connection to the three generations among

4 Thanks to my colleague Melvyn Woody for bringing out this point.

whom we dwell, if we are lucky. The ageing body is the site of 'organic' time, and the more one aspires to agelessness, the more one loses that 'rooting'.

Bioconservatives bring out the limits of the ideal of authenticity when it is interpreted primarily in terms of creativity. To become who we are requires gratitude for the gifts that enable us to live most deeply. Foremost among these are our families and communities that empower us to experience our biological decline as an opportunity to take responsibility for future generations who will inherit the world from us. The most tragic feature of our culture is not that it hasn't yet found the elixir of life, but that it has so removed the elderly from places where they can feel their connection to the young. The body – lived as ageing – sets the pace within, but it is geared to the urgency of passing the mantle on to those who will be there in a world without us. Our creativity needs to be linked to what Erik Erikson called 'generativity', and this requires letting go for the sake of newcomers who deserve their moment in the sun. It is not enough to say that we should be grateful for mortality because it gives us a deadline for deciding what really matters to us. If we are serious about our time, it's important, too, that the deadline be set by the ageing body in accordance with the natural rhythms of time and the cycle of generations.

I end with a story that I know may be interpreted as 'ageist', but I tell it in the spirit of Sherwin Nuland's grandmother, Bubbeh. At the age of 90, the great screenwriter-director Billy Wilder hobbled up to the podium to give his acceptance speech upon receiving an Oscar for lifetime achievement. Here is the entirety of his address:

> A man goes to a doctor and says anxiously, 'Doc, I can't pee any more.' The doctor, perplexed, looks at the man and asks him, 'How old are you?' And the man says, 'Ninety.' 'Well,' the doctor replies, 'you've peed enough.' Thank you very much. (e.g. Wilder 2002)

References

Arendt, Hannah. 1958. *The Human Condition.* Chicago: University of Chicago Press.

Aronson, Ronald. 2007. 'Thank Who Very Much'. *The Philosophers' Magazine Online*, 27 July.

Bailey, Ronald. 2006. 'Anyone for Tennis, at the Age of 150?' *Times Online*, 8 April.

Bostrom, Nick. 2006. 'Why I Want to be Posthuman When I Grow Up'. *Future of Humanity Institute Papers.*

Callahan, Daniel. 1987. 'Medicine and the Conquest of Aging'. In *Setting Limits: Medical Goals in an Aging Society*, edited by Daniel Callahan, 52–81. New York: Touchstone.

———. 2007. 'Nature Knew What It Was Doing'. *Cato Unbound*, 10 December.

Caplan, Arthur. 2005. 'Death as an Unnatural Process'. *European Molecular Biology* 6: 72–5.
de Grey, Aubrey. 2007. 'Old People Are People, Too: Why It Is Our Duty to Fight Aging to the Death', *Cato Unbound*, 3 December.
Harris, John. 2007. *Enhancing Evolution: The Ethical Case for Making Better People.* Princeton: Princeton University Press.
Jonas, Hans. 1984. *The Imperative of Responsibility: In Search of an Ethics for the Technological Age.* Chicago: University of Chicago Press.
———. 1996. *Mortality and Morality: A Search for the Good after Auschwitz.* Evanston: Northwestern University Press, 1996).
Kass, Leon. 2002. 'L'Chaim and Its Limits: Why Not Immortality?' In *Life, Liberty and the Defense of Dignity*, ed. Leon Kass, 257–74. San Francisco: Encounter Books.
———. 2003. 'Ageless Bodies, Happy Souls'. *The New Atlantis* 1: 9–28.
Nagel, Thomas. 1979. 'Death'. In *Mortal Questions*, edited by Thomas Nagel, 1–10. Cambridge: Cambridge University.
Nuland, Sherwin. 1994. *How We Die: Reflections of Life's Final Chapter*. New York: Knopf.
Parens, Erik. 2005. 'Authenticity and Ambivalence: Toward Understanding the Enhancement Debate'. *Hastings Center Report* 35(3): 34–41.
Sandel, Michael. 2007. *The Case against Perfection: Ethics in the Age of Genetic Engineering.* Cambridge, MA: Harvard University Press.
Wilder, Billy. 2002. 'Kings of Comedy.' *Time Magazine*, 31 March.
Williams, Bernard. 1973. 'The Makropulos Case: Reflections on the Tedium of Immortality'. In *Problems of the Self*, edited by Bernard Williams, 82–100. Cambridge: Cambridge University Press.

Chapter 5
Some Paradoxes Linked to Risk Moderation[1]

Nathalie Frogneux

> They go on with their daily occupations, feeding, contemplating, building, resting, playing, raising their children, calmly and effortlessly seeing to the business at hand. (Goffman 1959, 238)

Jonas found himself confronted with the paradox of the invisible and imperceptible catastrophe and tried to convince us that the risk is major and quite real: the paradox of a sentiment that readily motivates us, the paradox of predicting a future that should not take place, the paradox of perceiving a future vulnerability felt now and, finally, the paradox of wanting to see ourselves as responsible. Jonas, in fact, sought to raise our awareness of technological perils in 1979, a far cry from today. The global catastrophe has now become all too perceptible, if only for the fact that we encounter it via (allegedly still) local catastrophes such as the Chernobyl nuclear accident in 1986 or the Fukushima natural and nuclear power disaster in 2011; or else through regional changes which may well have their roots in global (climatic) modifications.

Aware that an overall idea of threat anticipation would be setting his sights too high, Jonas hoped that small catastrophes would be enough to make us wake up to the risk and make us change our attitudes. 'Nature is sending us reprimands and I hope that a series of small natural disasters will bring us around to reason in time, so that we are spared from major catastrophes' (Jonas 1993, 61). However, today we have to admit that seeing real local damage has not been enough to make us change our attitudes or adopt new socio-political options. Thus, while we are no longer dealing with ignorance of the threat, we are confronted with a denial of its breadth and seriousness.[2] Yet we are convinced that the same paradoxes carry

1 Translated from the French by John Cronin.

2 Peter Kemp insists on three forms of barriers 'to the good will of a climatic crisis consciousness': physical; structural and economic; psychological and ideological. We synthesize this in the following way. (1) Physical barriers, or might we say scientific, are due to the difficulty of perceiving physical changes whose causal link to human activity is hard to establish scientifically and is so for three reasons: (a) because the causal links are invisible, unperceivable and are not unquestionably proven on scientific bases; (b) subsequently, because the complexity of changes within ecological systems are always multi-factorial; (c) and finally because of their unperceivable character and deferred effects. (2) The second barriers, which Kemp calls structural and economic, are socio-economic and institutional

over from risk ignorance to denial of its scale and thus that the questions Jonas asked are not obsolete. We feel that revisiting the interventions that allowed Jonas to awaken our sense of responsibility and raise the imperceptible to a perceptible level is worth while. In other words, noting that the risk, its potential victims and its overseers had become invisible, Jonas developed mediations to gain the upper hand on that invisibility: (1) Cassandra's paradox, (2) Pascal's wager to incline us to moderation, (3) a heuristics of fear designed to reveal those who are weak and count for us, (4) a declining scale of vulnerability to build confidence and reverse the utilitarian scale, and (5) the real vulnerability of infants, allowing our return to a relationship of transmission with regard to future humanity. We might nevertheless ask ourselves whether the mistrust Jonas harbours with regard to imagination and the emotions might not be the cause of certain problematic points in his thought: Aren't emotions an essential source for trying to open new paths and to resist through creativity? Moreover, his methods seem only to be applicable by those who are already won over to what they want to achieve.

Cassandra's Paradox

Renewing ties with the moral tradition criticized by Nietzsche, Jonas presents fear 'as the best substitute for virtue and true wisdom' (Jonas 1984a, 45; 1984b, 57) and even affirms that 'the appropriate feeling is a mixture of fear and guilt' (Jonas 1992, 141), employing anticipative shame and remorse. This is undoubtedly where the fracture occurs between those accepting and those refusing the argumentation of *The Imperative of Responsibility*. The opposition between those who accept the forecast of misfortune and those who reject it is certainly not new; it is thematized in the anticipation of the Trojan War and the threat hanging over Nineveh.

Jonas is aware of dealing with the heart of Cassandra's paradox: Priam's daughter knows but that knowledge remains vain, for her fellow-citizens won't

and block individual initiatives because of their inertia. 3) Lastly, and these are the most insurmountable, the psychological or ideological barriers: (a) a fatalism declaring any action to be in vain since the catastrophe is inescapable; (b) the 'insignificance complex', which would have it that any action, individual or collective, is derisory given the extent of the task; (c) the short-term view, which supposes that interest and compassion with regard to future generations does not go beyond two or three generations. See Kemp 2010. See also on this subject Garvey 2008, and in particular his paragraph entitled 'psychological resistances', 234–41. Basing himself on Hillman 2004, he enumerates 10 subterfuges which contribute to refusing the facts in blatant bad faith: (1) 'I don't believe in climate change', 2) 'Technology will be able to stop climate change', (3) 'I blame the government (mine or another)', (4) 'Reproaching the risk denouncer for his lack of coherence' (kill the messenger); (5) 'It's not my problem', (6) 'I can't do a thing about it'; (7) 'how I live is my business', (8) 'There are much more urgent (socio-economic) problems to be dealt with'; (9) 'I *do* do something (sorting waste)', (10) 'We have already made a lot of progress in this area'.

listen to her and she fails to convince them. She is sometimes understood not as she who announces the future, but as she who prophesies a misfortune in vain: the fall of Troy. The Trojans know, but don't believe her and don't act. Such is the curse Apollo has cast upon her: her knowledge of the danger and the truth falls on her contemporaries' deaf ears, rejecting her as 'useless Cassandra' or denouncing her 'cries of Cassandra', whose sole effect is to spread panic through the city. Comparing himself to her, Jonas harbours few illusions either as to his own possibilities of convincing people of the veracity of his remarks or as to the practical effectiveness of his predictions[3]. How is one to overcome the paradox of a truth which cannot be assumed because it predicts the inescapable in the hope of mobilizing one's contemporaries so that they might prevent it? 'The prophecy of doom is made to avert its coming, and it would be the height of injustice later to deride the "alarmists" because it did not turn out so bad after all' (Jonas 1984a, 120). Unlike scientific experiments which can count on repetition and comparison, the time of the *human experiment* is irreversible. That is why, if the catastrophe does not occur, we will never be sure that an actual danger was indeed avoided.

We therefore need to distinguish two truth dimensions in prophecy, one involving contents, that of prediction, and the other being effectiveness in prevention. In a strict sense, forecasting may be understood as the anticipated description of a state of the world on which neither the prediction nor the observers have any influence: that is the case of tragic destiny or physical systems, like predicting a solar eclipse. In a second sense, however, when it can be understood by the agents involved, the prediction is a warning of the worst-case scenario, so that efforts might avoid its ever occurring. In this case, we are dealing with a performative act whose aim is to invalidate its content. Jonas situates his remarks as being of this type of prediction. 'I personally believe that the warner would be doomed to a Cassandra role' (Jonas 1974, 98). In this case, Cassandra suffers from the fact that her clear-sighted oracle is self-refuting, but its refutation is its victory, since it cannot claim at once to achieve its goal and to predict the future. This type of prophecy has the duty of being self-negating, since it is no more than hypothetical knowledge

---

3 On the question of alarm, see Goffman 1959, 2 Behavior in *Public* Places. Goffman stresses the fact that the surveillance may be maintained by a few individuals who are more receptive to the sometimes minimal signs others ignore. In this way, and provided that the delegating of responsibilities is clearly recognized, not everyone need be awake. 'Those guarded can devote all their time to ordinary occupations; the guard who permits this result may be selected for his particular competence and his readiness to sacrifice his interests for the groups' embetterment' (our translation from the French edition, 233). It even seems inherent to this guardian function that it may be assumed by some and not by all. Opposed to this, Bernard Sève and Jacques Taminiaux criticize the notion of a fear to which some would be sensitized early on, as well as its political consequences. See the excellent article by B. Sève, 'La peur comme procédé heuristique et comme instrument de persuasion' (1993) and Taminiaux 1991.

understood as prevention. Indeed, the prevention supposes that the undesirable event is possible so that it does not take place.[4]

Certainly, Jonas' talk is unpleasant to our ears and may seem to result from a pessimistic psychology. But what exactly can one reproach a prophecy of misfortune which does not take place with? Undoubtedly, precisely with spreading a panic that paralyses action. However, Jonas, who preaches moderation, hardly fears – and even seeks – to exert this effect on threatening technological and scientific processes.

Cassandra against Pascal

At antipodes from Cassandra's pessimistic figure, we find Blaise Pascal's, although both of them call for action in the present because of an imperceptible future. At the beginning of *The Imperative of Responsibility*, Jonas criticizes Pascal's famous wager for remaining blind as to the value it places at risk and points out the need to reveal the potential loss that such a gesture commits itself to in remaining exclusively riveted on an anticipated benefit. Through analysis of this 'dreadful metaphysical bet' (Jonas 1984a, 13), Jonas criticizes the fundamentally acosmic character of a technological logic which unceasingly bets on the future and refuses to estimate the stakes it lays down. Indeed, it is only thanks to an extreme under-evaluation, or even a negation of present values, that such a wager can be attempted.

Pascal's whole argument consists in making a wager he describes as finite to obtain an infinite good: eternal life.[5] The disproportion between what is wagered and the benefit is such that any rational person capable of figuring the odds cannot allegedly help but take the risk, and hence to wager and bet, affirms Pascal. Actually, as Jonas underlines, what is bet and the gain are not only disproportionate, but incommensurable; what makes it possible for Pascal to take a mortal leap and write that 'the finite is annihilated in the presence of the infinite, and becomes

4 This prophecy bears similarities to the dissuasive intention which consists in threatening the enemy with the worst under certain conditions, so that the conditions under which the worst would take place never come about. Consequently, the dissuasive intention is also self-invalidating or self-refuting. On the contrary, the self-fulfilling prediction or prophecy announces, while supposing, a future state of the world due to the agency of adverse parties, whose realization it provokes. This prediction includes and anticipates its own effect, i.e. it can claim a double victory, on the ethical and metaphysical level. A warning or a wish: these two types of prophecy are performative language acts having new effects on the world.

5 Let us note that, for his part, Jonas refuses the assumption of an individual eternal life. Indeed, Jonas shows that actions performed with a view to recompense in the hereafter can only destroy morality. See 'The Abyss of the Will', in Jonas 1974, 342. See also on this subject 'Immortality and the Modern Temper' (Jonas 1966) and 'The Concept of God after Auschwitz: A Jewish Voice' (Jonas 1996, 131–43).

a pure nothing' (Pascal 1958, 66). Far from a moderate version of faith which consists in stressing that the life most pleasant to God is also what the believer describes as eternal life, this wager relies on a devalorization of the stakes, life on earth, whose value is null (or tending towards zero). Indeed, looked at closely, Pascal claims, the pleasures of social life are negligible and insignificant. 'I will tell you that you will thereby gain in this life, and that, at each step you take on this road, you will see so great *certainty* of gain, so much *nothingness* in what you risk, that you will at last recognize that you have wagered for something *certain* and infinite, for which you have given nothing' (Pascal 1958, 68). The wager's justification is ultimately to show that the gain is *always higher* than what is bet, since what is bet is null. Pascal's wager thus relies on an acosmic and even anti-cosmic axiom that Jonas can no longer accept since his critique of gnostic dualism and its demundanization tendency (*Entweltlichungstendenz*).[6] He refuses Pascal's starting point: 'The stake is one's entire earthly existence with all its possibilities of enjoyment and fulfillment, whose very renunciation is made the price of eternal salvation' (Jonas 1984a, 13). However, applying this utopian reasoning in the context of modern thought on technological advancement is doubly dangerous. First of all, in the case of Pascal's wager, it relates to a radically individual and egocentric good. It is thus indeed a utilitarian calculation of individual interest correctly understood. But the economic-technical-scientific system makes us run collective, and even global, risks, in a universe of 'uncertainty' (Jonas 1984a, 31) and for an 'indefinite future' (Jonas 1984a, 9).

While Jonas refers to uncertainty, what he surely has in mind is the undetermined world in which risks can never be taken in an absolute manner, but always relatively. In other words, the potential risk of an infinite – that is, irreversible or global – loss, should first of all be eliminated. The principal flaw in Pascal's wager is placing nothingness in play twice over: on the one hand, by reducing the stakes of life in the world to a value equivalent to zero and, on the other hand, by getting into a game wherein the gain is possibly null, what the ancient Cassandra knew but the modern Pascal didn't.

The Imperative of Responsibility may be seen as a precursor to the precautionary principle which rules this double pitfall out, since it in fact recognizes that what is at stake is always positive, life on earth, and that no claim can be advanced with the probability of a pure and simple loss. It is only under these two conditions that risk-taking is ethical: in removing the stakes and gains from the incommensurability (in which all players who think they have nothing to lose reside), resituating them in the proportionality (of one who appreciates his stake at its just worth and fears losing it).

In other words, this principle quite simply 'forbids any *va-banque* game in the affairs of humanity' (Jonas 1984a, 38). In an uncertain world, Cassandra is right and Pascal wrong, for the terms of probability are reversed: no matter how infinitesimal, the stakes are infinite compared to a gain which might prove to be

6 On this subject, see Jonas 1988 and 1958.

null. 'This 'go-for-broke' calculation of risks, objectionable also in other respects, is in error already by the fact that, in proportion to the *nothing* which is here accepted among the risks, every something [...] is of infinite magnitude; and thus the second alternative [...] also bears the risk of *infinite* lost.' (Jonas 1984a, 37–8). Jonas reproaches Pascal for not having evaluated his wager's goal under another mode than 'the empty assertion that it [eternal life] is the ultimate value' (Jonas 1984a, 14). But of course it can only be – at best and under the assumption that an eternal life exists – a relative value, since that of life in this world is juxtaposed to it.

In so far as his faith offers him certainty of eternal life, Pascal does not wager: he calculates and counts. His 'wager' is for him the first application of probabilities outside the domain of parlour games.[7] On the other hand, those whose faith is less solid or less radically acosmic do wager.

Paradoxically, turning Pascalian acosmism back into 'radical cosmism', Jonas takes up the notion of staking everything, which this time is God's doing. In effect, if, in a gesture of sovereign freedom, God risks everything – that is, his whole being – it is because a life marked by the future is superior to a static and immutable being. 'In the beginning, for unknowable reasons, the ground of being, or the Divine, chose to give itself over to the chance and risk and endless variety of the becoming. And wholly so: [...] In such self-forfeiture of divine integrity for the sake of prejudiced becoming, no other foreknowledge can be admitted than that of *possibilities*, which cosmic being offers in its own terms' (Jonas 1996, 134). And it may be that God loses his initial bet there, because men unfailingly prove to be poor keepers of this earthly adventure – which is nonetheless worth undertaking.[8]

But as to human activity endangering this precious future, the stakes should be limited and will hardly be able to include the 'great causes' and in no case the 'very great causes', meaning 'the really great, irreversible ones, which go to the roots of the whole human enterprise' (Jonas 1984a, 31). The world's worth is indeed high and non-renewable, for nature proceeds in a groping way in 'making very small bets' very many times over. Consequently, its piecemeal gains are minimal, but added up can produce a major and necessarily slow evolution. Accordingly, its losses are slight and limited because they never involve more than small stakes and remain non-cumulative. This is, in some sort, the prudence and wisdom of natural cosmic-biological evolution. By this slow and extremely fragmented process, nature minimizes its losses and correlatively maximizes its chances of winning.

---

7 Thus, in a strict sense, this Pascalian wager paints a picture of a risky universe, the field of predilection of insurance specialists, characterized by the fact that the agent knows which events may take place in the future and knows the probability of each one of them occurring. *The* paradigmatic and simple example of the probability calculus is the game of heads or tails. The notion of risk elaborated in the context of games of chance (which has led to probability theories and betting) justifies taking measured risks.

8 On this subject, see our study (Frogneux 2002).

In contrast, technology proceeds in taking much greater risks, in placing much more sizeable stakes, which are moreover the fruit of a slow, natural complexification whose loss is irreversible. Through this ample and rapid way of progressing, technology incurs losses that are much greater than nature's and much greater than its gains.

Above and beyond the size of the stakes, Jonas reproaches Pascal's gambler's posture because he claims that a completely hypothetical gain is certain. And yet, every indication would lead us to think that today's economic-technical system places us in Pascal's gambler's position in two ways. On the one hand, because we put a present, major and non-renewable good into play (Jonas 1984b, 38) in the name of an anticipated and always hypothetical progress; on the other hand, because the undefined dynamic of technological progress leads us not to the utopian progress anticipated, but to catastrophe. Confronted with this irresponsible attitude, Jonas retorts that an action's goal should be evaluable with full knowledge of the facts and is even intrinsic to ethical decision-making; however, the world and causality's opacity make any long-range forecasting in a complex world impossible. Against these extreme forms of utopian thinking, ultimately nihilistic, a return to a commitment of costs that are proportionate to benefits is called for. So what are our reasons for granting more credit to the future described by Cassandra than by Pascal?

The Paradoxes of a Rational Fear

For Jonas, fear appears to be a major element of the theory of responsibility in confronting an invisible danger. On the one hand, inasmuch as it imparts new information, it teaches us about danger and boldness avoidance; on the other hand, in motivating us to action, it saves us from cowardice. The first essential moment of the responsible attitude, it is nonetheless not the whole of ethics. Jonas insists on this: he does not preach fear for its own sake or a 'fright principle',[9] but as a method for mobilizing '*the imperative of responsibility*'. That is why he points out and underlines its heuristic and practical dimensions. It presents the following characteristics: (1) it is disinterested fear for others' sakes and not for myself and my own physical integrity; (2) constructed and methodical, it is not a feeling; (3) it relates to a future reality and the object of dread must thus be constructed; (4) rational and not impassioned, it deals with man's image and not with a singular suffering attested to; (5) it does not paralyse but rather motivates action.

9 Jonas proposes a heuristics of fear or fright (*Heuristik der Furcht*). The French translator of *Das Prinzip Verantwortung*, Jean Greisch, chose, however, to sometimes translate *Furcht* by *peur* (fear) and sometimes by *crainte* (fright). In the French-speaking context, also see his study (Greisch 1998). Among this theory's bitter critics in the French-speaking milieu, we mention Dominique Lecourt, Dominique Bourg, Luc Ferry and Catherine Larrère (1997), particularly Chapter 6.

Fright wakes us from our slumbers in emerging from the torpor an overly widespread and unquestioned current of thought has plunged us into. An alert or alarm in a world enfeebled by technicist ideology, it introduces reflexivity and motivates action. Indeed, it is the very fact of being able to remain in a stable environment without questioning it that sinks us into dangerous habits. On this subject, Jonas recalls his memories of the outbreak of World War I: 'Whoever is old enough still remembers the misplaced enthusiasm the youth of a materially saturated bourgeoisie greeted World War I with' (Jonas 1984b, 365) and 'with the stupidity proper to childhood, I had the feeling that something had finally happened' (Jonas 2003, 26, our translation). The young Jonas saw his mistake and that his world was being turned upside down only when he saw that the swimming pool was closed.

Driving us on to face a correctly evaluated danger courageously, fear should give rise to vigilance; that is, it should combine with theoretical and practical reason, triggering an awareness leading to an investigation of the consequences of our actions and a feeling of responsibility.

This fear is apprehension for others and only motivates us to act in that respect. Unlike the Thucydidean model of fear in the Peloponnesian Wars or Hobbes (in those cases fear of a violent death), it is not fear for oneself. It is fear for others, a decentred and disinterested fear. Based on the model of éléos rather than *phobos*, resembling what Aristotle describes in the *Poetics* as the chorus's sympathetic fright in the Attic tragedies – certainly an ineffective fright since the chorus watches the heroes' loss in a spectator role without being able to alert them in time. 'Everybody knows that the vision of tragedy can accomplish things, and comparison with the scene allows us to add anticipative "pity" to that "fright" vis-à-vis a posterity condemned in advance' (Jonas 1992, 141).

This methodical fear is also heuristic because it teaches us about what remained invisible: good and value. Jonas begins with the observation that the negative has a greater revealing capacity than the positive, for it allows a more rapid and surer revelation of what value or good leaves in the shadows and confusion. 'Moral philosophy must consult our fears prior to our wishes' (Jonas 1984a, 27). Indeed, lies reveal the value of truth, injustice that of justice, death the value of life, disease that of health and sleaze the value of probity. Jonas is in notable agreement with Aristotle and Ricœur on this point: 'And evil forces its perception on us by its mere presence, whereas the beneficial can be present unobtrusively and remain unperceived, unless we reflect on it' (Jonas 1984a, 27). Hence a threat (*Bedrohung*) which attacks a value and so is taken seriously as an objective danger reveals what had been taken for granted for being obvious. Tendencies, attraction and appetite can less readily determine a hierarchy of values than fear of losing those values, for they generally remain evanescent and partial.[10]

10 We note that Jonas' entire critique of utopia in Chapter 6 of *The Imperative of Responsibility* is based on his critique of desire. For his critique of attraction, we might also think of the blinding fascination Heidegger exerted on his students and which Jonas 'found repugnant' (see Jonas 2003, 108 and also Greisch 1991).

Accordingly, goodness and prevailing values appear at once as a result of the representation or proof of their opposite, evil. A threat readily highlights a value we adhere to emotionally, and it is just because of that tie that we fear it might disappear or be lost; hence fear motivates us to act. Rationally constructed, the object of this fear escapes the pitfalls of singular, perceived situations. 'And we need the *threat* to the image of man [...] to assure ourselves of his true image by the very recoil [*Erschrecken*] from these threats' (Jonas 1984a, 26–7). Thus Jonas is wary of the effects of compassion and emotions alone in the domain of responsibility. Basing an ethics on compassion alone would be likely to risk attaching oneself too exclusively to the question of suffering, to the detriment of man's image. Opposed to an ethics of well-being, Jonas maintains a qualitative difference between life and living conditions which, whatever their roughness, can never call the value of life as such into question, whether that be within the context of medical responsibility (Jonas 1992, 135) or in defining death (see Jonas 1978).[11]

Let us now reconsider the paradox of the undefined threat. The problem with this 'spiritual' or ethical fear lies particularly in its lack of spontaneity, and hence the uneven character of its mobilization. Knowing and fearing is not enough; people capable of bringing about change must learn and act. But don't you have to be already affected by a fear in order to foster mobilization? For who will be sensitized by such an injunction if not the overseers, already attuned to the future? 'This [what to avoid] is perceived first and teaches us, by the revulsion of feeling which *acts ahead of knowledge*, to apprehend the value whose antithesis so *affects* us' (Jonas 1984a, 27; italics ours).[12] Therefore it is indeed the feeling of fear that the worst might happen that provides new knowledge. '*We know the thing at stake only when we know that it is at stake*' (Jonas 1984a, 27). There is a circularity here that he leaves unresolved.

Jonas himself makes use of this sort of heuristic, crossed between a spontaneous desire anchored in a lack and its evaluation thanks to the threat of losing what we have. Is life's worth better revealed through fear of death or a spontaneously expressed positive desire? The apparently widespread dream of an infinitely long and limitless life is quickly shown for what it is. Indeed, that which is desirable is less an infinite life than the prolongation of days giving it meaning. Yet it is because our days are counted that they count. And an infinite life is desirable neither from an individual nor from a collective point of view, since it would notably have as a hypothetical collateral effect impeding the arrival of newcomers to the world in the name of a massive occupation by old existences.[13] Hence the idea that we might live an endless life as a good can be corrected by the menace of days become meaningless, consequently remedying excessive fears of (individual

11 Cf. German version (Jonas 1985).

12 If we learn about value more quickly through its opposite, this is sometimes linked to the pure negation of what seems to us an anti-value, although revolting against injustice does not thereby allow us to define justice.

13 See on this subject Jonas 1996, 87–98. Cf. German version (Jonas 1992, 100).

death). It is only under the threat of a negative (death disappearing) that a value can be rightly evaluated (human mortality is a good).

Hence such fears deserve to be described as heuristic for providing ideal and philosophical knowledge: a theoretical knowledge of values and ethical principles which Jonas carefully distinguishes, on the one hand, from practical wisdom in the application of these principles – which must needs be political in a technological culture where the actors are necessarily collective – and, on the other hand, from the factual knowledge produced by the empirical sciences which allows forecasting future states of humanity and the world.

> The fact that such extrapolations are no more than conjectural, and each can be opposed plausibly by others without conclusive estimation of the relative probabilities, we found to be innocuous for the doctrine of principles, which needs no more than demonstrated possibilities. But it must be admitted now that this same uncertainty of all long-term projections becomes a grievous weakness when they have to serve as prognoses by which to mold behavior – that is, in the practical-political application of whatever principles were apprehended with the help of the heuristic casuistry. (Jonas 1984a, 30)

Fear does not inform us about future states of the world, but about our values.

Certainly, in conformity with a Leibnizian type of metaphysics, ideal knowledge of ethical principles depends partly on empirical knowledge about the real, the possible and the resulting forecasts, since it is in proceeding to a comparative futurology through alternative hypothetical forecasts (as in a decision tree) that negativity will be taken into account.[14] As an intentional emotion, the feeling of fear allows us to prefigure loss. It is thus in our being horrified at the fate of someone imagined as having suffered an irrevocable loss that we can evaluate the present situation via the future anterior. It is thus a matter of advancing an assessment on a future hypothetical: 'contrary to all logic and all method, in this domain, knowledge proceeds from that against which it has to protect itself' (Jonas 1984b, 63).

Let us therefore stress that threat anticipation does not give free rein to delirious flights of imagination assailing us with false images or fantasies of possibilities: the sort that make us dread what doesn't deserve to be and keeps us in a panicky fear that reason rightly dreads as its worst enemy. Indeed, panic troubles spirits like the god Pan, from whom it takes its name. Jonas relates reason and fear and resorts to a bracketing of emotion, favouring instead the knowledge rational representation provides. Instead of talking about imagined threats, he rather refers to threats of an 'imagined and distant evil' (Jonas 1984a, 28), 'dies vorgestellte *malum*' (Jonas 1984b, 65) and proposes turning our attention to 'thought experiments'

14 All of Jean-Pierre Dupuy's work on enlightened catastrophism consists, on the contrary, in considering the future as necessary and not as the place of numerous possibilities (see Dupuy 2002).

(Jonas 1984a, 29) (*Gedankenexperienceen*, Jonas 1984b, 67), thereby deepening our philosophical wisdom and eliminating certain pointless and vain questions. Moreover, just because ideal knowledge of principles and empirical knowledge of possibilities correct one another, thought experiments have real relevance for the acquisition of philosophical knowledge on the foundations of ethics.

Consequently, in his heuristic detour through negativity, Jonas suggests that fear can come from a detached knowledge of emotions and thus limit itself to mere representation.[15] Similarly, in *The Phenomenon of Life*, he shows how the image – as representation – is constructed beginning with the objectifying capacity of the regard and hence the capacity for abstraction, opening the way to thought, language and the possibility of creating the unreal (see Jonas 1996, 135–75). Hence the goal is to distinguish 'the possibilities of misfortune founded in a sufficiently serious way' (that is, rationally) from 'frightful fantasies [*Furchtfantasien*]' (Jonas 1984b, 72). This caesura between fear and panic, thus enabling him to rationalize anticipative fear, relies on mistrust with regard to imagination, which seems unsuited for finding solutions to the crisis. 'And yet inventing skill in the service of human welfare often reveals itself as in conflict with human dignity' (Jonas 1996, 50). Perhaps in thus opting for a rational representation cut off from its sensitive and imaginary bonds, Jonas finds himself caught up in the non-problem which consists in reconciling an intellectual construction with sensitivity:

> The imagined fate of future men, let alone that of the planet, which affects neither me nor anyone else still connected with me by the bonds of love or just of coexistence, does not of itself have this influence upon our feeling. And yet it 'ought' to have it – that is, we should allow it this influence by purposely making room for it in our disposition. (Jonas 1984a, 28).

That's what he will do with the paradigm of vulnerability a newborn infant represents.

Yet, if fear constructs images following a rational method, doesn't it become impossible to render it its emotional dimension – because the obligation to allow oneself to be affected by representations can only be understood by those for whom representations are always emotional and intentional?[16] But Jonas seems conscious of this problem when he talks about the fright (*Erschrecken*) caused by representing a threat; he undoubtedly recognizes that a separation between rational fear and the emotion of fear is impossible. At the end of *The Imperative of Responsibility*, too, he seems to reduce the voluntary and intellectual

---

15 A supplementary proof of what is an essential distinction for Jonas between, on the one hand, representation (*Vorstellung*) as projecting for a thought experiment and, on the other hand, imagination, i.e. inventive and creative *phantasia* (*Einbildungskraft – Imagination*), appears in a text devoted to the difference between man and animal (see Jonas 1996, 75–86). Cf. German version (Jonas 1992, 34–49).

16 On this point, see Castoriadis 1997. For Castoriadis, the imaginary is always indissociably representative-emotional-intentional.

character of this fear, granting it an emotional dimension: 'Fear is an obligation [...] a justified fear, not pusillanimity; maybe even anguish [*Angst*], but not anxiety [Ängstlichkeit]; and in no case fear [*Furcht*] or anguish [*Angst*] for its own sake. Avoiding anguish [*Angst*] where it is called for would in effect be anxiety [Ängstlichkeit)]' (Jonas 1984b, 392).[17] As Heidegger underlined (Heidegger 1986, §30), fear (*Furcht*) is focused on an object as opposed to anguish (*Angst*), which remains undetermined and objectless. Jonas undoubtedly borrows this distinction: the object of fear is what we produce through a thought experiment, whereas anguish lies in waiting when we know that the worst may occur without our being able to identify its exact nature. On the other hand, what he dreads is anxiety, undoubtedly due to its psychological character, for it paralyses and, in putting off action, may seem fundamentally anti-ethical.

However, this bond is still too tenuous and the problem will involve reconnecting with the emotional dimension of fear – initially put aside. In fact, to the extent that the objective danger is *felt* as a real or probable threat, and to the extent that a sentiment accompanies the prediction of a future hypothetical harm, negativity may reveal its opposite.[18] Whence his (disappointed) hope that local catastrophes might be enough to modify our behaviour.

Risk Internalization and Inverting Utilitarianism

Because technology puts us in a situation of no longer deciding with knowledge of, but in 'ignorance of the facts', we in fact find ourselves in a context similar to that of an experiment. As in a scientific experiment, we are unaware of the effects of the acts carried out, but the comparison stops there because, unlike what happens in the context of 'controlled trials', we do not master our actions, because, on the one hand, the context is not limited and, on the other hand, we cannot identically repeat what goes on irreversibly in reality (and all the more so if it is

17 Our translation from the German text. The American edition of *The Imperative of Responsibility* is not an exact replica of the German edition. On the one hand, it includes a book published separately in German and hence also in French: 'Macht oder Ohnmacht der Subjektivität'. On the other hand, the end of the translation differs slightly from the German edition, notably regarding what might be called 'a little anthropology of Jonas', found in the book's last pages, in section III of chapter 6.

18 In Stefan Zweig's novel entitled *Angst*, Irene lets herself get into an extramarital adventure out of sheer indolence, and the subsequent fear of losing everything, i.e. of losing her reputation and her social life, makes her understand the point to which her lover counts less than her life as a married woman. Irene's husband, Fritz, also thinks that fear may awaken a new consciousness in his wife and enable her to opt for what is most precious, since he commissions an actress to frighten her. However, the novel is well named *Angst* and not *Furcht* (fear), for, terrorized, Irene is drawn into a progressive paralysis of her thought and gestures. Can a heuristic fear (*Furcht*) avoid a paralysing panicky fear (*Angst*) and, if so, how?

on a global scale).[19] Consequently, Jonas seeks a means of moderating the stakes in this 'experimentation' (Jonas 1974, 105–31).

His critique of Pascal's wager and his refusal to lay massive or total stakes down are still not enough for evaluating what reasonable stakes would consist in when acting in an uncertain situation. Hence, in an article devoted to the question of experimentation on humans, he proposes evaluating the risk level which may reasonably be assumed. However, scientific forecasts are not enough here: they need to be associated with the testimony of people competent in evaluating, meaning honest and reliable people. Only those with a sense of responsibility will adhere to this risk scale.

The point is to show that the stakes consented to in view of an expected and, by definition, never certain gain cannot help but be weak or in any case never higher than the hoped-for gain. On the other hand, the stakes invested to preserve or save a precious asset may very well be high and even required of certain individuals by the society. Thus Jonas clearly distinguishes utopian salvation from safeguarding. Saving the day via success does not authorize taking major risks, but preserving and safeguarding an endangered asset merits major risk-taking. Only a way of thinking which depreciates the real world thereby put at risk can confuse the two meanings of the word 'save': based on a devalorization of our world, the first is soteriological or meliorist, while the second is conservative or therapeutic, aimed at restoring a lost former state. However, for Jonas, our condition should neither be saved nor improved; no epoch prepares for the following: 'That genuine man is always already there and was there throughout known history' (Jonas 1984a, 200; Jonas 1984b, 387).

The question is thus the following: Can certain individuals be sacrificed in the name of a common good? Two cases may be envisaged: obligatory conscription for war (and the restoration of peace), and conscription for experimentation (and improvement of living conditions). But we are transposing his question.

He proposes a method capable of specifying a 'so-called common or public good and its potentially superior claims, to which the individual good must or might sometimes be sacrificed, in circumstances that in turn must be counted among the unknowns of our question' (Jonas 1974, 109).[20] He thus seeks a measurement of the proportionality between what is wagered and the desired

19 We are not gamblers with inexhaustible stakes and the experiment cannot be repeated elsewhere. Thus, when Jonas makes the assumption that an intelligent and extraterrestrial form of life might exist elsewhere in the universe, he concludes that, however great the empirical difference between its existence and its non-existence, and however remarkable the intellectual interest of such a discovery, it would in no way modify the philosophical knowledge of our responsibility as to terrestrial nature and the foundations of the ethics of this responsibility (see Jonas 1996, 165–97).

20 Hasn't Jonas all too easily and wrongfully been reproached for having a religious interpretation of society, whereas, like Ivan Illich, for example, he shows that the reasoning accompanying certain utopian reflections presents striking parallels to religious thinking.

gain. Three principles are required to do this: the principles of identification, understanding and motivation, which will be applied as strictly as possible according to the rule of 'decreasing order' for risk-taking. In fact, by ensuring that those who identify with a cause whose stakes they are able to understand and which motivates them personally are the first engaged in risk-taking, we can 'supervise the imperceptible steps' (Jonas 1974, 121) of technological innovation. The call to experimentation and innovation is thus addressed in priority to the researchers and innovators themselves. Thus individuals who most strongly identify with the goals pursued by research and who are (socially and intellectually) the freest in their choices as well as the most motivated and enlightened in having a maximum of up-to-date knowledge in the area are the first concerned with the new methods and technologies.[21]

Hence the second procedure for reinvigorating our sense of responsibility consists in applying a scale in which the least vulnerable should run the greatest risk: this is the rule of a descending order of exposure, a descending scale of permissibility due to an increase in vulnerability.[22] Jonas challenges the fact that creative human relationships of responsibility and solidarity should follow the law of the market and social utility. In effect, this requires reversing the equation according to which what is available can be used, in other words of ensuring that the most vulnerable, who are also the most numerous, will also be the best protected and will finally be the last exposed. In human affairs, the market's utilitarian law replaces that of the duty of elites, 'noblesse oblige' – that is, the law of responsibility according to which power necessarily implies duty: 'accepting the lowest price last (which is excused only by the greatest urgency of need), and paying the highest price first' (Jonas 1974, 121–2).[23] Hence, contrary to market law, Jonas proposes developing an attitude of protection and care. What is vulnerable, fragile, uncertain, wounded or endangered should be protected in proportion to its vulnerability. When lives are involved, the sophism 'the desperate case is an expendable case' should be denounced (Jonas 1974, 125). The *inflexible* principle that 'total helplessness demands total protection' (Jonas 1974, 126; italics ours) replaces it.

---

21 Certainly, this principle of self-recruitment does not resolve everything, for certain innovations may concern people who never fall under the category of researchers. To take only a few examples: young children, the severely handicapped, people at the end of life. Another mode of mediate identification might appear as a version approximating the principle of self-recruitment, but never with the same certainty index and never with the same integration of goals.

22 Jonas in fact proposes developing a rule allowing us to reconcile the need for testing new molecules on human beings with that of respecting them as subjects. This involves responding to the scandals of a medical-pharmaceutical industry which had practised massive research projects in Africa on fragile and readily available populations.

23 Admittedly insufficient as a principle of justice, this principle is limited to reducing injustice.

It is only with a good deal of prudence that we can move down from people informed about the new technologies and known risks, towards people less intellectually or financially motivated, towards people subjected to economic pressures (either because they are poor or because they hope for important benefits) or are (intellectually) unable to resist expert authority. The descending scale allows us to ascertain that the risk weigh first on those who are able to evaluate it before assuming it themselves.[24]

But since this scale seemingly holds an interest which largely exceeds the context of medical experimentation, in that we are now within a global context of technological-scientific experimentation, everything seems to indicate that it will also allow us to evaluate the relationship between technical-scientific gain and risk. It allows us to see whether those who know and understand technologies, including the known and hidden risks they involve, consider that the gain is greater than the potential damage, if the gain is worth while and especially whether the correlative risk is assumable. This scale thus introduces an element of reflexivity within the community of experts and decision-makers.

Of course, this method is not only hard to use but, additionally, is not infallible. Indeed, one must always count on the fact that researchers may be idealistic dreamers ready to involve themselves in hare-brained or dangerous schemes. That an architect may be willing to live in a house he has built himself or that a doctor may take his own medicine is not in itself a guarantee that his contemporaries are safe from the slight madness of convinced and impassioned inventors, even if individual follies may be corrected by the collective involvement of innovators and decision-makers. As we see, Jonas is still wary of fantasies and passions.

But if the researchers' commitment level does not always rhyme with the harmlessness of their inventions, meaning that if this scale should be considered with circumspection in its positive application, on the other hand, its negative application is certainly valid: the innovators' and disinterested deciders' non-involvement in their innovation may be taken as a proof of the innovation's risky character, either for intrinsic reasons or for its being insufficiently secure given the present state-of-the-art, or futile as to an imagined gain.

To those who might regret that certain creative opportunities may end up being smothered in this way, Jonas responds that an absence of gain is always better than the loss of a good obtained through the hard struggle of natural evolution's slow processes. Moderation inevitably presupposes forgoing some possibilities.

Here again it is clear that his intention is not to prevent all technological advance, but to measure the interest and proportionality of the risk incurred in this

24 In this case, if experimentation on human beings involved a new treatment in oncology, those initially subjected to it would be the medical researchers in oncology, then the oncologists, then the research doctors in medicine and other specialization areas, the pharmacists ready to market the products, followed by the assistants in oncology, and finally the students.

undetermined world.[25] This scale is precisely what allows us to assume a position of 'chargé d'affaires' – that is, he who takes risks for others. As with royal food tasters, if the chef is not à table, he has to taste his dish before a witness, and if he cannot taste it himself because the dish is not yet ready, certain members of the cooking team have to serve as overseers and signal any irregularities as to the ingredients and procedures used.

This scale might be rebaptized the 'risk internalization scale', or perhaps the deciders' reliability scale.[26] Only risks taken by those understanding them (as far as possible),[27] those who foresee the benefits and those who are free to refuse them deserve to be brought to public debate. On the contrary, those unwilling to run the risks they are ready to let others run clearly indicate by their attitude that the imagined advantages would be insignificant or null. Thus the experts' involvement in their own technology becomes a clear and explicit barometer of their evaluation of the technology and their reliability.

Anticipating Vulnerability Requires Perceiving Vulnerability

Now let us reconsider the method by which the time gap between us and future generations can be reduced. As a responsibility paradigm regarding the defenceless, Jonas proposes the example of the infant, allowing us to join being and duty in an obvious way, as he puts it. But it is also a way of bringing all the unseen and unforeseeable vulnerabilities back around to a perceived vulnerability. This responsibility paradigm presents the perceptive evidence needed in morals. Jonas affirms: 'Look and you know' (Jonas 1984a, 131). By his very breathing, the newborn addresses an irrefutable injunction to his entourage: 'you have to keep it alive'. According to Jonas, the newborn is unable to address an explicit request and does not oblige us; he does not engender immediate feelings of compassion, empathy or love but, between feeling and duty, a sentiment of responsibility which may then be extrapolated to those we don't see, for they have yet to be born.

---

25 'I say, it is defensible and right to draw when the research objective is worthy enough; and it is a prime duty of the research community […] to see that this sacred source is never abused for frivolous ends' (Jonas 1974, 122).

26 Of course, that would not apply to those rectifying a difficult situation or engaged in institutional reforms, but rather to innovators.

27 Naturally, this scale does not inform us on the unknown and unforeseeable risks for the experts themselves. It cannot function in cases where the anticipated effects will touch neither the experts themselves nor the people with whom they may identify (their own children or grandchildren), as in cases of a technology with effects only felt at a much later date. Thus this scale does not permit us to completely answer the question we asked ourselves – what risks do we make future generations run – but only to reduce the scope of those risks somewhat.

Yet here again, paradoxically, while he motivates our perceptions to awaken a feeling of responsibility, Jonas opts for reason rather than the emotions. 'Thus no mention also is made of sympathy, pity, or whichever of the emotions may come into play on our part, and not even of love' (Jonas 1984a, 131). Jonas therefore indicates a feeling not limited to the situation of a singular encounter and dependent on the partners' proximity. When compassion or empathy incites the entourage to care for the newborn, it is not a matter of instincts and natural feelings, which are usually enough to foster a protective attitude. With the newborn, Jonas in fact proposes a paradigm allowing us to break free from the dogma of the separation between being and duty, since 'a de facto existent immanently and evidently contains an ought for others' (Jonas 1984a, 131). It is indeed a question of visibility that is at play here in its obvious force and hence of the perception affecting us. Hence the theoretician's objection, insinuating doubt about this obviousness in stressing that this child is in the final analysis only a cluster of cells presenting a physiological activity, must be rejected: Jonas refuses the visibility of this imperative's being questioned by the theoretical mathematician's deconstructive intellect, through the abstraction of a disciplinary regard.

> And naturally, even the brightest visibility still requires the use of the visual faculty for which it is meant: it is to this that our 'Look and you will see' is addressed. To contend that this beholding of the given in its fullness possesses less truth-value than the evidence of its last residue in the filter of reduction is a superstition which only lives upon the success-prestige which natural science enjoys outside the cognitive domain it has staked out for itself. (Jonas 1984a, 131).

But there is more to this responsibility paradigm than newborns; it is more about a being of another cohort than about a remote descendant. Hence he is not in the strong, and extremely problematic, sense a being of a 'future generation', but of a descent resulting in future generations belonging to a continuum within humanity. Jonas thereby mobilizes the relationship of co-membership in humanity and *transmission* against a competitive rapport towards future humans; he thus underlines the continuity of cohorts which are always partially contemporary. Imagining future generations as non-contemporary is also engaging in abstractions.

Curiously, the paradoxes underlined by Jonas seem to be weighty paradoxes in the sense that simple rational knowledge and individual will don't seem able to overcome them. It all comes across as if it were unceasingly a question of resisting an egoistic tendency bringing us back around to short-term concerns, to intellectual laziness or, worse, to a desire not to know, to the sluggishness of our personal and social, economic and political habits, to serene bad faith. Hence these 'paradoxes' of responsibility for future generations are not strictly linked to the first generation of ethics for the future, meaning to the moment of our becoming aware of what's at stake, but are rather constitutive of our capacity for sensing our responsibility when we realize what's at stake. To that extent, Jonas is right in reminding us that overseers are needed with the courage to pronounce an unpopular word that will often be proven wrong by later events. He himself thus incarnates the figure of the *warner* and resistant swimmer against the current.[28] Jonas' work on Gnosticism made him quite aware of the saviour figure whose knowledge ends up foiling the world's falseness and illusion. But here knowing is not enough to obtain salvation: you must motivate action. Isn't that one of the dimensions of the philosopher's work, one that he himself fully assumed?

References

Castoriadis, Cornelius. 1997. *The Imaginary Institution of Society: Creativity and Autonomy in the Social-historical World.* Cambridge: Polity Press.

Dupuy, Jean-Pierre. 2002. *Pour un catastrophisme éclairé.* Paris: Seuil.

Frogneux, Nathalie. 2002. 'Une aventure cosmothéandrique: Hans Jonas et Luigi Pareyson'. *Revue philosophique de Louvain* 100(3): 500–526.

Garvey, James. 2008. *The Ethics of Climate Changes: Right and Wrong in a Warming World.* London: Continuum.

Goffman, Erwin. 1959. *The Presentation of Self in Everyday Life.* Garden City: Anchor Books.

Greisch, Jean. 1991. 'De la gnose au *Principe responsabilité*: un entretien avec Hans Jonas'. *Esprit* 54: 5–21.

———. 1998. 'L'*heuristique de la peur* ou qui a peur de Hans Jonas?' In *Une parole pour la vie. Hommage à Xavier Thévenot*, edited by Geneviève Médevielle and Joseph Doré, 103–22. Paris: Cerf.

Heidegger, Martin. 1986. *Sein und Zeit.* Tübingen: Niemeyer.

Hillman, Mayer. 2004. *How Can We Save the Planet?* London: Penguin Books.

Jonas, Hans. 1958. *The Gnostic Religion: The Message of the Alien God and the Beginnings of Christianity*. Boston: Beacon Press.

———. 1966. *The Phenomenon of Life: Toward a Philosophical Biology*. New York: Harper & Row.

———. 1974. *Philosophical Essays: From Ancient Creed to Technological Man.* Englewood Cliffs: Prentice Hall.

———. 1978. 'The Right to Die'. *Hastings Center Report* 8(4): 31–6.

———. 1984a. *The Imperative of Responsibility: In Search of an Ethics for the Technological Age*, translated by Hans Jonas. Chicago and London: University of Chicago Press.

———. 1984b. *Das Prinzip Verantwortung*. Frankfurt: Insel.

———. 1985. 'Techniken des Todesaufschubs und das Recht zu sterben'. In *Technik, Medizin und Ethik. Praxis des Prinzips Verantwortung*, edited by Hans Jonas, 242–68. Frankfurt: Insel.

28 On this subject, see the text entitled 'Against the Stream: Comments on the Definition and the Redefinition of Death' (Jonas 1974, 132–40).

———. 1988. *Gnosis und spätantiker Geist. I Die mythologische Gnosis.* Göttingen: Vandenhoeck und Ruprecht.
———. 1992. *Philosophische Untersuchungen und metaphysische Vermutungen.* Frankfurt: Insel.
———. 1993. *Dem bösen End näher. Gespräche über das Verhältnis des Menschen zur Natur*, edited by Wolfgang Schneider. Frankfurt: Suhrkamp.
———. 1996. *Mortality and Morality: A Search for the Good after Auschwitz*, edited by Lawrence Vogel. Evanston: Northwestern University Press.
———. 2003. *Erinnerungen.* Frankfurt und Leipzig: Insel.
Kemp, Peter. 2010. *Citizen of the World: The Cosmopolitan Ideal for the Twenty-first Century*. Amherst: Prometheus Books.
Lecourt, Dominique, Dominique Bourg, Luc Ferry and Catherine Larrère. 1997. 'Précaution'. In *Du bon usage de la nature. Pour une éthique de l'environnement.* Paris: Aubier.
Pascal, Blaise. 1958. *Pensées*. New York: E.P. Dutton.
Sève, Bernard. 1993. 'La peur comme procédé heuristique et comme instrument de persuasion'. In *Aux fondements d'une éthique contemporaine. H. Jonas et T. Engelhardt*, edited by Gilbert Hottois, 107–25. Paris: Vrin.
Taminiaux, Jacques 1991. 'Sur une éthique pour l'âge technologique'. *Le Messager européen* 5: 187–202.
Zweig, Stefan. 2011. *Angst*. Frankfurt: Fischer.

Chapter 6
Inclusion – A Moral Imperative, but Also Socially Desired? An Essay in the Ethics of Responsibility[1]

Holger Burckhart[2] and John-Stewart Gordon[3]

Introduction

This chapter examines the question of whether in public life the (at least verbally) ubiquitously desired inclusion of people with impairments and those with special developmental needs can be demonstrated in moral-philosophical discourse as ethically imperative, or whether it can only be shown to be socially desired.

To this end, light will be thrown on the problem in three systematic, historical steps.

The first section reconstructs the philosophical discourse of rationality as a discourse of exclusion of questions concerning disability and the disabled. The second section shows, first of all, that the traditional moral-philosophical concepts of flourishing, of a duty-bound or happy life miss the perspective of the impaired person and of disability. Second, on one hand it will be shown that even in the modern discourse paradigm, the impaired person comes to the fore merely as an 'argument' or 'object', but not as a subject or as someone with arguments. On the other hand, it must be investigated whether the outcome of communicative competencies is suitable to answer the initial question as to whether inclusion – conceived as full participation – is ethically imperative. Apart from ethical aspects, philosophic-anthropological aspects also play an important role in this context.

In the third section, as a consequence of the results of reconstruction, we outline a sketch in which the approach of an ethics of responsibility in discourse ethics – and thus a combination of Hans Jonas' thoughts with those of Karl-Otto Apel and Gunnar Skirbekk – forms the starting-point. We believe that it is possible

---

1 Partly translated from the German by Dr Michael Eldred, artefact text & translation, Cologne.

2 Dedicated to the students attending my lectures and seminars who motivated me for the topic discussed in this chapter as well as important impulses to pursue the issue.

3 This chapter originated in the context of the research project on 'Global Bioethics. Human Rights and Disability' financed by the Hermann und Marianne Straniak Stiftung and the Forschungskolleg 'Zukunft menschlich gestalten' of the University of Siegen.

to show that a properly understood concept of eupraxia, together with a dialogic notion of responsibility, could render the social participation of people who are factually excluded in everyday life as morally uncircumventable in the context of the life-world.

The result to be attained is that inclusion is ethically grounded and imperative – but social acceptance still remains our task.

The topic of inclusion is currently at the forefront in diverse social contexts, particularly in education (Colker 2013, Danforth and Gabel 2006, Wallimann-Helmer 2012). Some people believe that inclusion is merely an extended concept of integration, in particular the integration of people with special developmental needs. For others, however, the concept of inclusion concerns the issue of full participation in society according to all its facets. It contains migration, integration and social participation as well as questions about the living situation in society in general.

Although we generally defend a broad concept of inclusion, in the following we will occasionally deal with inclusive education as well. Here, however, a strict distinction must be made between integration and inclusion for the proper perspective of both conceptions associated with the concept to be adequately grasped.

Schematically speaking, integration means additive accumulation towards a common sum or aim, whereas inclusion proceeds from the community and starts with realities and realization-formats for growth, stabilization and further development of communities thus constituted. If integration assumes a starting-point of factual segregation, conversely inclusion paradigmatically presupposes starting from the supra-individual difference of each individual in a community, encompassing everybody. In reference to education, integration presupposes that particular students with impairments attend regular schools if they are – in general – able to adjust to the educational setting of the school in question, while inclusive education requires the educational sector to adjust to the special needs of students with impairments, in order to educate them in the same class as non-impaired students.

Why is this change of perspective so difficult socially? Why do we prefer to stick to integration, and regard inclusion as a thoroughly positive, but unrealistic, utopia? There are many reasons for this, including social, individual-psychological and socio-psychological, cultural, and historic-cultural reasons, but also bold philosophical reasons of a systematic-historical kind. We will examine these in three consecutive steps and then propose a solution.

The Philosophical Discourse of Rationality as a Discourse of Exclusion

If one looks at the tradition of early Western philosophy, at the time when questions concerning human beings were not yet posed starkly at all (if the *homo mensura* postulate is left to one side), the human being is initially a theme in contexts of political and ethical action. In particular, we might mention Plato's *Republic* (1997b) and Aristotle's *Nicomachean Ethics* (1995a) here. Fruitful for our question is, then, the issue posed in various contexts concerning the whence and whither as well as constancy in the alternation of life and death – most notably found in Plato's *Phaedo* (1997a) and Aristotle's *On the Soul* (1995b). The human being is defined as part of living nature, as *zoon logon echon*, as *animal rationale et sociale*, whose related generic feature is defined via the specifically human psychic configuration. This pre-anthropological conception is a first step on the way to excluding people with mental impairments. The soul or psyche as the principle of life, that is, as the first and last ground of possibility, determines the species-being of human, animal and plant – both within themselves and against each other. A human being is defined as capable of reflection. Without the argument from potentiality – as it is used today, in order to answer questions regarding being not yet able, or no longer able, to reflect – the severely mentally or linguistically impaired fall into the category of the non-human. This is reinforced in ethics, but also in Aristotle's metaphysics, where competence to engage in dialogue and discourse – that is, the reflective discourse of grounding through argument – is highlighted as being the special active hallmark of 'rationality/reason'.

As is well known, this continued in the Christian and Modern Age discussion in the context of the *imago dei* assumption of the special human being, to whom God has given the world to shape.

Into the philosophical discussion Kant (2002) steps decisively with his double determination of human being, when he distinguishes between *animal rationale* and *animal rationabile*, as well as between morality and moral law – which every reasonable being should (be able to) follow – and the plane of character and virtue that is essentially based on socialization. This separation is an important indication that things are moving in the right direction, but does not yet reach the goal, because ultimately Kant sees the starting-point of the *ens perfectissimum*, the perfect living being, as a yardstick. Instead of this perfect difference in unity, Kant (2002), too, proceeds from a fundamental difference between rational beings and those who lack the capacity of rationality when he claims that only rational beings have dignity in so far as they are capable of acting morally – that is, of acting autonomously. In this respect, autonomy is the foundation of the dignity of each rational being. Beings who are endowed with dignity are – according to Kant – required to treat themselves and other rational beings not only as mere means (Kant 2002). Furthermore, in Foucault's *Birth of the Clinic* (1973) or *Madness and Society* (1965), we can also acknowledge the consequences just as we can with Nietzsche's morality of masters and slaves (2006, trans. 1994).

This very brief history of the discourse of rationality from an anthropological perspective shows that such an exclusion unquestionably has to do with the particular history of Western philosophy.

The Impaired Person – Amoral? – Communicatively Competent?

In a twofold step, let us look at these questions. Can people with restricted reflective competence be responsible, in a moral sense? We treat animals, or at least we should treat them, according to morally acceptable standards. This holds true for the broad spectrum of the conservation of species and domestication through to medically required experiments on animals. To cite Gunnar Skirbekk (2012), animals are moral objects, but not moral subjects or beings capable of making arguments. This means that animals should be protected because we as human beings have an interest or reason not to harm them, for example by virtue of their vulnerability. This anthropocentric argument, however, does not ascribe animals a moral status independently of the existence of human beings.

Is it any different for the mentally impaired, or at least the severely mentally impaired? Factually, no (if rationality is the cornerstone of morality), but pragmatically, yes. Pragmatically, yes, because the mentally impaired still remain human beings independently of any particular medical impairment, and therefore they are protected by laws that forbid treating them in an inhuman or undignified way. Unfortunately, however, the factual argument predominates: the mentally disabled do not appear to be moral actors and are also, with good intention, not held responsible, and this holds true, as is well known, even in pertinent contexts of criminal law. This, however, is once again an individual exclusion, and the classical ethical concepts of utilitarianism, deontic ethics and the ethics of happiness of all kinds are asserted 'in favour of' such exclusion (e.g. Graumann 2012). The behaviour of the impaired should, indeed it must, not (be able to) correspond precisely to these ethical types; at best, it should be ensured that they are free of suffering and should be able to experience themselves to a maximum extent. With regard to step 1, the mentally impaired are even excluded from ethically grounded options for action, because these are based thoroughly on rational reflection and thus on behaviours providing reasons and exercising reason. The impaired would thus also be systematically excluded from the perspective of ethical action.

The former practice of the medieval court fool and, nowadays, the practice of special schools, etc., exemplify this impressively (albeit in a negative way). In practice, society basically treats people with mental impairments as 'special cases' with 'special conditions', and it thereby classifies the mentally impaired as *amoral* and as greatly restricted in their ability to communicate. Only by appealing to an approach that draws on communicative competence – with the classical facets of Searle's speech-act theory (1969) and Wittgensteinian language games (2001) – for those with restricted semiotic capabilities as well, and which, at the same time, takes up the concept of moral action, will people with mental impairments not be denied human status. Instead – like every other human being, indeed, every living being, in its uniqueness as a difference within a whole – the impaired can be taken as a starting-point.

Participation as a Basic Right: Hans Jonas' Perspective from the Ethics of Responsibility

Let us begin this constructive section with a question concerning an ethics that fulfils our endeavours. If, for once, one does not break down the happy and flourishing life – eupraxia – into reflective hierarchical acts at whose end the reflective form of life lies as happiness itself, and if one breaks down, for once, reflective insight into the validity of ethical law and the resulting categorical imperative of its application to moral action, then one quickly comes to different, but not necessarily higher and lower, life-formats. One comes to life-formats of differing practices with similar and individual equally valued ethical components, instead of hierarchies. This, however, is woven neither into classical ethics nor into classical conceptions of reason. But if one turns away from such substantive conceptions of ethics and reason or rationality, and turns toward procedural conceptions of ethics, then the problems we have confronted so far can be answered positively, and the unquestionably correct aspects of traditional approaches – such as rational justification and dialogic acceptance of responsibility – can be incorporated. Particularly important are concepts relevant to our context, as presented by Jürgen Habermas in his works *Theorie des kommunikativen Handelns* (2011, trans. 1985), *Faktizität und Geltung* (1998a, trans. 1998b), and *Zukunft der menschlichen Natur* (2005, trans. 2003), as well as by Karl-Otto Apel in his *Diskurs und Verantwortung* (1990), and finally, with a pragmatic, so-called praxeological perspective, as presented by Gunnar Skirbekk in *Rationality and Modernity* (1993), *Praxeologie der Moderne* (2003) and *Herausforderungen der Moderne* (2012). All of these works can be read as supplements to Hans Jonas' *Das Prinzip Verantwortung* (1979, trans. 1984).

Without question, it was Hans Jonas who critically brought conceptions of traditional ethics, together with questions of an anthropological nature concerning the theory of rationality, into the discussion. Here we do not have to argue about the well-known critique of his metaphysico-ontological foundations, but rather we must sharpen the focus on the *shared* task of shaping a future worthy of human life, one which holds true independently of culture, talent, or physical or mental fitness, for a life *worthy of a human being* in general. Coupled with the semiotic act-perspective that Habermas (1985) introduced into the debate, this means acting in the mode of mutual respect before the actions of the other as other, a mode which then requires the art of translation and not the practice of exclusion. It also requires that we couple both thinkers, which Apel (1990) has undertaken with his approach to discourse ethics when he conceives of dialogical practice as constitutive of meaning and validity and also as unsurpassable – perhaps not indispensable – with regard to legitimacy. We know very well about the latter in the mode of violence and factual exclusion from participation. A principle of discourse of such a kind offers itself as a yardstick for social inequality, for instance, in discourses on education.

One might object that an attempt to use a sophisticated version of discourse ethics, even in connection with Jonas' notion of responsibility, seems unfruitful in the context of disability and education. The underlying assumption is that in order to be an equal member of the ethical discourse one needs to fulfil certain criteria, such as a minimum standard of rationality and sufficient communicative skills which – simply speaking – most people with (severe) mental impairments do not have. Therefore, mentally impaired people (as well as animals) are not members of the ethical discourse (although they can be represented by another person), even though they can have a certain particular moral status which the members of the ethical discourse ascribe to them. In other words, if the members consensually make the well-informed decision to exclude mentally impaired students from the regular school system, then this is – according to the theory – just.

At first sight, this line of reasoning seems to be sound, but at second glance one might question the objection by appealing to Jonas. For example, one could in general question the idea that rationality should be used in order to ascribe moral status. This is only one suggestion – admittedly a very popular one – among many other proposals, such as Albert Schweitzer's approach (1991) where he claims that all living beings are part of the moral community, deserving the same respect. Even though rationality is the necessary precondition of being held responsible for one's actions, it nonetheless must not be a sufficient criterion in order to be a full member of the moral discourse and community. For example, little children, who are not of course fully rational, and people with dementia, who are no longer fully rational, both enjoy human rights without sharing the burden of the corresponding duties. That is, there is no reciprocity involved in this relationship. Likewise, one could also argue for the claim that mentally impaired people are always full members of the moral community (with all rights) and therefore should also be part of ethical discourse.

The question is, then, how mentally impaired people could be part of the ethical discourse as such, if they are unable to actively participate in the decision-making process by virtue of their lack of rationality. The response is simple and straightforward. Following Jonas, we believe that the notion of responsibility is of utmost importance and must reflect the whole process of consensual ethical reasoning and decision-making. Two points should be mentioned that back up this claim. First, rational human beings are members of the ethical discourse and should be seen as *active* participants. Mentally impaired human beings, instead, are *passive* participants, who should be seen as members of the ethical discourse independently of their inability to actually partake in discussion. Second, their particular perspective is brought to the fore by the normative structure of the discourse itself, which is based on core features such as dialogic responsibility, care, relational bonds and eupraxia. Whether this should be further strengthened by additional representatives or advocates in the ethical discourse who speak in the name of the mentally impaired is, at least pragmatically speaking, a reasonable idea but – as has been argued – *not* part of the theoretical justification.

Referring to education, based on the above-mentioned analysis, it is logically impossible to circumvent the uncircumventable at a theoretical level of justification. That is, one is no longer able to justify integrated education (i.e. exclusion) by appealing to the consensus of the members of the ethical discourse. According to our view, it is practically impossible to constantly act against one's own better knowledge on a practical level without becoming immoral or less authentic. In order to remain a morally serious person, one is – therefore – required to fulfil the demands of inclusion, and particularly inclusive education.

Conclusion

With Jonas, and beyond him, we can then finally ascertain, along with Gunnar Skirbekk (2012), that the challenge of modernity lies in participation; and realizing it requires:

- taking seriously the difference between cultures and religions as of equal kind and equal value, instead of discrediting them with (perhaps) unintentional blasphemy;
- splitting the reconciliation of religions and modernity neither into one-sided secularization nor into dogmatic religiosity, but, rather, valuing both from the perspective of intercommunicating channels and accepting both in their individual character;
- respecting the difference between democracies as a difference between life-formats without undermining basic standards of democracy; as well as
- dissolving every form of ethical gradualism insofar as it is hierarchical, and transforming it into an individual, universal, ethical potentialism, in which everyone can take part in so far as they are accessible to communicative competence. In this system, everyone has a right to participate alongside those who bear responsibility and who, accordingly, can potentially act ethically and be made morally accountable for their actions.

Against this background, difference in the sense of exclusion becomes inapplicable, in favour of difference as a starting-point whose common third element is that, fundamentally, communicative competence is ascribed to those who are different as their 'human nature'. And this determines the difference from those for which we are ethically exclusively responsible in a one-sided way, such as the animate and inanimate ecosphere or biosphere. Neither of these can call us to account. Their claims, however, must be represented by advocates, just as Hans Jonas also teaches us how we can be sensitized to the circumstance that between us, as bearers of responsibility, and the bio/ecosphere, there is an Aristotelian gradual difference, but no difference in principle. If all this is drawn before the brackets of our social practice as human beings, cooperating with and also rivalling each other, but also as human beings vis-à-vis animate or inanimate nature, then the life-world (i.e. quasi that which is within the brackets) is suffused and impregnated with participation – in which difference is constitutive of the diversity and quality of life, since communicative competence is also ascribed to those who are different by virtue of 'human nature'.

Starting from difference conceived as a diversity, of those who are morally and communicatively of equal kind and equal value – that is, starting from the situation of a counterfactually anticipated discursive universality (Skirbekk 2012) – makes talk of participation and the claim to participation not only possible and sensible, but also necessary in an ethical and social sense.

References

Apel, Karl-Otto. 1990. *Diskurs und Verantwortung: Das Problem des Übergangs zur postkonventionellen Moral*. Frankfurt: Suhrkamp.

Aristotle. 1995a. 'Nicomachean Ethics'. In *The Complete Works of Aristotle*, edited by Jonathan Barnes, 1729–867. Princeton: Princeton University Press.

———. 1995b. 'On the Soul'. In *The Complete Works of Aristotle*, edited by Jonathan Barnes, 641–92. Princeton: Princeton University Press.

Colker, Ruth. 2013. *Disabled Education: A Critical Analysis of the Individuals with Disabilities Education Act*. New York: New York University Press.

Danforth, Scot and Susan L. Gabel. 2006. *Vital Questions Facing Disability Studies in Education*. New York: Peter Lang.

Foucault, Michel. 1965. *Madness and Civilization: A History of Insanity in the Age of Reason*, translated by Richard Howard. London: Tavistock.

———. 1973. *The Birth of the Clinic: An Archaeology of Medical Perception*, translated by Sheridan Smith. New York: Pantheon Books.

Graumann, Sigrid. 2012. 'Freiheit als Entwicklungskonzept und das Menschenrecht auf inklusive Bildung'. *In Chancengleichheit und 'Behinderung' im Bildungswesen*, edited by Ivo Wallimann-Helmer, 86–106. Freiburg im Breisgau: Karl Alber.

Habermas, Jürgen. 1985. *Theory of Communicative Action*, translated by Thomas McCarthy. Boston: Beacon.

———. 1998a. *Faktizität und Geltung: Beiträge zur Diskurstheorie des Rechts und des demokratischen Rechtsstaats*. Frankfurt: Suhrkamp.

———. 1998b. *Between Facts and Norms: Contributions to a Discourse Theory of Law and Democracy*, translated by William Regh. Cambridge: MIT Press.

———. 2003. *The Future of Human Nature*, translated by Hella Beister and William Regh. Cambridge: Polity Press.

———. 2005. *Zukunft der menschlichen Natur: Auf dem Weg zu einer liberalen Eugenik?* Frankfurt: Suhrkamp.

———. 2011. *Theorie des kommunikativen Handelns*. Frankfurt: Suhrkamp.

Jonas, Hans. 1979. *Das Prinzip Verantwortung: Versuch einer Ethik für die technologische Zivilisation*. Frankfurt: Insel Verlag.

———. 1984. *The Imperative of Responsibility: In Search of an Ethics for the Technological Age*. Chicago: University of Chicago Press.

Kant, Immanuel. 2002. *Groundworks for the Metaphysics of Morals* [1785], translated by Allan W. Wood. New Haven: Yale University Press.

Nietzsche, Friedrich. 1994. *On the Genealogy of Morality*, translated by Carol Diethe. Cambridge: Cambridge University Press.

———. 2006. *Zur Genealogie der Moral*, edited by Volker Meid. Stuttgart: Reclam.

Plato. 1997a. 'Phaedo'. In *Plato. Complete Works*, edited by John M. Cooper, 49–100. Indianapolis: Hackett Publishing.

———. 1997b. 'Republic'. In *Plato. Complete Works*, edited by John M. Cooper, 971–1223. Indianapolis: Hackett Publishing.

Schweitzer, Albert. 1991. *Die Ehrfurcht vor dem Leben: Grundtexte aus fünf Jahrzehnten*. Munich: Beck.

Searle, John. 1969. *Speech Acts: An Essay in the Philosophy of Language*. London: Cambridge University Press.

Skirbekk, Gunnar. 1993. *Rationality and Modernity: Essays in Philosophical Pragmatics*. Oslo: Aschehoug AS.

———. 2003. *Praxeologie der Moderne*. Weilerswist: Velbrück Wissenschaft.

———. 2012. *Herausforderungen der Moderne*. Berlin: Logos.

Wallimann-Helmer, Ivo, ed. 2012. *Chancengleichheit und 'Behinderung' im Bildungswesen*. Freiburg im Breisgau: Karl Alber.

Wittgenstein, Ludwig. 2001. *Philosophische Untersuchungen*, edited by Joachim Schulte. Frankfurt: Wissenschaftliche Buchgesellschaft.

PART 3
On Religion, Ethics and Natural Philosophy

Chapter 7
God in the World of Man: Hans Jonas' Philosophy of Religion[1]

Michael Bongardt

Religions served as an important point of reference for Jonas his whole life long – for his personal life and even more so for his scholarly work.[2] Hans Jonas never disassociated himself from his Jewish identity. Born into a liberal Jewish family, he encountered among his relatives stricter forms of Jewish life, although these always remained alien to him. Early on, he joined the Zionist movement and during his studies was often active with groups of his fellow Jewish students. Jonas became defined by his Jewish origins through external forces, the unspeakable brutality of Nazi persecution, which killed his mother and drove Jonas into exile. He expressed his commitment to defeating the Nazi regime and his support for the existence of the State of Israel not only as an intellectual, but also as a soldier. He maintained friendships with Jewish scholars throughout his whole life – from his academic beginnings in Germany to the New School in New York, the émigré university where he taught. Yet, it was in his talks with Rachel Salamander in 1989 that he revealed the fact and extent to which the Jewish tradition provided the foundation for his life and thought (Jonas 2003, 339–47).

However, whether or not or to what extent Jonas felt bound to Judaism is of no significance in assessing his academic work. At best, it explains his critical receptiveness for religious phenomena of the past and present, as well as his particular interest in the significance of Jewish thought in terms of both spirituality and the history of religion. As such, Jonas consistently stressed in his academic work that he did not regard himself as a theologian, but rather as a philosopher. He questioned religious texts according to their philosophical content, but also examined philosophical texts in terms of their hidden metaphysical premises and allusions. He characterized only a very few of his reflections as 'speculative theology' (Jonas 1987, 131) and clearly separated these from his philosophical thought. With this strict differentiation of both perspectives and the greater emphasis that Jonas accorded to philosophy, his work quite definitely exhibits parallels to the thought of Emmanuel Lévinas, his fellow student from Freiburg, who was only two years his younger. Lévinas also clearly differentiated between his philosophy,

1 I have to thank John Bergeron, Berlin, for the very thorough translation of my text into English.

2 For the biography and history of the work of Hans Jonas, see Böhler 2010.

which was almost entirely concerned with the subject of transcendence, and his biblical and Talmudic studies (Lévinas 1992, 13–17).

The subjects of research pursued by Jonas in the history and philosophy of religion extended far beyond the scope of Jewish tradition. Jonas regards religious systems and mythical traditions first and foremost as forms of self-interpretation of human life (Jonas 1965, 80–89). On the basis of Jonas' elaborately detailed proposition of the unity of all life, it is possible to formulate still further: Jonas sees religions as the self-interpretation of life, achieved in man through his abilities to self-reflect and interpret. As such, his concern is that formulated in the title of my chapter: 'God in the World of Man'. Here, God appears as an idea of man in his attempt to interpret the world.

Such interpretations are in no way trivial. They have a direct impact on the orientation and actions of people in the world. The value attributed to the world by man and the beliefs in God and gods that men have developed have the highest practical relevance for life. Whether man views his earthly existence as a gift or a curse can be recognized by how he behaves towards the earthly reality with all of its living beings.

The significance of this relationship between the religious self-interpretation of man and his concrete life is something that Jonas only gradually came to realize. External events, including the Nazi regime, the arms race, and insight into the real danger of an ecological catastrophe, have undoubtedly contributed to this realization. This helps to explain the various phases that can be recognized in the thought Hans Jonas with respect to the philosophy of religion. This development spans from his early preoccupation with Christian theology and research into Gnosticism to the development of a philosophical biology and the 'Imperative of Responsibility'. These concerns were accompanied by investigations into the significance of Jewish thought, both past and present. The philosophical insights of Hans Jonas are remarkably fruitful when he inquires into the metaphysical preconditions and consequences not only of the thought of others, but also of his own positions. He thereby does not manage to arrive at the reality of God, but does come to reach some 'metaphysical suppositions' (Jonas 1992b). He even ventures to further deliberate these suppositions within a theological perspective, namely, under the precondition, posited by faith, that a God exists. He then asks whether and how this 'God in the world of man' can exist and be present. Thereby, Jonas once again proves himself to be a philosophical thinker who swims 'against the stream' (Jonas 1974, 133–40) of his time. The stages of his intellectual development can be clearly differentiated in terms of the subject of thought. Yet, it is not possible to separate them temporally, as the transitions are fluid.

The following text will present the main focal points of Hans Jonas' thought in their essential intentions and results. These will be interspersed with reflections and comments in an attempt to make clear why Jonas had to move beyond previously attained insights and search for new approaches. An image of this religious and philosophical thinker thereby emerges which, despite all its consistency, remains impressively multifaceted.

A Christian Point of Departure: Three Thinkers from Marburg

How did it come about that two of the earliest academic works of Hans Jonas focused on the apostle Paul (Jonas 1974, 335–48) and Augustine (Jonas 1965)? Many regard Paul as the true founder of Christianity, who transformed the Jewish 'belief of Jesus' into the Christian 'belief in Jesus' (Buber 1950). Augustine, an authoritative exegete of the epistles of Paul, stamped Christian theology with his anthropological pronouncements on sin and grace for many centuries.

How and why Jonas became occupied with the two key figures in the history of theology of the Western Church can be initially explained by his two most important teachers. When, as a university student, Jonas followed Martin Heidegger to Marburg in 1924, he there met Rudolf Bultmann. Yet, one should first call to mind the situation in which these three very different thinkers challenged and enriched each other's thought. In the years following the First World War, Germany experienced a period of profound disorientation. The previous social order had been shattered and traditional customs and conventions came under question. Heidegger emerged in this situation with the claim of establishing philosophy anew. He aimed to conceptualize a new ontology on the basis of an existential analysis of human 'being'. In the process, he explicitly turned against all previous systems, including, as a matter of course for Heidegger, religion,of which Christianity is a part. Despite this, he adopted numerous concepts from Christian anthropology in order to articulate his ideas (Jonas 2004a, 43). The proximity of his analysis of human existence is conspicuously close to the insights of Søren Kierkegaard. Yet, Kierkegaard's steadfast attachment to the Christian understanding of God and salvation was sacrificed by Heidegger for a purely immanent philosophy set in this world. For his part, Bultmann saw the necessity of a new beginning for Christian theology. Bible criticism of the eighteenth and nineteenth century was concerned with the classification of biblical texts in the context of their emergence and development, and the conclusions derived from these endeavours subsequently served as the basis of exegesis.[3] Whether and how these texts by antique authors could still be regarded as holy revelation became the decisive issue for theology. Also requiring fresh examination was whether and/or how these texts could provide the faithful with access to God (Bongardt 2009, 149–58). Between 1924 and 1927 Heidegger developed the fundamental ideals of *Being and Time* (1986) his main work, which had been stimulated in many respects by the thought of Bultmann. At the same time, Bultmann was attempting to employ Heidegger's existential teachings to gain new meaning from biblical texts and he developed his method of 'demythologization'.[4] Hans Jonas, their common student, dedicated himself to exploring Paul and Augustine from an explicitly philosophical perspective. In the process, he not only provided his teachers with a significant stimulus, but also began the first steps along his own path on the philosophy of religion.

3 On contemporary criticism of Bible criticism and the history of religion, cf. Schweitzer 1913.

4 Cf. in a programmatic review: Bultmann 1965.

Paul and Augustine: The Aporia of Human Freedom

Early Christianity professed a belief in Jesus Christ as the saviour of mankind and hoped for an eschatological completion of this salvation beyond the realm of history and time. In particular, Paul attached great importance in demonstrating the universal significance of Christ and the belief in Christ as saviour. This could succeed only by making plausible the need of all mankind, without exception, for salvation. According to Paul, the plight of mankind lies in its sins. With this soteriological interest, he thereby presents the thesis: 'For all have sinned and fall short of the glory of God' (Romans 3:23).[5] It is a thesis which cannot truly expect unquestioning approval.

Jonas approaches Paul's theology in an equally unconventional and remarkable manner. He completely sets aside the question as to whether and/or how Jesus' death on the cross delivered mankind from its sins. 'About this possibility philosophy has nothing to say' (Jonas 1974, 341). Instead, Jonas aims to examine with the aid of an 'existential analysis' (Jonas 1974, 335)[6] whether the anthropological claims of Paul express such a fundamental experience and constitutive state of human existence in order for them to be accredited with Paul's assertion of universal validity. Jonas therefore assumes that human suffering can exist and that it can be recognized and described independent of the prospect of salvation (cf. in principle: Jonas 1974, 237–60). Jonas has chosen a key text from the New Testament, Romans chapter 7, in order to prove his point. Here, Paul employs the first-person singular to describe the inner turmoil of man in what Jonas claims is a representation not only of the concrete historical person of Paul, but of 'man as such' (Jonas 1974, 336). 'For I do not perform the good which I will, but the evil I will not, that I do' (Jonas 1974, 338). The subsequent text leaves no doubt that man is himself responsible for this ambivalence and cannot accuse an external force of leading him astray from the chosen path.

Jonas attempts to elucidate this rather enigmatic text with an analysis of human desire.[7] The precondition for desire in freedom is the self-awareness of man, constituted through reflection on one's own thought and actions. Man recognizes himself as a counterpart to all the objects of the world and to himself. He discovers that he can react to these objects as to himself. His behaviour is not determined, but rather he faces an abundance of possibilities. Man must therefore come to a decision and his will comes into play. Man can and should choose – not only the concrete goal of a particular action, but, more primordially, he must choose himself as a volitional agent. 'It must be noted that the reflection of the will is itself volitional, the will is at once the willful positing and affirmation of itself. The formula, therefore, reads [...] *volo me velle*' (Jonas 1974, 338). Yet, according to

5 Cf. in addition e.g. Wilckens 1978, 170–202.

6 This takes place with direct reference to Heidegger.

7 Cf. in the following the detailed interpretations of the text by Lenzig 2006, 19–49; Bonaldi 2008.

Jonas, it is exactly at this point that the dialectic of human freedom breaks down. On the one hand, man desires to realize his freedom through concrete actions and thereby go beyond himself. On the other hand, he has the tendency to refuse exactly this self-realization of freedom. If he follows it, then he ends up turning back to himself in ever-new reflections and objectifications. The 'volo me velle' thereby transforms into a 'cogito me velle' (Jonas 1974, 340) – instead of an action, one is left with thought, in which human freedom remains imprisoned. Jonas stresses that this self-entanglement of human freedom is its own deed and responsibility. It takes place independently of how one's own 'ought' is construed – whether it is through a divine command or an autonomous Kantian law. The de facto universality of this snare internal to freedom can be understood in light of the 'giddiness' (Jonas 1974, 344) that takes hold of freedom when it glimpses into the abyss of its own possibilities. Self-objectification, which Jonas, in other locations, describes as 'vanity' (Jonas 1965, 44) with respect to a concrete act, should stem this giddiness. This explains the inner turmoil depicted by Paul, which Jonas acknowledges as an apt description of human freedom. Jonas' existential analysis refers, through Heidegger, back to Kierkegaard, for whom the concepts of 'self-choice' (Kierkegaard 1987, 227–30) and 'giddiness' (Kierkegaard 1983, 60)[8] play a central role. With respect to the conception of man before God, developed by Augustine over the course of his life, Jonas was clearly more critical (Jonas 1974).[9] In a detailed exegesis of the text in which Augustine repeatedly comments on Romans 7, Jonas demonstrates how Augustine loses sight of the dialectic of human freedom and transforms it into a developmental logic of freedom (Jonas 1965, 64, 74). Augustine felt challenged by his theological opponent Pelagius to identify the relationship between human freedom and divine grace. The conflict ended with Augustine expressing confidence that grace enjoyed precedence, even sole efficacy. This position has far-reaching consequences. If a man has not yet received 'the state of grace', it means that he does not share the belief of the Church in Christ and cannot recognize, desire, nor do good (Jonas 1965, 71). He can't even yearn for faith. Because he lacks every form of freedom, he is also unaware of its dialectic. Yet, the free grace of God, which is not subject to this dialectic, is the sole operating force in the man of faith. By identifying 'original sin', passed on through the act of procreation, as the reason for the lack of freedom in man, he abandons an idea so important for Paul, namely, that man's actual lack of his freedom is the consequence of freedom. Jonas refuses to become involved in these Christian controversies.[10]

8 The current English language edition of Kierkegaard's work translates the concept with the term 'dizziness'.

9 In addition, Lenzig 2006, 51–63; Müller 2008, 17–25; and, not least, the introduction by Robinson 1965, 11–22.

10 Kierkegaard (1983, 22–7) had already discovered the internal aporia of original sin: what did not take place out of freedom cannot be counted as sin. A detailed analysis of Augustine's understanding of freedom and sin is offered by Häring 1979, who takes up many of Jonas' motifs.

However, he views Augustine's 'dogmatism' (Jonas 1965, 24–5), in contrast to the Paul's Epistle to the Romans, as inadequate to describe the permanent challenge of man in his experience of freedom.

By way of conclusion, it should be pointed out that there is a problematic accent in Jonas' analysis of freedom. According to Jonas, the task to be fulfilled by freedom is to live 'within the execution of its self-chosen action' instead of being 'its own observer' (Jonas 1974, 340). This formulation is ambiguous. This could be understood as a translation of Kant's inculcated duty to do the good for the sake of the good, without expectation of divine reward or the possibility of self-praise. The sentence can also be read in the spirit of Heidegger, whose concern is that man comes into his 'ownedness' when given over not to ethical tasks, but rather those that are powerfully stipulated.[11] The possible consequences of such an understanding would exhibit themselves within only a few years after Jonas drafted his exegesis of Paul.

Some of the insights that Jonas arrived at so early in his career would prove central to his later thought in religious philosophy. Human freedom, chosen in self-consciousness, is the indispensable precondition for ethically responsible actions. It should be stressed that the beliefs that men had and still hold of their relationship to God is of considerable significance in the discovery of this freedom – even though Jonas discerns these beliefs only as a horizon in his investigations of Paul and Augustine, while refraining from examining them in detail.

Man in the World: From Anthropology to Cosmology

Even the hermit, who, in his solitude, attempts to understand God, is at the same time a man in the world and is intricately bound to natural and social interconnections. As such, Jonas refers to '"Welt" und "Selbst" in ihrem korrelativen Verhältnisse als ein Urthema aller faktischen Selbstdeutung' (Jonas 1964, 14).[12] And for this very reason, Jonas felt in necessary to augment his insights on human self-understanding attained through his work on the apostle Paul and the interpretations of Augustine by conducting research into the human understanding of the world at that time. With this as his goal, he turned to Gnosticism, a subject that had previously concerned him in his short doctoral dissertation (Jonas 1928).

For centuries, Gnosticism had been regarded as an early Church heresy, the rejection of which resulted in the development of Christian orthodoxy. It was only in the late nineteenth century that research into the history of religion arrived at the conclusion that Gnosticism was a much more all-encompassing phenomenon, which could also be observed beyond those cultures influenced by Hellenism.

11 This criticism is also expressed by Bonaldi (2008, 224). However, he wrongly understands such a resoluteness without content as a position held by Paul.

12 '"World" and "self" in their correlative relationship is a basic theme of all de facto self-interpretations' (trans. J.B.).

Despite the lack of critical sources – the library of Nag Hammadi had not yet been discovered and the majority of Gnostic texts had to be reconstructed from the polemics against it by the Church Fathers – Gnosticism subsequently became the object of extensive and controversial research. This led to significant changes in the picture that scholarship had held of antiquity and, not least of all, the first centuries of Christianity. What became manifest was an understanding of the world that stood in tension and contradiction not only to Christianity and Judaism, but also to Hellenistic conceptions of the world, the cosmos and society.[13]

Gnosticism in Antiquity and the Present: The Nullity of the World

Gnosticism became a major preoccupation for Jonas for more than 40 years. He not only was extremely familiar with contemporary research in philology, form and content, and history relating to Gnosticism, he also took an active role in its development. Not all the details need to be elaborated upon for our purposes. It is sufficient to present a picture of the motives behind the Gnostic understanding of the world as summarized by Jonas. Above all, the task at hand is to present Jonas' interpretations of the relevant texts and assess their significance for the philosophy of religion (cf. the following: Jonas 1992a, 42–7).[14]

The clearest attribute shared by all Gnostic myths and systems, which are extremely diverse in their specific forms, is a radical dualism. According to the Gnostics, the cosmos, the tangible world as a whole, stands completely opposed to the absolute, transcendent God, who has nothing to do with the world. They regarded this division as so strict that even the creator of the world, the 'demiurge', does not belong to the sphere of God. This strict division is bound to an unequivocal ascription of value – the world is the complete and negative antithesis to the divine reality, that which should not exist, the dark realm lacking in spirit. As to how this division came about, Jonas offers us two very different answers. One group of Gnostic texts, which finds its clearest expression in Persian Manichaeism, starts from the assumption of a primordial confrontation between enemy powers. Their struggle against each other constitutes concrete events in the world (Jonas 1992, 210–16). Other systems, probably having arisen in Egypt and Syria and flourishing in the Gnosticism of the Valentinians, see the origin of the division in the divine sphere itself. Ever more sophisticated myths about a multiplicity of intermediate stages were employed to reveal the manner and the reasons for this division (Jonas 1992, 179–84).

Despite its absolute transcendence, the divine is tragically ensnared in the tangible world. Whether of its own accord (Jonas 1992a, 113–16), as a result of

13 Cf. to this overview of the history of research on Gnosticism: Jonas 1928, 1–91; also Rudolph 2003.

14 In this work, written for a wide public, as in both volumes of Jonas 1928, it is clearly shown how the various Gnostic myths develop the themes named here.

conflict in the divine sphere (Jonas 1992a, 185–9), or through an unavoidable mirroring of the divine light in the darkness, resulting in the formation of substance (Jonas 1992a, 57–62), traces of the pneuma, sparks of the divine spirit, have found themselves in the world. Here, they are imprisoned, tied to matter and all of its energies. The location of this earthly imprisonment of the spirit is to be found in man himself.

The concern of the Gnostics is to resolve this problem of amalgamation, both at the level of the individual man and also in terms of the drama of world history. Man should ascend to the divine, as that is the true home of the pneuma within him. This overcoming the world though the ascendance of mankind is not understood as individual salvation. The final goal is the dissolution and destruction of the world as a demonic reality in order to re-establish the sole unity of the divine. This goal is achieved when all elements of the pneuma have returned to the divine sphere (Jonas 1992a, 194–7).

In order to understand how this return should come about, the fundamental nature of this imprisonment must first be made clear. The Gnostics regarded ignorance as the true suffering of mankind. Despite the fact that the pneuma resides in him, man knows nothing of the pneuma, the divine or the absolute transcendent. The similarly ignorant demiurge employs all of his powers to keep mankind in his ignorance. This is why man needs an intermediary, a saviour, who can rescue him from the suffering of his ignorance. The insight given – gnosis – is the way to achieve deliverance.[15]

The distinctiveness, even uniqueness, about Hans Jonas' research in the field of Gnosticism is not yet apparent in his arrangement of Gnostic motifs. Jonas' concern is far greater. He investigates the Gnostic texts in a similar fashion to that of the testimonies of Paul and Augustine – in the form of an 'existential analysis'. His aim is 'a philosophic one: to understand the spirit speaking through these [Gnostic, M.B.] voices' (Jonas 1992a, xvii). Jonas is thereby convinced that a particular existential experience and interpretation lies at the basis of and is expressed through the various Gnostic systems. Beyond the dualism, the yearning for salvation, and the negative assessment of the world, he sees 'the transcendental acosmic principle in man, normally hidden and undiscovered in his earthly preoccupations, or only negatively betraying in a feeling of alienness, of not completely belonging' (Jonas 1992a, 158).

There must be a reason for this feeling of being a stranger in a strange world – a feeling that is characteristic of Gnosticism and that permeates its mythic forms. Jonas finds its roots in the shift from the Greek polis to the Roman–Hellenistic world power. In the polis, every individual had his recognizable place, which he occupied and which gave meaning to his life. The Hellenistic Stoics attempted to universalize these ideas. The Stoics believed that divine reason guaranteed

15 Jonas cites the Gnostic 'formula of salvation' from the so-called Gospel of Truth: 'Since Deficiency came into existence because they did not know the Father, so when they know the Father, Deficiency, at that same instant, disappears' (Jonas 1992a, 197).

order in the world, in which everyone had their place. Through the use of reason, every person is able to recognize this order and their place in it. Through such knowledge, man finds repose and meaning. Yet, according to Jonas, the individual living in a vast empire can no longer experience the meaningful order as expressed by Stoic philosophy and is thereby deprived of this sense of meaning. In the place of the security of the familiar polis appears the abstract membership in an order that is not fundamentally denied, but which is experienced as meaningless. The cosmos as a whole becomes alien. If there really is a home, then it can only lie in an absolutely other reality. According to Jonas, it is this experience of alienation that finds such an incisive and pragmatically reinforced expression in Gnosticism (Jonas 1992a, 241–65).

This fundamental Gnostic position also serves as an explanation, says Jonas, for the explicit opposition of Gnosticism to Judaism. The idea of a good creation is no longer possible. The God of Israel as revealed in the Bible is identified by the Gnostics as the demiurge (Jonas 1992a, 133 f.).[16] The Gnostic creator figure is indeed the author and guarantor of cosmic order, yet it is not God, but rather the absolute and negative other to God.

The relationship of Gnosticism to Christianity is, by contrast, considerably more ambivalent. The Christian apocalyptic expectation of a soon-to-occur end of the world and, above all, the figure of an intermediary and saviour, revered by Christians as Jesus Christ, were positions that could mesh with Gnostic ideas. Contact between Christians and followers of Gnostic groups apparently resulted in a frequent mutual exchange and acceptance of one other's views – even to the extent of giving up essential elements of Christian beliefs in creation, as can be seen in the case of Marcion (Jonas 1992a, 130–46).[17]

Of particular significance for Jonas are the ethical consequences that follow from the Gnostic understanding of man and the world. They are not unequivocal, but rather extremely contrary. Alongside Gnostic ascetical ideals that attempted to minimize attachment of the spirit to anything earthly stood libertine concepts: as knowledge is the only thing relevant to salvation and there is no reason to be good in a bad world, the Gnostic could act with reckless freedom and enjoy all that one could enjoy in this world (Jonas 1992, 270–81).

With his research into Gnosticism, Hans Jonas developed and tested his hermeneutic techniques, which were governed by the principle of existential analysis. He succeeded in revealing the Gnostic texts as construing and enabling a specific experience of existence. In his analysis of their image of God, he discovered the world of the people who conceived it. Yet, he still remained an

---

16 A strong rejection of the thesis that Gnosticism has Jewish origins can be found in Jonas 1974a, 277–90.

17 Even the subtitle of the American edition of the introductory volume on Gnosticism, 'The Beginnings of Christianity', draws attention to the precarious relationship between Gnosticism and Christianity, which to this day arouses controversial discussion.

outsider among experts on the history of religion – their 'objektgeschichtliche'[18] research consciously abstained from offering hermeneutic approximations of past self-conceptions. Yet, Jonas also clearly distanced himself from classical philosophy of religion with its methodology, as it tends to concern itself with the philosophical development of metaphysical ideas rather than with examination of religious-historical testimonials.

A Fatal Nihilism: The Downfall of Humanity

In 1952 a text by Hans Jonas was published in which he offered a provisional assessment of his research into Gnosticism. For more than 20 years, he had been occupied with this religious phenomenon. He had long since been forced to leave Germany. The break with Heidegger on account of his proximity to National Socialism, for which he never expressed regret to Hans Jonas, had taken place years ago. Jonas' text focuses on a 'reciprocal illumination' (Jonas 1992a, 320–40) of Heidegger's philosophy and Gnosticism. It has been sufficiently clear the extent to which existential analysis had helped Jonas in attaining his own insights on Gnosticism. Conversely, the question of whether Jonas' interpretation of Gnosticism could lead to back to Heidegger's philosophy might simply be a case of 'circularity' (Jonas 1992a, 320) of concepts and argumentation.[19] Yet, Jonas hereby arrives at a radical critique of Heidegger's thought and depiction of modernity. Heidegger is very close to Gnostic motifs when he sees man as thrown into the world – as a being for whom the world remains alien and meaningless. According to Heidegger, the task of man is to lead an authentic, self-determined life in anticipation of his end. However, he views death as a step into nothingness, not into eternity. Heidegger denied the absolute transcendence of Gnosticism – he represents a 'dualism without metaphysics' (Jonas 1992a, 340) One could equally formulate this position as a Gnosticism that offers no salvation. As such, Heidegger's man lives in a remarkable meaningless present between 'having been thrown' (Jonas 1992a, 334) in the world and death. The world has no value for him; rather, it is simply present. Existence for Heidegger is 'a merely formal resolution ('Entschlossenheit') to be, without a *nomos* for that resolution, becomes a project ('Vorlauf') from nothingless to nothingless' (Jonas 1992a, 338). These words make it clear that Jonas had distanced himself from the open understanding of freedom he had previously maintained in his exegesis of Paul.

Jonas was formulating his severe criticism of Heidegger at a time when the philosopher was attempting to develop the idea of a transcendence in immanence and to think of the appearance of 'Seyns' (the being) as the future for mankind. Some years later, Jonas criticized any Christian theology that hoped to establish a link with this position of Heidegger. God and its self-revelation, the God of the

18 'Object-historical' research (Jonas 1964, 12).

19 For Jonas' criticism on Heidegger, see Brumlik (1992, 312–47).

Bible is not thinkable in terms of Heidegger's philosophy (Jonas 2004a, 49, 56–7). Conspicuous is the fact that in this text Jonas repeatedly accuses Heidegger of 'Heidentum' (paganism) (Jonas 2004a, 41) and not atheism. Paganism is commonly understood to be a religion, although not one that leads to salvation. Whether believers in Gnosticism arrive at the desired goal of absolute transcendence is, in principle, something that cannot be known. That Heidegger's appeal to adopt a 'resoluteness' not bound to ethics played into the hands of an inhuman regime is, however, demonstrable. Already in 1952, Jonas feared for the worst as to what the future might bring in calling attention to the notion of an 'indifferent nature' (Jonas 1992a, 339) resulting from the 'abstraction of natural science'.

As such, he saw himself and philosophy as facing a new task. It had to be established whether 'a third way is open [...]' to the modern spirit, 'one by which the dualistic rift can be avoided and yet enough of the dualistic insight saved to uphold the humanity of man' (Jonas 1992a, 340).

The Unity of the Living: Philosophical Biology

The above-quoted conclusion to Jonas' essay on nihilism could be read as the heading to the subsequent work of Hans Jonas. There was no abrupt end to his work on Gnosticism, yet it did move from centre stage.[20] Increasingly, in its place came commentaries on ethical matters and, in particular, a long-term project towards the development of a philosophical biology. This was meant to serve as the 'third way', which would recognize man as part of nature and the world, without dismissing his unique ability to also understand himself apart from the world. As other contributions to the present volume concern themselves in greater detail with this aspect of Jonas' work, only a sketch of his basic ideas will be offered at this point.[21] In his studies towards 'Organismus und Freiheit', Jonas makes reference to the theory of evolution, which he attempts to interpret philosophically. In the process, he gathers together a number of related approaches, ranging from the German-language 'Philosophy of Life' to Whitehead's process philosophy. Jonas turns his attention primarily, but not exclusively, to the development that began rather late in the history of the cosmos – the evolution of life. The step from inorganic matter to the first organisms is something fundamentally new in the world. We are dealing here with a form of being that can maintain itself only through an exchange with its environment, through metabolism. With regard to

20 The commemorative volume dedicated to Jonas on his 75th birthday also had Gnosticism as a theme. It paid tribute to Hans Jonas in that it connected new aspects of research into Gnosticism with his specific interpretation of Gnosticism (Aland 1978, 13). The importance of research into Gnosticism for the intellectual development of Hans Jonas is also documented by Wiese 1999. It offers a very succinct exposition of the ambivalent fascination that Gnosticism provoked, and not only for Jonas.

21 In Jonas 1973 a translation and revision of Jonas 1966 was published in German.

these organisms, Jonas makes an unusual decision, which would prove pioneering for all his subsequent work. He characterized the specific distinguishing feature of all living beings as transcendence and freedom (cf. in particular: Jonas 1974, 185–205; Jonas 1996, 59–74). However, this qualitative difference to the inorganic world has come at a high price. The reliance of life on its environment is always one of dependence and fragility. Jonas describes the development of life as a process in which the radius of activity of living being steadily grows. Adaptation to the environment and the shaping of the environment supplement each other. This makes both possible and necessary an ever-greater variety of life forms. New qualities emerge – sensitivity to pain, focused attention, the first forms of consciousness, and emotions. Over the course of these developments, man also comes into being. In man, life achieves a qualitatively new stage. The brain has reached such a state of complexity that it permits the development of a self-consciousness, 'but as something essentially new, not as something that simply emerges gradually' (Jonas 1996, 77). Humans are able to recognize themselves as the free initiators of their actions. This freedom allows them to act in opposition to their environment. Their actions are not only reactions. They create their world as a world of their interpretative conception and as a consciously designed social world. Yet, as part of nature, being only one stage in the development of life, man is able to reflect upon and, in his actions, encounter this nature and his own bond with it. This remarkable ability is coupled with a responsibility that no other living being is both awarded and burdened with – the responsibility for life (Jonas 1996, 176–7). Briefly sketched, this is the 'third way' that Jonas cleared between an unbridgeable dualism and a naturalistic monism, which no longer recognized the *specificum humanum*.

The Will to Live: On the Threshold to Transcendence

By already ascribing transcendence and freedom to the basic forms of life, Jonas succeeds in securely binding man into the world of nature. These binds cannot be broken even when consideration is given to man's self-reflexivity and spirit. These attributes are part of the continuity of living beings and, at the same time, explain how the experience of alienation can arise, from which Gnosticism derives its strict dualism and Heidegger develops his notion of an indifferent world. However, Jonas can postulate this continuity only by employing the concepts of transcendence and freedom in an extremely weak sense. 'Transcendence' is the 'transcendence of need, which breaks the isolation of inner identity to embrace a circumference of vital relationship' (Jonas 1996, 69). 'Freedom' means no more than the ability to turn outwards to the environment. Metabolism 'is the first form freedom takes' (Jonas 1996, 60; also Lenzig 2006, 120–41). Neither consciousness of freedom nor the demand that a free action must have its origin in the actor can or should be required here. Such a weak concept of transcendence does not even approach the periphery of metaphysics. Philosophical biology is not meant to be metaphysics. This is a limit that Jonas stresses time and again.

Yet, occasionally, he ventures over this limit. Far closer to the religious-philosophical and the metaphysical tradition of philosophical thought than was the case in his research into Gnosticism, Jonas questions the implicit, or at least possible preconditions and consequences of the understanding of humanity and the world that he has developed. He does not avoid the questions that follow from his investigations. Jonas quite deliberately refers to his attempt to once again survey the field of possible religiosity as 'speculation' (Jonas 1992b, 7).

Origin and Recollection: God and World

Jonas unfolds his 'metaphysical speculations' in three independent thematic areas, which are nevertheless related to one another in a number of ways. They all deal with philosophical reflection on the phenomenon of life.[22] Jonas is hereby concerned first with the origin of history and the world, and then with its purpose or goal, if not outright with its completion. Most of all, however, he addresses his deliberations on the possibility and reality the direct intervention of God in history.

Man can ask where he comes from. He thereby discovers the long history of the earth and of life as his prehistory, with which he is inseparably bound. And on the basis of natural scientific knowledge and without turning to metaphysical speculation, he can say that this history led up to him. He can read this history as history of mankind, of being human.

In light of this insight, Jonas regards it as legitimate to view mankind as the purpose or at least a purpose of evolution (cf. Jonas 1966, 26–37; Jonas 1984, 51–7; Schieder 1998, 26–55). He draws upon the antique notion of final cause, which, in the modern era, has been completely displaced by the effective concept of causality as employed in the natural sciences. In order to rehabilitate the concept of purpose, Jonas employs it – as he has previously done with the concepts of freedom and transcendence – in an extremely reduced sense. According to Jonas, this reference to a purpose merely states the connection between goal and development. It does not presuppose that this purpose requires a subject who had previously set this as his goal. Nor is a purpose shown to be legitimate only in that it presents the finishing point of a development. Arguably, this makes it possible to speak of a teleological development.

Jonas maintains the irrefutability of a second thought – if the spirit of man has developed out of the long history of becoming, then the possibility of this development must have already been included at the very start of becoming (Jonas 1996, 172). If the initial conditions of becoming had excluded this

22 Cf. the following: Uhtes 2006, 44–65; 127–59; Brune 2004, 259–82; Gronke 2008, 269–90. A good overview of the various discussions on Jonas' metaphysical interpretation of philosophical biology is offered in Müller 2008, 105–18.

development, then it would never have come about. This thought leaves room for a scenario where the first rudimentary possibilities in an inestimably long chain of ever-new resultant concrete possibilities led to the constellations from which life began and in which spirit awoke. The apparent fact that no similar development has taken place elsewhere in the immeasurable vastness of the cosmos demonstrates that this development exhibits no inherent necessity.

It is only at this point that Jonas turns to a classical metaphysical thought, which he formulates as a question: 'Can something that is less than mind be the cause of mind?' (Jonas 1996, 180). He thereby does not deny that a development beginning with lifeless matter can lead to spirit. He remains true to his rejection of a strict dualism. Yet, this is only possible, as previously mentioned, under the precondition that this possibility already existed in matter. When we say 'that matter from the very beginning is mind asleep, so we must immediately add that the really first cause, the creative cause, of mind asleep can only be mind awake. [...] So the anthropic evidence [...] lead us now to the postulate of a mental, thinking, transcendent, supertemporal being at the origin of things' (Jonas 1996, 181). According to Jonas, this thought is not meant to serve as a proof of God's existence. Yet, it is meant to create space in opposition to the dictates of a dualism in the tradition of Descartes or a monism in the tradition of Spinoza, which has been understood and absolutized in a naturalistic fashion by science. And this space is to provide for the conceivability of a creative spirit. As will be demonstrated, this thought will also play a role in Jonas' other metaphysical themes.

Man can inquire not only into the past, but also into the future. Is it enough to see himself as the purpose and goal of those developments that have led to him? Does not the question almost inevitably arise as to the goals that man has for himself? Jonas does not avoid this question (Jonas 1966, 262–81). He dismisses, however, the typical answers and eschatological conceptions. According to Jonas, it is almost impossible to consider an individual subsistence beyond bodily existence. Man is namely characterized by the indisolvable bond of body and spirit. For the same reason, the conception, popular in antiquity, that space, time and physicality are mere appearances, which man and soul leave behind in death, can no longer be held today. Finally, the hope of an otherworldly justice, which rewards the good and punishes the evil, has lost its naivety and, thereby, its possibility. 'Indeed the here cannot be traded for a there – such is our present stance' (Jonas 1966, 267).

Irrespective of such faded hopes, and not just in the eyes of Jonas, there are those moments in the life of man that point beyond ourselves. 'In moments of decision, when our whole being is involved, we feel as if acting under the eyes of eternity' (Jonas 1966, 268). This sounds unmistakably like Heidegger's call to authenticity in his 'project to death' (Heidegger 1986, 263). Yet, Jonas refuses Heidegger's return to the finiteness of the individual. Instead, he takes the bold step of separating the actor from his action. According to Jonas, the individual has no hope or prospect of immortality. It is, however, conceivable that the decisive deeds of man remain preserved. Jonas here employs the Jewish notion of the 'Book of Life' (Jonas 1966, 271) in which these deeds are recorded. It remains open as to what kind of final balance this book would present at the possible end of history. With reference to a Gnostic myth, Jonas even goes one step further. It is from the deeds of men in history that the becoming God achieves his form. 'In the temporal transactions of the world, whose fleeting now is ever swallowed by the past, an eternal presence grows, its countenance slowly defining itself' (Jonas 1966, 274).

In a later continuation of the thought that events can be preserved in eternity, Jonas develops a 'supplement to the so-called proofs of the existence of God' (Jonas 1992b, 173–89). What concerns him here is a strictly epistemological problem. He opens with the question of whether it is possible to make a true statement about something in the past. He is not interested in the always thorny question of the verifiability of a statement about the past.[23] Rather, he focuses on the different and more fundamental question of whether statements about the past can possibly be true at all. If truth means the correspondence of statement and object, then a problem arises at the moment when a statement is made about an object that is no longer present, hence, no longer exists. Jonas suggests a solution, which he views as strictly transcendental (Jonas 1992b, 189) – as it is aimed at the conditions for the possibility of such a statement. 'Wenn wir postulieren, daß es die Unterscheidung von wahr und falsch in Bezug auf Nicht-mehr-Existentes, Vergangenes gibt und wenn ihre paradoxe Rechtmäßigkeit unabdingbar unsere Zeitlichkeit begleiten muß, damit wir sie mit Sinn leben können, bleibt schließlich nur der Rekurs auf irgendeine Art der Präsenz dessen, was je gewesen ist.'[24] Jonas has thereby built a bridge to the previously developed thought of the 'immortality' of human deeds. Yet, Jonas goes even further. For one thing, he no longer speaks only about this excellent decision with respect to eternity, but now completely in general about 'everything that has been'. For another thing, he surpasses the metaphors of the book and of images. 'Ein Gedächtnis an sich ist kein vollziehbarer Begriff. Ein Gedächtnis muß seinen Sitz in einem *Subjekt*, in einem *Geist* haben. Und der transzendentale Zweck unseres Postulats verlangt, daß es ein *vollkommenes*, sowohl fehlloses wie universales Gedächtnis ist, folglich ein *universaler und vollkommener Geist*.'[25] This continuation of the idea of an eternal memory is tied to the talk about spirit, without which the potential of matter to bring forth spirit would be unthinkable. In terms of the philosophy of religion, this

23 On the fundamental possibility of understanding testimony from the past, see the previously mentioned text: Jonas 1974, 237–60.

24 'If we postulate that there is a difference between true and false with respect to [...] that which no longer exists or has past, and if their paradoxical legitimacy must indispensably accompany our temporality in order that we may live with meaning, then there remains no other recourse than some kind of presence of what has already been' (Jonas 1992b, 184; trans. J.B.).

25 'A memory in itself is not a concept that can be implemented. A memory must have a location in a *subject*, in a spirit. And the transcendental purpose of our postulate demands that it is a *perfect*, as well as unmistakable and universal memory, consequently a *universal and perfect spirit*' (Jonas 1992b, 186; trans. J.B.).

thought stands for the conceivability of a God who remembers history. Yet, stresses Jonas, he cannot advocate the reality of this God. These reflections are namely a 'supplement' to thoughts, no longer considered to be proof, on the conceivable reality of God.[26] What is clear is that this conception of God, in contrast both to Gnosticism as well as Heidegger's thinking about being, is unmistakable in its proximity to the Jewish interpretation of the biblical testimony of God.

It is not possible to go any further within the perspective of the philosophy of religion. It is no surprise, then, that the last of Jonas' thematic areas to be considered here is that of speculative theology.[27] Jonas' thought here ensues from a reality of God that is only accessible through faith. The basic question of the text is whether God intervenes in history and world events. Elsewhere, Jonas critically grappled with the fundamental possibility of God acting in the world (Jonas 1996, 144–64). His warned his teacher and friend Rudolf Bultmann in this text from taking 'demythologization' too far and, in its name, setting aside all discussion of God's historical actions as mere myth. At the very least, the possibility of God to reveal himself must be preserved if faith within the biblical tradition is to be maintained (Jonas 1996, 160–61). In order to philosophically secure the possibility that God – and man as well – could freely intervene in the course of world events, Jonas pointed out 'that the laws of nature are quite compatible with neutral threshold situations, zero points of indifference, as it were, from which as from a divide the further process could take several directions' (Jonas 1966, 157). However, Jonas fails to provide the proof of how an action based in freedom could intervene in such situations. Nevertheless, it is important for the context of interest here that Jonas offers a philosophical perspective for the possibility of God's action in the world. As such, the decisive objective of his theological argumentation in 'The Concept of God after Auschwitz' is that God, after he made possible and initiated the becoming of the world, renounced making any use of his potential for action. Jonas sees himself obliged to think in such a manner. The three attributes of God that Jonas sees as definitive for the religious tradition – 'absolute goodness, absolute power, and intelligibility' (Jonas 1966, 139) – can be united without discrepancy only when one takes seriously what took place in Auschwitz and that God did not intervene. The myth in which Jonas – completely in line with his philosophical biology – describes the becoming of the world (Jonas 1966, 134–6) is so well known that it does not need to be summarized here. In his interpretation

26 In an apparent, yet explicitly only suggested proximity to the argumentation, Spaemann 2007 encounters the thought projected into the future that then looks back at the elapsed present. In contrast to the approach presented here of trying to understand Jonas' attempt as a facet of a 'speculative theology,' Polidowa 1995 attempts to prove the inconsistencies of the various lines of thought pursued by Jonas.

27 The central text in this respect is *Der Gottesbegriff nach Auschwitz* published in 1984 and which became well known after Jonas read the paper on the occasion of an honour ceremony in Tübingen. However, the basic thoughts had already been given in a lecture in the United States in 1961 – with practically identical text.

of the myth, Jonas outlines an image of a God who renounces his omnipotence and withdraws himself in favour of his creation. It is a God who caringly attends to the becoming and, above all, the freedom of his creation in the words and deeds of those who believe in him. He has placed the fate of the world in the hands of mankind and is himself affected by this fate. 'It is man's now to give him. And he may give by seeing to it in the ways of his life that it does not happen or happen too often, and not on his account, that it "repented the Lord" (Genesis 6: 6–7) to have made the world' (Jonas 1966, 142).

Hans Jonas' proposal provoked extremely controversial reactions from both Jewish and Christian theological communities. Some accepted it with a sense of relief, as it offered them the possibility to bid farewell to an image of God that made their belief difficult, if not impossible. The necessity of the theodicy question not only has Jonas doubting the image of God as the all-powerful arbiter of world affairs. Yet, the position was also greeted with loud and massive dissent. Does not the thesis that God renounces his omnipotence on behalf of the freedom of man and the world result in giving up the core of the biblical belief in God? Does not the Bible picture God as the saviour, who leads Israel out of the Egypt and, according to Christian beliefs, raised Jesus from the dead? What is left to hope for if one can't even believe that at the end of time God will deliver salvation to the just? This is not the place to present the controversy in detail or to attempt some form of conciliation.[28]

Within the framework of presenting Hans Jonas' works on the philosophy of religion, it is more interesting to look back again at 'The Concept of God after Auschwitz'. How can the main themes of Hans Jonas' work be discovered again in this key text?

With more clarity than the Christian theologians of his time, Jonas had worked out the basic problem with the theology of Augustine. In his teachings on original sin and grace, the Church Father attempted to dispel the dialectic of human freedom. The high esteem in which he holds divine freedom and grace leads to the complete denial of human freedom. Jonas takes away the foundation of this thought, namely by not regarding human freedom and divine grace as being in competition with each other. The freedom of mankind and the world is itself a gift that God in his freedom has given.[29] Although man cannot dispel the dialectic of his freedom through a belief in this merciful God, the problem of self-objectification can be left behind. Freedom and faith once again find themselves in the state of tension described by Paul.

The myth of a 'becoming God' (Jonas 1966, 137) is, as Jonas himself indicates (Jonas 1966, 54), taken from the Gnostic vision of the world. The suggestion there is that the total process of world events serves only the self-realization and

28 For a summary of the discussion, see Baum 2004; Schiwy 1995; Koslowski and Hermanni 2001; Metz 1995.

29 For a Christian conception of divine grace and human freedom without competition, see Rahner 1967; Menke 2003; Pröpper 2011.

salvation of God (Jonas 1992, 196). Does the 'speculative theology' developed by Hans Jonas therefore stand in the shadow of Gnosticism, the consequences of which Jonas so massively criticized? Those making this claim have allowed themselves to be deceived by the images that Jonas employs and they overlook the fundamental difference between Jonas and the Gnostics. In their dualistic worldview, the cosmos is the exclusively negative counterpart to God, created by God's eternal adversary or by a power fallen from the divine realm. Jonas has conceived his myth in order to retain the love of God, as it is maintained in the Bible, as well as the positive value of creation – against all the reasons to despise the world and its creator. 'And God saw every thing that he had made, and, behold, it was very good' (Genesis 1:31). The contrast with Gnosticism could not be any greater.

This is most clearly seen in the anthropology held by Jonas. He regards man not as a stranger in the world, thrown into a fundamentally hostile environment. It is not man's goal to escape this prison as soon as possible and irrevocably. Jonas sees man as part of the world willed by God. He has emerged from it and can even understand himself as its purpose. And yet he differs from everything else in the world through his spirit and freedom. This is why he can and must bear responsibility for this world. If and how he fulfils this task has consequences not only for him and the world, but, spoken from a theological perspective, for God as well.

Life, Responsibility and Religion: A Delicate Relationship

In conclusion, one more critical question is posed with respect to the thought of Hans Jonas as presented here. How is it that Jonas, quite unlike most of the other philosophers of his time, gave so much emphasis to the philosophy of religion and metaphysical thought? Curiously, the critique of religion and the rejection of metaphysics which played such a great role in the philosophy of the nineteenth and twentieth centuries remained at the margins of his entire work. Far more frequently than, for example, Kant, Feuerbach and Nietzsche, Jonas drew on the works of antiquity and, in a thoroughly critical manner, built upon their understanding of metaphysics and religion. With his 'metaphysical suppositions', he once again confirmed his status as an exceptional case in the philosophy of the twentieth century.

It would be inappropriate, however, to accuse Jonas of naivety on this account. He knows and accepts the limits to metaphysics set by Kant (Jonas 1992b). He does not question Kant's insight into the impossibility of proving the existence of God (Jonas 1966, 177) and knows very well the persistent hypothetical character of religious-philosophical thought. Nonetheless, he exploits the remaining possibilities for thought within these strict limits.

The question remains as to why this form of thought was so important for Jonas. One might dare to conjecture at this point. Perhaps, Jonas was so energetically concerned with religion because he understood how dangerous it could be. His research into Gnosticism led to insights into the highly problematic ethical and anthropological consequences of a strict dualism. Dogmatic atheism leads back to an uncritical, exclusive natural scientific-monistic thought, which Jonas confronts with its own, though admittedly unconscious, metaphysics. The curious link between religious criticism and neo-paganism in Heidegger is another important motif for Jonas in his search for intellectual alternatives (Brumlik 1992, 241–347). Against the background of his intensive research, Jonas managed to achieve a responsible religion on the basis of religious, scientific and existential-analytical thought with an ethical impulse. Not only was Jonas shaped by Jewish tradition (Jonas 1974, 21–44, 165–82), he also emphasized its important contribution to the fulfilment of this task. As such, no one can reproach him for this position, even those who do not also stand in this tradition.

In light of all this, the question posed by Jonas as to whether ethics is possible without religion (Jonas 1984, 22–3; Jonas 2004b) is both remarkable and in need of interpretation. Here, he is certainly not taking aim at the existence of God as one of Kant's postulates of practical reason. Kant sees the existence of God, who alone can guarantee the harmony of morality and happiness, as a demand of practical reason. Jonas explicitly turns against this thought in his deliberations on immortality (Jonas 1966, 266–7). His question on the link between ethics and religion aims in another direction. The deduction from 'being' to 'ought' in modern philosophy is shown to be a 'naturalistic fallacy' and the suspicion of illegitimacy confirmed. However, Jonas regards another insight as being more important than this philosophical verdict. The claim that the world, life and man are worthy of protection is not readily an object of experience. The dualism of Gnosticism, Heidegger's position of 'having been thrown', and Augustine's theology of sin could all be regarded as expressions of the kind of precarious experiences that lead to doubt concerning the positive value of the world and human existence. They shake the foundations of an ethics that demands taking responsibility for life.

Opposed to such appearances, the biblical tradition testifies to the belief in a God who, out of love, wanted the world and mankind in it. This belief recognizes the world as valuable and sees mankind as bearing the duty to care for it. At a time in which the destruction of the world through the hand of mankind was recognized as a real danger, Hans Jonas saw his task as one of reminding his contemporaries of their duty. He thereby regarded a religion committed to life as a welcome ally.

References

Aland, Barbara, ed. 1978. *Gnosis. Festschrift für Hans Jonas.* Göttingen: Vandenhoeck & Ruprecht.

Baum, Wolfgang. 2004. *Gott nach Auschwitz. Reflexionen zum Theodizeeproblem im Anschluß an Hans Jonas.* Paderborn: Schöningh.

Böhler, Dietrich. 2010. 'Einführung zur kritischen Gesamtausgabe'. In *Kritische Gesamtausgabe der Werke von Hans Jonas*, edited by Dietrich Böhler, Michael

Bongardt, Holger Burckhart, Christian Wiese and Walther Ch. Zimmerli, vol. 1, xv–lxxix. Freiburg, Berlin and Vienna: Rombach.

Böhler, Dietrich and Jens Peter Brune, eds. 2004. *Orientierung und Verantwortung. Begegnungen und Auseinandersetzungen mit Hans Jonas.* Würzburg: Königshausen & Neumann.

Böhler, Dietrich, Horst Gronke and Bernadette Herrmann, eds. 2008. *Mensch, Gott, Welt. Philosophie des Lebens, Religionsphilosophie und Metaphysik im Werk von Hans Jonas.* Freiburg, Berlin and Vienna: Rombach.

Bonaldi, Claudio, 2008. 'Der Mensch vor Gott: Hans Jonas' Interpretation der paulinischen Erfahrung'. In *Mensch, Gott, Welt. Philosophie des Lebens, Religionsphilosophie und Metaphysik im Werk von Hans Jonas,* edited by Dietrich Böhler, Horst Gronke and Bernadette Herrmann, 209–25. Freiburg, Berlin and Vienna: Rombach.

Bongardt, Michael. 2009. *Einführung in die Theologie der Offenbarung.* Darmstadt: Wissenschaftliche Buchgesellschaft.

Brumlik, Micha. 1992. *Die Gnostiker. Der Traum von der Selbsterlösung des Menschen.* Frankfurt: Eichborn.

Brune, Jens Peter. 2004. 'Verstehen des Lebendigen? Vom Gottesstandpunkt zum Diskurspartner'. In *Orientierung und Verantwortung. Begegnungen und Auseinandersetzungen mit Hans Jonas,* edited by Dietrich Böhler, 259–82. Würzburg: Königshausen & Neumann.

Buber, Martin. 1950. *Zwei Glaubensweisen.* Zürich: Manesse.

Bultmann, Rudolf. 1965. 'Zum Problem der Entmythologisierung'. In *Glauben und Verstehen. Gesammelte Aufsätze,* vol. 4, edited by Rudolf Bultmann, 128–37. Tübingen: Mohr.

Gronke, Horst. 2008. 'Phänomenologie und Ontologie – Wie philosophiert Hans Jonas? Ein Versuch'. In *Mensch, Gott, Welt. Philosophie des Lebens, Religionsphilosophie und Metaphysik im Werk von Hans Jonas,* edited by Dietrich Böhler, Horst Gronke and Bernadette Herrmann, 269–90. Freiburg, Berlin and Vienna: Rombach.

Häring, Hermann. 1979. *Die Macht des Bösen. Das Erbe Augustins.* Zürich, Cologne and Gütersloh: Benziger, Mohn.

Heidegger, Martin. 1986. *Sein und Zeit.* Tübingen: Niemeyer.

Jonas, Hans. 1928. 'Der Begriff Gnosis'. Ph.D. thesis, Philipps-Universität Marburg.

———. 1964. *Gnosis und spätantiker Geist. 1. Teil,* 3. Auflage, Göttingen: Vandenhoeck & Ruprecht,.

———. 1965. *Augustin und das paulinische Freiheitsproblem. Eine philosophische Studie zum pelagianischen Streit.* Edited by James Robinson. Göttingen: Vandenhoeck & Ruprecht.

———. 1966. *The Phenomenon of Life: Towards a Philosophical Biology.* Chicago, London: The University of Chicago Press.

———. 1973. *Organismus und Freiheit. Ansätze zu einer philosophischen Biologie,* Göttingen: Vandenhoeck & Ruprecht.

———. 1974. *Philosophical Essays: From Ancient Creed to Technological Man.* Chicago, London: The Chicago University Press.

———. 1984. *The Imperative of Responsibility: In Search of an Ethics for the Technological World.* Chicago and London: The University of Chicago Press.

———. 1992a. *The Gnostic Religion: The Message of the Alien God and the Beginnings of Christianity.* London: Routledge.

———. 1992b. *Philosophische Untersuchungen und metaphysische Vermutungen.* Frankfurt, and Leipzig: Insel.

———. 1996. *Mortality and Morality: A Search for the Good after Auschwitz.* Evanston: Northwestern University Press.

———. 2003. *Erinnerungen.* Nach Gesprächen mit Rachel Salamander. Vorwort von Rachel Salamander. Geleitwort von Lore Jonas. Hg. u. m. einem Nachwort versehen von Christian Wiese. Frankfurt am Main und Leipzig: Insel.

———. 2004a. 'Heidegger und die Theologie'. In: *Orientierung und Verantwortung. Begegnungen und Auseinandersetzungen mit Hans Jonas*, edited by Dietrich Böhler and Jens Peter Brune, 39–58. Würzburg: Königshausen & Neumann.

———. 2004b. 'Wie können wir unsere Pflicht gegen die Nachwelt und die Erde unabhängig vom Glauben begründen?' In *Orientierung und Verantwortung. Begegnungen und Auseinandersetzungen mit Hans Jonas*, edited by Dietrich Böhler and Jens Peter Brune, 71–84. Würzburg: Königshausen & Neumann.

Kierkegaard, Sören. 1983. 'Der Begriff Angst'. In *Gesammelte Werke*, part 11, edited by Emanuel Hirsch and Hayo Gerdes. Gütersloh: Mohn.

———. 1987. *'Entweder / Oder II. '* In *Gesammelte Werke*, part 2, edited by Emanuel Hirsch and Gerdes Hayo. Gütersloh: Mohn.

Koslowski, Peter and Friedrich Hermanni, eds. 2001. *Der leidende Gott. Eine philosophische und theologische Kritik.* Munich: Fink.

Lenzig, Udo. 2006. *Das Wagnis der Freiheit. Der Freiheitsbegriff im philosophischen Werk von Hans Jonas aus theologischer Perspektive.* Stuttgart: Kohlhammer.

Lévinas, Emmanuel. 1992. *Ethik und Unendliches*, edited by Paul Engelmann. Vienna: Passagen.

Menke, Karl-Heinz. 2003. *Das Kriterium des Christseins. Grundriss der Gnadenlehre.* Regensburg: Pustet.

Metz, Johann Baptist, ed. 1995. *'Landschaft aus Schreien'. Zur Dramatik der Theodizeefrage.* Mainz: Grünewald.

Müller, Wolfgang Erich. 2008. *Hans Jonas. Philosoph der Verantwortung.* Darmstadt: Wissenschaftliche Buchgesellschaft.

Polidowa, Sebastian. 1995. 'Gottesbegriff und Gottesbeweis. Zur philosophischen Theologie bei Hans Jonas'. In *Jahrbuch für Philosophie des Forschungsinstituts für Philosophie*, vol. 6, edited by Peter Koslowski and Richard Schenk, 123–41. Vienna: Passagen Verlag.

Pröpper, Thomas. 2011. *Theologische Anthropologie*, vol. 2. Freiburg: Herder.

Rahner, Karl. 1967. 'Natur und Gnade', In *Schriften zur Theologie*, vol. 4, edited by Karl Rahner, 209–36. Einsiedeln: Benziger.

Robinson, James M. 1965. 'Einleitung', In *Augustin und das paulinische Freiheitsproblem. Eine philosophische Studie zum pelagianischen Streit*, edited by James Robinson, 11–22. Göttingen: Vandenhoeck & Ruprecht.
Rudolph, Kurt. 2003. 'Hans Jonas und die Gnosisforschung aus heutiger Sicht'. In *Weiterwohnlichkeit der Welt. Zur Aktualität von Hans Jonas*, edited by Christian Wiese and Eric Jacobson, 93–107. Berlin and Vienna: Philo.
Schieder, Thomas. 1998. *Weltabenteuer Gottes. Die Gottesfrage bei Hans Jonas*. Paderborn: Schöningh.
Schiwy, Günther. 1995. *Abschied vom allmächtigen Gott.* Munich: Kösel.
Schweitzer, Albert. 1913. *Geschichte der Leben-Jesu-Forschung*. Tübingen: Mohr.
Spaemann, Robert. 2007. *Der letzte Gottesbeweis.* Munich: Pattloch.
Uhtes, Regina. 2006. *Metaphysik des Organischen. Zum Verhältnis von Philosophie und Wissenschaft in Jonas' Philosophie des Lebens vor dem Hintergrund der organischen Philosophie Whiteheads.* Bochum, Freiburg: Projekt.
Wiese, Christian. 1999. 'Revolte wider die Weltflucht', In *Die Botschaft des fremden Gottes*, edited by Christian Wiese, 401–29. Frankfurt: Insel.
Wiese, Christian and Eric Jacobson, eds. 2003. *Weiterwohnlichkeit der Welt. Zur Aktualität von Hans Jonas.* Berlin and Vienna: Philo.
Wilckens, Ulrich. 1978. *Der Brief an die Römer*. Cologne: Benziger.

PART 4
The Ethics of Technology and Moral Responsibility

Chapter 8
What Is Natural about Natural Functioning? Examining an Indirect Argument in Favour of Teleological Naturalism

Micha H. Werner

Introduction

In his philosophy of nature as well as in his ethics, Hans Jonas challenged basic assumptions of the modern world view by defending a (meta-)ethical position we may call 'teleological naturalism'. Prompted by Jonas' article 'Medical Art and Human Responsibility' (Jonas 1985),[1] this chapter asks whether a plausible interpretation of medical practice could add, albeit in an indirect manner, some plausibility to this heavily contested (meta-)ethical position. Contra its first appearance, the discussion (and different interpretations) of medical practice is not sufficient to render teleological naturalism plausible. It does, however, hint at certain connections between our evaluations and what we regard as 'natural'.

The Modern Condition

The transition to modernity is marked by a fundamental change in the perceived relation between nature and values. Prior to the end of the Middle Ages, the dominant view in Western thought had been that the natural was also the valuable. For Aristotle as well as for the Stoics, nature had its own intrinsic goals, and realizing these goals was considered good in itself. This *teleological naturalism*[2] has been endorsed by the mainstream of Christian philosophy, which basically added only an additional

1 All quotes from German sources have been translated by the author.

2 The term 'naturalism' is known to be highly ambiguous. In the present context, I will use the term 'teleological naturalism' exclusively to refer to a complex conception which includes: (a) the assumption that the development of (biological) nature and/or the functioning of biological systems can be explained by its/their orientation towards the realization of intrinsic goals; and (b) the assumption that statements about these intrinsic goals can provide a justificatory basis for evaluative and/or normative statements. What I mean by teleological naturalism is thus neither just a metaphysical position nor something identical to (meta-)ethical naturalism as such. It can instead be seen as a specific form of the

rationale for, and an additional layer to, it: since it is God who created nature, nature cannot but be good; and the grace of God does not abolish but rather perfects (*non tollit sed perficit*) the world of natural goodness. The hegemony of classical teleological naturalism came to an end, however, when nominalist philosophers such as Duns Scotus and William of Ockham challenged the alleged normativity of the natural, arguing that only God's authority establishes norms and defines what we (have to) consider good – a thought which subsequently was transformed by Hobbes into a secular theory of authority. Moreover, 'Ockham's razor' – the principle that our theories about certain phenomena must not contain any assumptions that are unnecessary for the explanation of the phenomena in question – has proved a deadly weapon in the fight against teleological interpretations of nature: if natural phenomena could be sufficiently explained as the result of *efficient* causes, any speculations about other kinds of influence – and especially about the influence of intrinsic goals such as Aristotle's *causae finales* – must be dismissed. Following this line of thought, empiricist philosophers and scientists such as Francis Bacon attempted to show that anything in nature could be explained causally. In the end, the position of both Ockham and Scotus, which had been considered heretical in their time, came to be the orthodox view in modern thinking. This view undoubtedly remains the orthodox view to this day. For the sake of clarity, however, it is necessary to distinguish between two primary assumptions. The first assumption concerns the scientific view of nature, including biological nature, in observing that teleological interpretations of nature are unfounded: natural entities do not truly 'have' inherent goals. The second assumption concerns the nature of normativity in saying that, even if the development of nature or the functioning of biological systems could be explained by certain intrinsic goals, these goals would not have evaluative or normative significance, at least not without further argument. That a natural entity aims at some goal does not imply that it *should* do so or that it *is good* for it (or for anything else) to do so. As David Hume (2005, 302) stated, we cannot simply infer 'ought statements' from 'is statements'; nor can we, according to George E. Moore (1994), analyse normative concepts in terms of descriptive (natural or metaphysical) ones.[3]

Jonas' Teleological Ethical Naturalism

Hans Jonas, never shy to argue 'against the stream' (cf. Jonas 1980), famously challenged this orthodox view. In his contributions to the philosophy of nature, he aimed to re-establish a teleological interpretation of (biological) nature (see,

latter: a form of (meta-)ethical naturalism which tries to derive true moral statements from true statements about the intrinsic goals of nature or natural entities.

3 For a summary of the critical discussion on Moore, as well as for a careful defence of his famous 'open question argument' in favour of the latter claim, cf. Darwall, Gibbard and Railton 1992; reprinted in Darwall, Gibbard and Railton 1997, 3–47.

especially, Jonas 1966, 33–7; Jonas 1996);[4] in his work on ethics, he defended the transition from natural goals to subjective values and, finally, to moral obligations (Jonas 1966, 282–4; Jonas 1984, chaps 3 & 4). Given the fact that Jonas thereby questioned two of the fundamental elements of the prevailing modern world view — the a-teleological interpretation of nature and the is/ought-dichotomy – it is not surprising that his positions were met with some scepticism. If one examines the philosophical literature concerning Jonas' writings on ethics, it is striking that, even among those authors who hailed the normative principles of Jonas' *Ethics for the Technological Age*, there was little support for something similar to Jonas' naturalistic foundation of these principles. These authors typically tried instead to separate Jonas' views on ethics from their naturalist bases and to provide an alternative foundation for his normative conclusions.[5] One could speculate that this might have been disappointing for an author who – as we know from the testimony of his wife, Lore Jonas[6] – considered *The Phenomenon of Life* his most significant contribution to the philosophical debate; Jonas anticipated the scepticism, however, which came to be associated with his views on teleological naturalism. In his *The Imperative of Responsibility*, he took two separate precautionary measures. First, he combined his 'neo-Aristotelian' teleological naturalism with 'phenomenological' intuitionist arguments in the tradition of Max Scheler (see Werner 1994). Second, he significantly restricted the scope of his ethical theory: his *Ethics for the Technological Age* was not meant to constitute a comprehensive system of morality but only to act as a kind of *supplement* to existing ethical codes, as a kind of emergency ethics that should help to prevent the extinction of 'genuine human life' (Jonas 1984, 11). This restricted scope seems to have had two advantages. First, since what we have to preserve is the (human) *capacity* to set and realize goals *as such*, Jonas does not need to be too specific about the *relative* value of different types of goals. Second, since goal-directedness *as such* is what is at stake, Jonas could make use of a kind of *precautionary reasoning* even on the most fundamental level of his ethical argument. This significantly lightened the burdens of proof on his philosophy of life. For even if we do not know for sure whether biological nature as such is actually oriented towards intrinsic goals and whether these goals are actually valuable, let alone objectively valuable, we must not risk the extinction of something that *might* be of objective value.

---

4 In the German version of 'Is God a Mathematician?' Jonas goes so far as to commit himself to the 'strong hypothesis' ('starke Hypothese') that a tendency towards freedom was already the 'underlying principle of the transition from dead to living matter' ('das gründende Prinzip des Überganges von lebloser zu lebender Substanz' – Jonas 2010, 1: 159).

5 For a typical example, cf. Böhler's efforts to provide a discourse-ethical basis for Jonas' ethical principles in Böhler 1994.

6 During a talk with students at Freie Universität Berlin, summer 1993 (cf. also Horst Gronke's introduction to Jonas 2010, 1: lxxxiv).

A Possible Defence of Teleological Naturalism?

In the present context, however, I neither want to discuss whether Jonas' teleological interpretation of nature as such is tenable, nor whether this interpretation of nature can serve as a justificatory basis for moral obligations, nor whether Jonas' efforts to accommodate scepticism about 'neo-Aristotelian' versions of ethical naturalism were successful and sufficient.[7] I instead wish to start from a point one could make in order to defend Jonas' rehabilitation of teleological naturalism: one could question whether we are actually *serious* in our rejection of teleological naturalism; that is, whether our modern 'ideology' is actually consistent with our everyday practices, or whether these practices can be sufficiently explained within the framework of our official scientific world view and its underlying philosophical premises. If we find that there is in fact an incompatibility between some of our practices (perhaps even including some practice-guiding theoretical considerations) on the one hand and our general commitment to the two basic assumptions of our scientific world view (the a-teleological interpretation of nature and the is/ought-dichotomy) on the other, this should at least give us pause and lead us to reconsider our position. We would of course still be faced with at least two options at that point: We could either (a) modify our practices so that they become compatible with our modern world-view, or (b) modify our world view so that it better fits our practices. We could perhaps even (c) accept some inconsistency within our framework of practical commitments and theoretical beliefs, as long as this inconsistency does not lead to serious problems. An inconsistency between some of our practices and the refusal of teleological naturalism, however, should at least give us some reason to reconsider the latter.

Let us therefore ask: Is there actually a human practice that is incompatible with those basic assumptions of the prevailing scientific world view: the a-teleological interpretation of nature and the is/ought-dichotomy? Or, framed differently, is there actually a practice that expresses a commitment to teleological naturalism? If we follow Jonas' own interpretation, one candidate suggests itself: medical practice. In his article 'Ärztliche Kunst und menschliche Verantwortung',

7 One reason for this is that I have already addressed (certain aspects of) these questions elsewhere. I attempted to illustrate that what I have referred to as the 'precautionary measures' taken in *The Imperative of Responsibility* do not suffice to meet scepticism about Jonas' ethical naturalism, and that the concept of a supplementary 'emergency ethics' leads to additional problems (Werner 1994; Werner 2008). In a later publication (Werner 2012), I attempted to show that one of the less-discussed steps in Jonas' justification of his 'categorical imperative' is inconclusive (just like similar arguments one finds in the 'neo-Kantian' accounts of Korsgaard and Gewirth): even if we grant that biological systems (or even nature as a whole) are oriented toward intrinsic goals, and if we grant, in addition, that these goals are of *subjective* value, we cannot conclude that the existence of goal-directedness as such or valuing as such is objectively valuable. (Moreover, even if we could, we would still have to show that there is a categorical moral *obligation* to preserve goal-directedness or valuing.)

originally published in 1983, Jonas leaves no doubt that, 'for the physician, the matter that is the subject of his art, that he "forms", is itself the ultimate goal: the living human organism as its own end' (Jonas 1985, 146). The goal of the medical art is, according to Jonas, 'already given by its object's "end in itself"', namely, the human organism's "health", and the latter is defined by nature. In this context, there is nothing left for him to invent, apart from the methods for reaching this goal' (Jonas 1985, 147).

It is obvious that Jonas interprets medical practice in terms of teleological naturalism. After all, Jonas suggests that the 'living human organism' itself has *intrinsic goals* and that physicians have a *duty* to help the organism in attaining these goals. In order to examine Jonas' position more closely, however, we must be as explicit as possible regarding its content. In detail, Jonas assumes:

1. that the object of medical practice is the living human organism;
2. that the living human organism is its own ultimate end in itself;
3. that the living human organism has its health as its own end;
4. that health is 'defined by nature'; and,
5. that the natural goal of the living human organism is also the goal of medical practice.

At first glance, (1) seems rather uncontroversial, hence the first thing that may be puzzling is the relation between (2) and (3). The problem is that Jonas refers to two separate things as the organism's 'own intrinsic end' ('Eigenziel', Jonas 1985, 147), 'end in itself' ('Zweck seiner selbst', ibid.) or 'ultimate end' ('der ultimative Zweck', ibid.): The *organism itself* and the organism's *health*. Both are obviously not the same thing, however: health is a specific *state* of an organism and not the organism itself. The problem could be alleviated by adopting a specific interpretation of the concept of health – e.g., as a state that contributes to the self-preservation of the organism. Although this interpretation would not render health an 'end in itself' but would rather assign to it an *instrumental* value, it would explain why, if we accept (2), health is *necessarily* of instrumental value for the organism. One may wonder, however, whether this interpretation of health as functionally related to the self-preservation of the respective organism is overly narrow. It is not any loss of health which endangers our existence as an organism – think of minor impairments to one's health, or think of infertility, which does not endanger or hinder the existence of the infertile organism but only its reproductive capacities. Moreover, diseases sometimes even contribute positively to self-preservation – the most-cited example being sickle-cell anaemia as protection against malaria. Perhaps it is possible to rebut such doubts with a more sophisticated functional interpretation of health (we will consider one candidate below), but the least we may say is that the relation between health and the organism's self-preservation is not as clear and obvious as Jonas has suggested.

One may also be puzzled about Jonas' statement (4) that health is 'defined by nature', for it seems that only a *person*, and not nature as such, is able to *define* anything. Perhaps we should interpret (4) as meaning a proper definition of health should be 'naturalistic' – that it should refer, in its *definiens*, to *natural* properties only and that it should avoid evaluative or normative terms. It would seem, however, that this would not truly capture what Jonas intended to say here. Perhaps we should instead take (4) to mean that our distinction between an organism's health and disease should reflect a difference that is essential to or significant for the respective organism itself. What that could mean, however, remains unclear. It would seem as though the most sensible interpretation would refer, again, to Jonas' statements (2) and (3): If it is true that (according to 3) any living organism is functionally organized to achieve or preserve its health, then we can identify and define what health is by examining the organism's functioning – it would then be the state that the functioning organism maintains. One obvious problem with this answer is that it presupposes a distinction between *normal* functioning and *dysfunction*: if we want to read off the defining characteristics of 'health' from the state that results from an organism's functioning, we must first make sure that the organism functions 'normally'. Since Jonas had already linked health to self-preservation, however, he seems to have introduced at least one element of a possible solution: it would be at least one step forward to interpret 'health' as the state an organism attains if its way of functioning contributes (or, were we to equivocate, would, under statistically normal circumstances, contribute) to its self-preservation. As we have noted above, this may not yet be a fully satisfying definition of health. What is more, our effort to make sense of (4) has contributed to an interpretation which, in the end, added nothing new to what we already knew from (2) and (3).

As for assumption (5), we may wonder whether we should understand it as an empirical, a conceptual or a normative statement. Jonas' subsequent arguments make clear that (5) is meant as *both* an empirical (historical) statement about the traditional goals of the medical practice *and* a normative statement about the *proper* goals of this practice – or rather about its prima facie goals, since Jonas argues these goals may sometimes be overridden by certain responsibilities physicians hold towards society. As a historical statement, (5) is certainly true – that physicians 'should work *with* nature, not *against* it', and the goal of medicine is 'to restore nature's balance and harmony by stimulating nature's own processes' (Skirbekk and Gilje 2001, 11) has defined the self-understanding of *Hippocratic* medicine. It is less obvious, however, to what extent (5) still captures the role of *current* medical practice, and this is one reason why Jonas also presents it as a *normative* statement.

Three Challenges

Starting from Jonas' assumption (5), we find that three independent challenges which must be met *before* one is justified in arguing that our current medical practice expresses an implicit (albeit perhaps unacknowledged) commitment to teleological naturalism.

First, the indirect argument in favour of teleological naturalism rests on the assumption that health is the goal of medical practice. The role of health as the overarching goal of medical practice, however, remains contested.

Second, the argument in favour of teleological naturalism rests on a specific interpretation of the concept of health. The definition of health, however, is even more strongly contested than is the guiding role of this concept in medical practice.

Third, the argument in favour of teleological naturalism rests on a specific answer to the question of *why* health (defined in a specific, naturalist manner) *should* be the defining goal of medical practice, since it is only in so far as the normative reasons why physicians should promote health result from the status of health as an intrinsic goal of the human organism that one's accepting of (5) can in fact be interpreted as an expression of commitment to teleological naturalism.

Let us now consider these three challenges.

The Current State of Medical Practice

That the preservation or recovery of health is no longer 'the' uncontested (exclusive) goal of medical practice is difficult to deny. Jonas himself was well aware of this fact. He explicitly pointed to cosmetic surgery and voluntary surgical sterilization as examples of medical interventions which are not conducive to health or are even detrimental to it. For Jonas, this is reason enough to regard these interventions as being located at the 'periphery of medicine' (Jonas 1985, 150) at best, as in the case of cosmetic surgery, or even as a clear breach of the Hippocratic Oath, as in the case of surgical sterilization (Jonas 1985, 152). While we must for the time being postpone discussion of Jonas' normative claims as such, it is relevant for our considerations regarding the first challenge stated above that Jonas is not alone in his evaluation of non-therapeutic medical interventions. Though his assessment of surgical sterilization will strike many practising doctors as overly harsh, the general idea that the *core business* of medicine is maintaining and restoring health and curing disease does still seem to express the prevailing *ethos* of the medical profession. There are, in fact, strong reservations among physicians regarding the concept of 'wish-fulfilling' (Buyx 2008) or 'preference-oriented' (Maio 2007) medicine, at least as the *prevailing* normative conception of medical practice. Still more relevant seems to be the fact that even those physicians who regard themselves as being engaged in 'wish-fulfilling medicine' refer to 'normality' as a guiding criterion for assessing their clients' wishes (Asscher, Bolt and Schermer 2012). Moreover, the still-prevailing self-understanding of doctors as primarily concerned with maintaining and restoring health corresponds with widely shared public expectations and legal regulations. Most publicly funded systems of medicine, for example, hold as a general rule (with few exceptions) that only those medical services which aim at curing diseases or maintaining health are paid for (Mazouz, Werner and Wiesing 2004). All in all, it seems that medical practice is still widely seen as directed towards individual health as its *primary* goal, and the influence of fundamental attacks on the role of health in medicine (Hesslow 1993; Wiesing 1998) seem to have been limited thus far.

This does not say much, however, as long as the concept of health itself remains ambiguous. In a radically 'normativist' and 'individualistic' reading of 'health', for example, there may be no difference between 'wish-fulfilling medicine' and medicine as a practice of maintaining and restoring health, since 'health' would then just be seen as any state that is desired by the respective individual (Siep 2003, 190). Such radically individualistic notions of health are clearly not what doctors and medical practitioners take for granted in medical practice and research. Moreover, it is easy to see that there must be at least *some* regularity about what individuals regard as their health if health-related science is to be possible at all. Without such regularities, we would have no idea *which* kind of knowledge we would have to collect in order to help individuals attain or maintain what they would regard as their health. This absurd consequence can be avoided by quite different conceptions of the health/disease distinction, however – not only 'naturalist' but also 'normativist' ones – as long as they allow for generalizations about when a specific physical or mental state should be considered, or will be regularly considered, as being 'healthy' or 'normal'. Let us then ask: What conception of 'health' (or of the distinction between health and disease, or between the normal and abnormal states of the organism) is taken for granted if one regards the medical commitment to healing as expressing a commitment to teleological naturalism? The most important ingredient of a correspondent conception is obviously the teleological interpretation of the (human) organism: The assumption that this organism is a *functional unity*, composed of organs as its *functional units*, whose proper operation contributes to the attaining or maintaining of certain species-specific *goals*. This does not necessarily imply that a suitable conception of health needs to be 'naturalist' in the specific sense of the word as taken for granted in discussion surrounding the health/disease distinction. After all, a main point of Jonas' philosophy of nature (and of other 'neo-Aristotelian' accounts such as those of Kateryna Fedoryka; cf. Fedoryka 1997) is simply that it cannot be easily categorized as either 'naturalist' or 'normativist' since it denies the underlying dichotomy: if natural organisms are teleological, goal-oriented systems, and if the goals of an organism are as such 'good', at least from the perspective of the organism in question, statements about the 'nature', the functional organization, of an organism are at the same time statements about 'values', about what is good, at least for the respective organism. Teleological naturalism does not imply a 'naturalist' interpretation of nature if 'naturalist' is taken to imply 'value-free'.

With regard to a possible argument in favour of teleological naturalism, we must consider two further points. First, if the respective interpretation of health should render teleological naturalism (as found in Jonas' works) plausible, the functional interpretation of biological organisms must tie the concept of a function to the concept of a goal. This is not trivial, since alternative concepts of biological functioning have been proposed. Obviously, we cannot fully discuss this complex issue here, but we may note that Christopher Boorse, by far the most influential proponent of a 'naturalist' interpretation of the health/disease distinction (Boorse 1975; 1976a; 1977; 1981; 1997), is also a defender of a goal-based interpretation of functions (cf. his forceful criticism of Wright's etiological approach (Wright 1973) in Boorse 1976b).

Second, in order to make a point in favour of teleological naturalism, one must endorse a specific interpretation of biological functioning which we may call 'objectivist' or 'realist': one has to assume that statements about the goals of an organism or its functional unities are descriptive statements which are truly independent of our interpretations of the respective organisms or organs *as* certain kinds of functionally structured entities. It is only then that one could derive statements about 'objective values' from statements about the teleological structure of organisms (*if* it were possible at all to derive value statements from statements about goals). Again, this is not trivial. As Kant (2007) famously argued, an alternative 'as-if-interpretation' of biological teleology is possible: one can hold the view that statements about the goals of biological organisms (and their organs) are ascriptions which constitute a certain *interpretive framework*. Assumptions about the goals of organisms are thus accordingly not seen as objectively true in the sense that they could be established by value-free natural sciences. These assumptions instead establish an interpretive framework that allows us to regard organisms *as* organisms (and to identify *a* specific organism as *that* specific organism) in the first place. Again, we cannot settle the issue here (for a brief overview of the complexities associated with functional interpretations of biological individuality, see Wilson 1999; 2000; for an overview of alternative views, see Clarke 2010). Were one to seek out a plausible interpretation of biological functioning, however, something akin to the Kantian 'as-if-interpretation' of biological teleology would seem to be a serious candidate. Moreover, since the decision between an 'objectivist' and an 'as-if-' interpretation of biological functioning is neutral as to what we are to regard as an organism's goals or functions, the as-if-interpretation seems to be, prima facie, just as suitable for the ends of medical science and practice as would be an objectivist interpretation.

As a preliminary conclusion, we may therefore say that the claim that medical practice expresses a commitment to teleological naturalism is seriously burdened by the requirement to defend not only a teleological interpretation of biological functioning (which would be in line with Boorse's prominent 'biostatistical model') but also an 'objectivist' interpretation of organismic 'goals'.

The Source of Normativity

Finally, even were we to accept that the goal of medical practice is to maintain and restore health, and even if we were to accept, in addition, that the concept of health rests on a teleological interpretation of biological organisms – and, moreover, that we have to accept an objectivist reading of teleology – even then, we must not take for granted that the medical commitment to healing expresses a commitment to teleological naturalism since whether this is the case or not depends on *why* physicians should maintain, restore or promote health.

It is only if:

1. the decisive *normative* reason for the medical commitment to healing lies in the intrinsic goodness of health, and
2. the decisive *evaluative* reason for the intrinsic goodness of health is simply that health belongs to, or can be derived from, the intrinsic goals of organisms

that we may take the commitment to healing as an indication of the truth of teleological naturalism.

At first glance both assumptions seem to be entirely plausible. Why else would doctors care for the health of their patients if not because of health's goodness? Why else should we value our own health if it were not because we are biological organisms who, by our very nature, strive for health (or perhaps who strive for self-preservation and reproduction as those goals to which, according to Boorse, health is conducive)?

Upon further reflection, however, we may recognize that the situation is far more complicated. Although both assumptions hint at certain aspects of a plausible story about the source of our commitment to healing, I think that, as stated above, they are both untenable. They both include a non sequitur.

First, it is far from certain whether we may infer normative statements about the *duties* of doctors from evaluative statements about what is *good* for some beings (in this case: the patients). I personally think that, following Prichard's (1912) critique of utilitarianism, the inference would be invalid even if 'good' were to refer to a concept such as the *universal* good of the whole moral community, although utilitarians may not be convinced. Even they would concede, however, that the professional or role-related moral responsibilities of the members of one group towards the members of another group – for instance, the responsibilities of physicians towards their patients – do not flow directly from what is good for the members of the latter group. Perhaps it would be good for me if my dentist were to give me half of her income but, unfortunately, that does not yet constitute an obligation for her. This is not to say, of course, that the fact that person A's φ-ing maintains, restores or attains something that is good for person B cannot play a role in a normative argument showing that A has a moral duty to φ. The full argument, however, will always be far more complex. A teleological naturalist, for example, would likely try to develop such an argument by referring to an all-encompassing hierarchy of natural goals wherein the relative value of each goal is determined. This was what Jonas imagined in the programmatic ethical epilogue to his *The Phenomenon of Life* (Jonas 1966, 282–4), but, as we have already seen, Jonas never fully realized this ambitious naturalist programme. What is more, if we realize that the argument 'φ-ing is good for B' can only be *part* of a normative justification of A's duty to φ, the indirect argument in favour of teleological naturalism which we are interested in loses its force, as we would then have to assume either (1) that physicians who are committed to healing express a commitment to a flawed, simplistic form of teleological naturalism, which does not seem to be a particularly strong argument in favour of a much more complex form of teleological naturalism; or (2) that their commitment to healing expresses a commitment to a complex hierarchical system of natural values and corresponding duties which, as an empirical hypothesis, seems rather implausible.

Second, it is far from clear whether we may infer *evaluative* statements about what is *good* for an organism from statements about the *goals* of the respective organism. One problem would arise if we were to accept the 'as-if-interpretation' of biological functioning: our statements about the goals of an organism would likely already express certain ideas about what is good for this organism, so that an argument from goals to goods would be in danger of becoming circular. Were we to accept the objectivist reading, however (as we have already been willing to do, albeit only for the sake of the argument), the inference from goals to goods would still seem to be problematic. In order to see what is at stake here, let us have an exemplary look at the differences between the naturalisms of Boorse and Jonas. Both authors assume that reproduction belongs to the natural goals of biological organisms. They also both mention the fact that reproduction is not always desired by human individuals (e.g., Boorse 1975, 52; Jonas 1985, 152); however, they draw markedly different conclusions from this observation. To Boorse, this fact simply illustrates the fact that normativism about the health/disease-distinction is unwarranted. While at a certain age being healthy implies fertility, we may not always find this aspect of our health desirable. That someone is healthy – that her organism is in a state that can be called normal or natural in so far as its functioning with regard to the goals of individual life and reproduction is on a level that is statistically normal for an organism of its reference group – does not imply that we actually desire to exercise that functioning. Moreover, it also does not imply that we *should* desire it. For Boorse, there is simply no direct link between the naturalness of a certain state of an organism and its desirability. Jonas, on the other hand, as is to be expected from a proponent of teleological naturalism, affirms the existence of such a link. This explains his (already mentioned) verdict regarding an individual desire for surgical sterilization and his conviction that physicians must not satisfy such desires. Although Jonas gives little weight to individual autonomy in this context, he leaves room for exceptions in the case of *collective* emergency (Jonas 1985, 153–7) – what he has in mind is a situation wherein catastrophic overpopulation endangers the flourishing of the whole human species – and this again may fit well with teleological naturalism. Which interpretation is more plausible, and which is in line with medical practice – Jonas' or Boorse's? Do we even have cause to abandon both forms of naturalism?

Discussion

It may seem that, after a long detour, the effort to develop an indirect argument in favour of teleological naturalism has led us back to our starting point: our goal was to determine whether we could take medical practice as expressing a commitment to teleological naturalism. Prima facie, this hypothesis seemed quite plausible, since (a) most physicians regard the health of their patients as the goal, or at least one of the most important goals, of medicine, and (b) health is traditionally seen – and is still interpreted by influential contemporary authors such as Boorse – as a *natural* state of biological organisms. We have had to realize, however, that even if other challenges could be met, (a) and (b) together were not yet sufficient to show that the commitment of physicians to healing implies that they regard naturalness itself as a goal, for (a) and (b) together do not show that physicians are committed to healing *because* they regard health as a *natural* state. Is this actually the case? Asking this question, we have to realize that there is neither consensus among physicians nor among philosophers of medicine. We therefore cannot avoid asking which interpretation *should* be adopted, which means that we must finally leave the path of indirect argument and instead must engage in substantive discussion. In the remainder of this chapter, however, limitations of space will allow me to draw only a rough sketch of a position which I deem plausible, and to hint at some of the most important arguments while I try to make sense and use of what we have discussed above.

Let us remember what the crucial issues are. We took medical practice as a test case in order to find out something about two main questions. First, does nature have intrinsic goals? Second, if so, are these goals normative for us? As for the first question, we have seen that prominent positions in the philosophy of medicine do in fact adhere to a teleological interpretation of biological organisms. As such, this interpretation seems plausible. First, there are good reasons to think that taking something as an individual organism regularly *means* to regard it as a functionally integrated whole. Second, both Jonas (1966, 108–26) and Boorse (1976b; cf. Searle 1995, 16–18) have developed sound arguments against reductionist interpretations of functioning which attempt to separate the concept of functioning from the concept of a goal. Along with Searle (1995), however, I think the most convincing way to make sense of the teleological structure of biological organisms is the 'as-if-interpretation'. Simply in so far as to *take* a specific individual organism *as* that specific individual organism *already implies* to take it as a functional unity that is directed toward certain goals, we are not then warranted in claiming that it is a 'brute', objective and concept-independent fact about that organism that it is directed toward the respective goals. Were we not to already have interpreted the organism in question as a functional unity (and hence to have ascribed certain goals to it), we would not then recognize it as this individual organism. While it is thus plausible to take individual life and reproduction as goals of biological organisms, as Boorse does, this is not a matter of a value-neutral observation, but instead involves an element of decision. As a side note, I should say that other elements of Boorse's interpretation of normality as naturalness also involve such elements – for example, certain assumptions about normal environments or assumptions about the adequate reference group, both of which are indispensable to Boorse's theory of natural functioning (cf. Lanzerath 2000, 117–25).

This gives rise to an argument against teleological naturalism: if those goals that we take as the 'natural' goals of biological organisms are not simply 'given' by nature as 'brute facts' but are instead constitutive of one way of looking at nature and identifying biological systems as individual organisms, they cannot serve as an independent basis of values or normativity. After all, the identification of these goals already involves some kind of decision.

Although one may object, does it not also seem odd to say that the identification of organismic goals such as self-preservation and reproduction are just a matter of 'decision'? Would this not imply that the basis of biological and medical research is arbitrary? Moreover, one may ask in a more 'Jonasean' way, does this interpretation really account for the phenomenology of organismic life, inclusive of our own experience 'from inside'? Just try to hold your breath for a longer time: can't you literally feel how the orientation towards self-preservation forces you irresistibly to respire?

It in fact seems as though we are here at a stalemate. On the one hand, it would be dogmatic to claim that individual life and reproduction 'just are' 'the' natural goals of biological organisms. On the other hand, it seems implausible to assume that our 'decision' to interpret biological organisms in this way is simply arbitrary. Can there be a middle ground? I think there are at least two independent points to be made; the first concerns the concept of biological individuality, the second is a point about the 'inside perspective' of teleology.

First, there are good reasons as to why a concept of biological individuality should identify at least the organisms of human beings as individual unities. The reasons for framing this as 'should' are not in themselves 'biological', but are rather reasons regarding the consistency of our self-understanding as autonomous persons: even before they come up with a specific account of biological individuality, biologists will have to regard their own organisms as a kind of functional unity, since it is only then – as constructivists such as Korsgaard would say, under a certain *normative* picture of their own identity as a unity (Korsgaard 2009) – that they can act, give reasons or respond to them, or take responsibility at all. This does not mean that a biology that would not or does not contain a concept of individual human organisms as unities would be strictly impossible or that it would be 'false' in a simple objectivist sense; it means simply that such a biology would lack a link to a concept that plays a crucial role in our pre-scientific practical self-understanding.

Second, one can tell a reductionist story about why we tend to value certain states of our organisms: obviously, some states of an organism and some of its patterns of behaviour are (or have been) evolutionarily advantageous. Hence it is also evolutionarily advantageous for a species if its members have a tendency to attain or maintain the respective states or to behave in the respective manner. To value a state or a pattern of behaviour is a means of possessing a tendency towards it. It is therefore evolutionarily advantageous for an organism to value those of its states or its patterns of behaviour which are evolutionarily advantageous. Natural selection therefore explains why we often value those states of our organism or patterns of behaviour that are (or have been) evolutionarily advantageous. One would of course have to say far more about both points, but I hope that the general idea is clear enough. In my view, both points together may in fact vindicate some sort of 'middle ground' between, on the one hand, the naturalist assumption that biological (human) organisms 'just are' directed towards certain 'natural' goals and, on the other hand, an implausible form of normativism according to which common notions of biological teleology are simply projections of arbitrary and rationally unwarranted value judgements. Both points together explain why we have *normative* reasons to regard at least our own individual organisms as functional unities and why we have a *natural* tendency to *value* those states of our organism that are regularly conducive – or rather, which have been regularly conducive during the history of evolution – to self-preservation and reproduction (cf. also Schramme 2002; Siep 2003, 141). This 'middle ground' obviously does not support teleological naturalism: the interpretation of our organism as such does not give us reason to think that we are *normatively bound* to strive for individual self-preservation or reproduction. It does, however, show why it is to be expected that we *normally* value our health and disvalue having a disease. Here, I disagree with Boorse, who calls the idea that diseases are prima facie undesirable 'obscure' (Boorse 1975, 53) – a significant statistical correlation may suffice. What is more, the prima facie relation between the concepts of health and disease on the one hand and normally expectable evaluations on the other constitutes a plausible relation between medical science on the one hand and medical practice (or medical art) on the other, a relation that is neither too loose (as in 'Boorsean' naturalism) nor too close (as in teleological naturalism). It explains why we regularly value states of our organism that are 'natural' according to an understanding of natural systems which, on a fundamental level, already expresses certain 'decisions', which, in turn, may express certain evaluative attitudes, which, again in turn, may be influenced by the evolutionary history of the organisms in question. This does not mean that we always value 'natural' states or that we *should* value them. (What about the 'natural' dysfunctions that are due to 'normal' ageing – does 'nature' actually give us a 'yardstick' for determining 'premature' death, as Jonas (1985, 150) explicitly claims?) Nature, even our own nature, does not actually tell us what to do. Any normative conception of our own identity, however, needs to comprise an evaluative interpretation of our own naturalness.

References

Asscher, Eva C.A., Ineke Bolt, and Maartje Schermer. 2012. 'Wish-fulfilling Medicine in Practice: A Qualitative Study of Physician Arguments'. *Journal of Medical Ethics* 38(6): 327–31.

Böhler, Dietrich. 1994. 'In Dubio Contra Projektum: Mensch und Natur im Spannungsfeld von Verstehen, Konstruieren, und Verantworten'. In *Ethik für die Zukunft: Im Diskurs mit Hans Jonas*, edited by Dietrich Böhler, 244–76. Munich: C.H. Beck.

Boorse, Christopher. 1975. 'On the Distinction between Disease and Illness'. *Philosophy and Public Affairs* 5(1): 49–68.

———. 1976a. 'What a Theory of Mental Health Should Be'. *Journal of the Theory of Social Behaviour* 6(1): 61–84.

———. 1976b. 'Wright on Functions'. *Philosophical Review* 85(1): 70–86.

———. 1977. 'Health as a Theoretical Concept'. *Philosophy of Science* 44(4): 542–73.

———. 1981. 'On the Distinction between Disease and Illness'. In *Concepts of Health and Disease: Interdisciplinary Perspectives*, edited by Arthur L. Caplan, H. Tristram Engelhardt, Jr. and James J. McCartney, 545–60. Reading: Addison-Wesley.

———. 1997. 'A Rebuttal on Health'. ,In *What Is Disease?*, edited by James M. Humber and Robert F. Albeder, 3–134. Totowa: Humana Press.

Buyx, Alena M. 2008. 'Be Careful What You Wish For? Theoretical and Ethical Aspects of Wish-fulfilling Medicine'. *Medicine, Health Care and Philosophy* 11(2): 133–43.

Clarke, Ellen. 2010. 'The Problem of Biological Individuality'. *Biological Theory* 5(4): 312–25.

Darwall, Stephen, Allan Gibbard and Peter Railton. 1992. 'Toward Fin de Siècle Ethics: Some Trends.' *The Philosophical Review* 10(1): 115–89.

———, eds. 1997. *Moral Discourse and Practice: Some Philosophical Approaches*. Oxford: Oxford University Press.

Fedoryka, Kateryna. 1997. 'Health as a Normative Concept: Towards a New Conceptual Framework'. *The Journal of Medicine and Philosophy* 22(2): 143–60.

Hesslow, Germund. 1993. 'Do We Need a Concept of Disease?' *Theoretical Medicine* 14(1): 1–14.

Hume, David. 2005. *A Treatise of Human Nature*, edited by David F. Norton and Mary J. Norton. Oxford: Oxford University Press.

Jonas, Hans. 1966. *The Phenomenon of Life: Toward a Philosophical Biology*. New York: Harper & Row.

———. 1980. 'Against the Stream: Comments on the Definition and Redefinition of Death'. In *Philosophical Essays: From Ancient Creed to Technological Man*, edited by Hans Jonas, 132–40. Chicago: University of Chicago Press.

———. 1984. *The Imperative of Responsibility: In Search of an Ethics for the Technological Age*. Chicago: University of Chicago Press.

———. 1985. 'Ärztliche Kunst und Menschliche Verantwortung'. In *Technik, Medizin und Ethik: Zur Praxis des Prinzips Verantwortung*, edited by Hans Jonas, 146–61. Frankfurt: Insel.

———. 1996. 'Evolution and Freedom: On the Continuity among Life-forms'. In *Mortality and Morality: A Search for the Good after Auschwitz*, edited by Lawrence Vogel, 59–74. Evanston: Northwestern University Press.

———. 2010. *Organismus und Freiheit: Philosophie des Lebens und Ethik der Lebenswissenschaften*, vol. 1, edited by Horst Gronke. Freiburg; Berlin and Vienna: Rombach.

Kant, Immanuel. 2007. *Critique of Judgement*, edited by Nicholas Walker, translated by James C. Meredith. Oxford: Oxford University Press.

Korsgaard, Christine 2009. M. *Self-constitution: Agency, Identity, and Integrity*. Oxford: Oxford University Press.

Lanzerath, Dirk. 2000. *Krankheit und ärztliches Handeln: Zur Funktion des Krankheitsbegriffs in der medizinischen Ethik*. Freiburg: Karl Alber.

Maio, Giovanni. 2007. 'Medizin auf Wunsch?' *Deutsche Medizinische Wochenschrift* 132(43): 2278–81.

Mazouz, Nadia, Micha H. Werner and Urban Wiesing. 2004. *Krankheitsbegriff und Mittelverteilung*. Baden-Baden: Nomos.

Moore, George E. 1994. *Principia Ethica: Revised Edition: With the Preface to the Second Edition and Other Papers*. Cambridge: Cambridge University Press.

Prichard, Harold A. 1912. 'Does Moral Philosophy Rest on a Mistake?' *Mind* 21(81): 21–37.

Schramme, Thomas. 2002. 'Natürlichkeit als Wert'. *Analyse & Kritik* 24(2): 249–71.

Searle, John R. 1995. *The Construction of Social Reality*. New York: The Free Press.

Siep, Ludwig. 2003. *Konkrete Ethik: Grundlagen der Natur- und Kulturethik*. Frankfurt: Suhrkamp.

Skirbekk, Gunnar, and Nils Gilje. 2001. *History of Western Thought: From Ancient Greece to the Twentieth Century*. New York: Routledge.

Werner, Micha H. 1994. 'Dimensionen der Verantwortung: Ein Werkstattbericht zur Zukunftsethik von Hans Jonas.' In *Ethik für die Zukunft: Im Diskurs mit Hans Jonas*, edited by Dietrich Böhler, 303–38. Munich: C.H. Beck.

———. 2008. 'The Immediacy of Encounter and the Dangers of Dichotomy: Buber, Levinas, and Jonas on Responsibility'. In *The Legacy of Hans Jonas: Judaism and the Phenomenon of Life*, edited by Christian Wiese and Hava Tirosh-Samuelson, 203–30. Boston: Brill Academic Publishers.

———. 2012. 'Ist Wertenkönnen Wertvoll?' In *Naturphilosophie als Grundlage der Naturethik: Zur Aktualität von Hans Jonas*, edited by Gerald Hartung et al., 187–214. Freiburg i. Br.: Karl Alber (in press).

Wiesing, Urban. 1998. 'Kann die Medizin als praktische Wissenschaft auf eine allgemeine Definition von Krankheit verzichten?' *Zeitschrift für Medizinische Ethik* 44(2): 83–97.

Wilson, Jack A. 1999. *Biological Individuality: The Identity and Persistence of Living Entities*. Cambridge: Cambridge University Press.

———. 2000. 'Ontological Butchery: Organism Concepts and Biological Generalizations'. *Philosophy of Science* 67: 301–11.

Wright, Larry. 1973. 'Functions'. *Philosophical Review* 82(2): 139–68.

Chapter 9
Ethics for the Technoscientific Age: On Hans Jonas' Argumentation and His Public Philosophy Beyond Disciplinary Boundaries

Jan C. Schmidt

Philosophy in the Public Arena

Hans Jonas is one of the outstanding public philosophers of the twentieth century: His future-oriented, anti-visionary philosophy had a tremendous impact on public and philosophical debates throughout the 1980s and the early 1990s.

Jonas has been credited with taking the recent situation of our life-world and our socio-technological culture seriously. He focuses on pressing life-world problems that show the ambivalence of technological advance. Jonas is not interested in putting forward a purely academic, disciplinary philosophy that addresses and reaches just a limited audience of experts: Good philosophy has to meet the present challenges and contribute – in one way or another – to societal problem perception, framing and solving. Philosophy needs to be good for something! It has a general duty to ensure the survival of the human species and the future of mankind: 'Care for the future of mankind is the overruling duty of collective human action in the age of technical civilization that has become "almighty"' (Jonas 1984, 136). His catastrophe prevention and emergency ethics encompasses a precautionary principle and, accordingly, a '"heuristics of fear", replacing the former projections of hope' (Jonas 1984, x), that has (since Francis Bacon's pioneering, but nevertheless ambivalent, works such as *Nova Atlantis* and his *Novum Organum*) been central to the modern epoch (cf. Schmidt 2011).

Although severely criticized by the scientific community of academic philosophers, Jonas' politically as well as philosophically influential book *The Imperative of Responsibility: In Search of an Ethics for the Technological Age* (first published in 1979) has been a forerunner for the idea of sustainable development and various political programmes of socio-ecological change (cf. Norton 2005; Schmidt 2000a, 2012). His (philosophically based and trans-disciplinary oriented) work has also induced an impressive wave of implementing science and engineering ethics in university curricula of disciplinary science and engineering education (cf. Harris et al. 2005).

Jonas' Approach

Indeed, by rethinking the foundations of modern ethics as well as by reframing the (pre-) concept of nature, Jonas advocates strong claims and provocative theses. His diagnosis, that we are confronted with an intrinsic ambivalence of technological advancement, formulated as early as in the 1970s, was based on the perception that we 'live in an apocalyptic situation' (Jonas 1984, 140) – facing a crisis with various 'threats' (Jonas 1984, ix). These threats are not caused solely by the unintended side effects of technology, including the misuse of technical systems, but rather by the success of science and technology itself. According to Jonas,

> [n]ot counting the insanity of a sudden, suicidal atomic holocaust, which sane fear can avoid with relative ease, it is the slow, long-term, cumulative—the peaceful and constructive use of worldwide technological power, a use in which all of us collaborate as captive beneficiaries through rising production, consumption, and sheer population growth—that poses threats much harder to counter. The net total of these threats is the overtaxing of nature, environment and (perhaps) human as well. (Jonas 1984, ix)

The emerging 'crisis', Jonas argues, is deeply rooted at the metaphysical foundation of contemporary culture – with its predominant way of perceiving and dealing with nature. Nature is becoming widely disposable and questionable. This overtaxes traditional ethics: ethics can no longer cope alone with these challenges. Moreover, the crisis challenges the metaphysical fundament of Western culture and calls for a revised view of nature ('metaphysics') and a change in the interrelationship of ethics, philosophy of nature and anthropology. Thus, the crisis 'push[es] the necessary rethinking beyond the doctrine of action, that is, ethics, into the doctrine of being, that is, metaphysics, in which all ethics must be grounded' (Jonas 1984, 8; see also Jonas 2009, 126): '[M]etaphysics must underpin ethics' (Jonas 1984, x). Major challenges require a fundamental reflection on and revision of the metaphysical bases and backgrounds. Anything else is too weak – so thought Hans Jonas over 30 years ago.[1]

In the present day, however, short-term pragmatic thinking seems to dominate public policy. Quick regulations in response to seemingly pressing problems are expected. Jürgen Mittelstraß speaks of a 'repair ethics': ethics is obviously far too reactive, hardly proactive or prospective. Seldom is it more than cosmetics and compensation. Yet global climate change, *Deepwater Horizon*, and *Fukushima* crisis – along with advances in synthetic biology and nanotechnologies, medical and neuro-technologies – renew the call for a much more deeply rooted ethics of nature and technology: Is it not an ongoing duty of any philosophical approach to

1 Cf. the most ambitious and comprehensive work on Jonas: Böhler et al. 2009. Introductions to Jonas' work include: Böhler 1994, Levy 2002, Müller 2003, Schmidt 2000a, 2007 and Wetz 1994. Some of Jonas' predecessors include: Schweitzer 1966, Picht 1969, Schulz 1972 and Passmore 1974.

reveal the underlying metaphysical assumptions, to open them to rational reflection and revision? Would philosophy not be well advised to express its neat relationship to the life-world and to society in programmatic terms: *shaping concepts of nature ('metaphysics'), underpinning ethics, building society*?[2] In short: What kind of ethics, philosophy of nature and anthropology do we need (and which one can we rationally justify) in order to progress *from* intra-philosophical justification discourse *to* philosophically reflective patterns of action and decision-making in the life-world and in society? (cf. Schmidt, 2000a, 2000b, 2007)

Certainly, such thinking is provocative today, although these programmatic theses – prominently presented in Jonas' *Imperative of Responsibility* – were broadly debated in the 1980s. Christoph Hubig called Jonas' book a 'philosophical bestseller' (Hubig 1995, 13). It contributed in a major way to the boom in philosophical ethics in the 1980s. Ethics sought to be more than (and different from) a 'bicycle brake on an intercontinental airplane', to cite the reproach directed at ethics by the sociologist Ulrich Beck (Beck 1988, 194). Ethics went public, was perceptible and audacious, it engaged and got involved. One expected it to deliver something and contribute to societal development – besides diagnoses of the times, analyses of origins and methods of argumentation even guiding answers for societal futures – in other words: a non-formal, normative 'orientational knowledge' (e.g. Wolters 1997). Jonas' public philosophy can therefore be regarded as an 'engaged philosophy', a term coined by Robert Frodeman in order to foster a reorienting of (disciplinary academic) philosophy (Frodeman et al. 2010).

Jonas' late work, which was pivotal to his third thematic period following his investigation of gnosis and philosophy of organisms, has earned an eminent status in the history of philosophy and also in cultural philosophical terms. His *Imperative of Responsibility* can be described as being both product and promoter of societal reflection; to a certain extent itself a mark of a 'reflective modernity' (Beck 1986). It represented a socio-historical milestone – or even caesura – which heeded the societal relations to technology, nature and self visible in the diagnosed socio-ecological and atomic 'survival crisis' and comprehended them as a challenge to philosophy.

Now, though, this socio-historical juncture characterizing the transition into the 'reflexively modern risk society' (Beck 1986) seems infinitely remote and alien to us today. So much has it become taken for granted that any hint of challange has vanished, leaving behind it an amorphous, unquestioning acceptance in which there appears to be practically no further point of contact. No other like Hans Jonas seems to have become such a symbol of this evidently concluded epoch – of an 'alarmism' (Luhmann 2006) now put behind us, stimulated by moralizing and metaphysically religious 'good men' in conjunction with culturally pessimistic and at the same time conservative-naturalistic talk of crisis and apocalypse-prevention in the face of alleged threats of doom. Former normativity seems to be deemed

2 This motto implicitly refers to the areas of science and technology studies (STS) that – notwithstanding their high relevance for a future-oriented shaping of science and technology within society – exhibit a lack of reflection on normative issues; e.g., Bijker and Law 1994.

falsified by present-day normality. Debates on risks are regarded as obsolete and superseded by programme of innovation. The ecological catastrophe, it seems, is not happening; genetic engineering and medical technology are lagging behind their utopian expectations; the *New Man* is not in sight – societal reality, individual life-world, man's biological constitution – all appear stable enough.

Postmodernism, pluralization and particularization also played their part in establishing a (purported) consensus about a radically 'post-metaphysical age' (Habermas 1992). Deconstructivism and constructivism dispelled the gravity of a problem-oriented objectivity – arguably exaggerated from an 'alarmistic' perspective – and portrayed the problems themselves as constructed: the hole in the ozone layer disappeared as a social phenomenon in the contingency of plural perspectives of socio–cogno constructions (e.g. Luhmann 1992, 2006). The 'power program' thinker Francis Bacon, who set out to 'conquer' (Schmidt 2011) nature, has also made a comeback. As a reflection of the societal climate, Jonas' approach seems to have vanished from philosophy. A normative anti-normativism emerged; a value-free description of allegedly non-referential phenomena (societal reality) seemed feasible *in* and *via* philosophy, of all things. Accordingly, Jonas' approach of putting central focus on the reflection on and revision of metaphysical considerations seemed to be the crystallization point of an old-fashioned style of philosophical thinking that is far from being in accordance with what *should* be considered as good philosophy.

In light of recent issues such as Fukushima or Global Climate Change, it might nevertheless be appropriate to reconsider whether Jonas' approach of establishing an interrelation between ethics, philosophy of nature and anthropology and his argument for a future-oriented responsibility on a global scale might not, after all, contribute to a critical analysis of the present state of affairs and our societal future. In the following, the main objections raised against Jonas will be reconstructed and critically assessed. It will be shown that most of the objections of the critics are not as sound as they claim to be – although Jonas' (context of) justification is somewhat weak. In particular, this chapter will underline the impact of Jonas' future-directed and problem-oriented approach on the recent debate on sustainability. Main ideas of his *Imperative of Responsibility* have been adopted by the Brundtland Report (UN General Assembly 1987) and are prevalent in the various concepts of sustainable development. A major objective of this chapter is thus to show that, and the way in which, Jonas regards 'ethics' and 'philosophy of nature' (not: 'natural philosophy') as twin sisters, or to be more precisely, that 'ethics becomes part of the philosophy of nature'.[3]

Objections: The Critics of Jonas' Thesis and Their Criticism

What did the critics hold against Jonas? In the early 1990s Lothar Schäfer maintained that 'we should not, and indeed must not, follow the propositions made by Jonas'

3 See the usage of the term 'philosophy of nature' in Jonas 2001, 282.

(Schäfer 1999, 96; my translation)[4] – a view which soon seemed to take hold in philosophy and in public. Schäfer accused Jonas of delivering merely 'religious answers' to dilemmas that are not religious but societal (Schäfer 1999, 28; my translation). The real task is to reshape the 'Bacon Project' – as Schäfer's book was entitled – to reformulate it for the future under modified conditions, and to undertake a critique of recent political economy. Johannes Wendnagel spoke of an 'untenable argumentative underpinning' (Wendnagel 1990, 7; my translation) of Jonas' *Imperative of Responsibility.*

Another major criticism of Jonas concerns significant problems with the application and implementation of his approach. According to Angelika Krebs, those like Jonas 'who press for a radical change, a paradigm shift, in our moral attitude toward nature, and brand anthropocentrism as the source of all ecological evil [...] are [...] wrong' and do not help to solve the problem (Krebs 1997, 379; my translation).[5] Gertrude Hirsch Hadorn discerns in Jonas' ethics a problematic 'secularized belief in God', a 'metaphysical speculation' with a philosophy of the 'absolute' leading to eminent 'problems of justification' that 'raise doubts about his philosophical responses to these issues' (Hirsch Hadorn 2000, 385/115/11/383/377; my translation): 'Jonas' Imperative of Responsibility', Hirsch-Hadorn writes, is 'onto-theological moral grounding without a moral definition. It leaves the interpretation of the orientational problem [and solution] of technological civilization [...] to arbitrariness' (Hirsch Hadorn 2000, 387; my translation). Heiner Hastedt identifies a 'tendency in Jonas' naturalistic ecological ethics to formulate in a vehemently moralizing way general and addressee-less postulates' that miss the 'societal dimension of the problem' and moreover themselves tend to exhibit 'inconsistency' in their arguments (Hastedt 1994, 178; my translation). Armin Grunwald believes that Jonas' reasoning is untenable analytically and that his ethics is socially irrelevant. 'Philosophical attempts to establish a "duty of mankind to exist" are therefore not only problematic because of metaphysical presuppositions, but also superfluous' (Grunwald 1996, 200; my translation). For Grunwald, the 'future path of an ethics of technology [...] is predestined: away from metaphysical justifications, an increasing liberation from Jonas' legacy of an "apocalypse-prevention ethic", [...] towards situative decision logic for the individual case [... and] towards a pragmatism of discursive conflict management' (Grunwald 1996, 202–3; my translation).

Some of the major objections against Jonas have thus far been outlined:

1. The *diagnosis objection* critiques Jonas' perception and diagnosis of the dilemma and the associated epochal break thesis.
2. The origin *analysis objection*, though it may share Jonas' diagnosis or his motives, does not identify any fundamental challenge to ethics, metaphysics or philosophy in general.

4 Schäfer explicitly deals with Jonas' line of argumentation in: Schäfer 1993.

5 See also in a more elaborated version: Krebs 1999.

3. The *argumentation and justification objection* accuses Jonas of fallacies, incorrect deductions and unfounded arguments.
4. Finally, the *practice objection* levels the accusation of ineffectiveness and irrelevance.

The criticism seems to be overwhelming. Yet, one might ask: Are the objections against Jonas as well founded and broadly recognized as they evidently appear to be? In the following, this chapter aims to present a critical and analytical reconstruction of the objections to Jonas' argument of 'responsibility for the future'.[6] This could show that – despite some deficits in its context of justification – the overall argument does exhibit a high degree of plausibility.

Diagnosis of the Recent Situation: What Is at Stake …

'[W]e live in an apocalyptic situation, that is, under the threat of a universal catastrophe if we let things take their present course' (Jonas 1984, 140). Jonas identifies an epochal break in the history of mankind. The Baconian ideal of infinite progress has given rise to a threat – not only because of unwanted and unintended side effects but, more fundamentally, because of the excessive magnitude of its success. Man's existence as a biological species and the human-societal existence of future generations are at stake. The 'original venture [of freedom]' prefigured in the organic draws attention (through man's deeds) to the possibility of not-being: the 'threat of its negative' (Jonas 2001, 5/4). That life is 'an experiment with mounting stakes and risks which in the fateful freedom of man may end in disaster as well as success' (Jonas 2001, x; see also xxiii–xxiv) – a 'progressive scale of freedom and peril' – is nowhere clearer than in the large-scale sciento-technological experiment with nature.

Jonas sees culturally established concepts of mankind, be they individual or societal, eroded by the 'altered nature of human action, with the magnitude and novelty of its works' (Jonas 1984, ix, similarly 9). Nature – conceived of as man's corporeal nature, as the growth of organic existence, as an external resource ('environment'), and as phenomenal, aesthetic nature – is becoming completely subject to disposal. 'The subjugation of nature with a view towards man's happiness has brought about, by the disproportion of its success, which now extends to the nature of man himself, the greatest challenge for the human that his own needs have ever entailed. Everything about it is novel and unprecedented in

6 Others have supported Jonas' approach and underpinned his argumentation, e.g.: Böhme 1999 and Dupuy 2005. In addition, J. Habermas refers to Jonas when criticizing the 'instrumentalist view of humans induced by gene technology' (Habermas 2002, 84–5). For a general account of the group of Jonas' supporters, see Böhler 1994 and the scholars of the Hans Jonas-Zentrum, Berlin.

character and magnitude. [...] That the promise of modern technology has turned into a threat forms the premise' for Jonas.[7]

A negative dialectic of freedom in our technological practices emerges. Jonas discusses the technoscientific progress from pre-modern *techne*, which basically revolved around instruments, tools and methods, to modern science-based technology. Mechanics, chemistry, electricity, information and communications technology, and bio-engineering have successively established themselves. Advanced technology potentiates nature's disposability and its 'vulnerability' (Jonas 1984, 6). The Aristotelian distinction between nature (*physis*) and *techne* – programmatically eliminated by Francis Bacon at the birth of the modern age – is becoming phenomenologically obsolete (Schmidt 2011). *Homo faber* is triumphing over *Homo sapiens* (Jonas 1984, 9). For Jonas, the boundary between nature and city (nomos, polis) serves as a guiding metaphor to underline his diagnosis. This boundary has become blurred and obliterated as a 'universal city' takes shape. 'The difference between the artificial and the natural has vanished'; free nature is being 'swallowed up in the sphere of the artificial' (Jonas 1984, 10). An ambivalent momentum in technoscientific advancement has emerged, with cumulative impacts and evolutionary hazards, revealing the 'vulnerability of nature' and the fragility of natural equilibriums. A negative dialectic of power over nature arises because 'every attempt to break the natural thralldom, because nature is broken, enters all the more deeply into that natural enslavement', as noted by Max Horkheimer and Theodor W. Adorno in a very similar tenor to that of Jonas (Horkheimer and Adorno 2002, 13).

Jonas, thus, starts – like Georg Picht, Walter Schulz and Carl Friedrich von Weizsäcker – with the anti-utopianist (anti-Blochian) shock that being is no longer a given and can no longer be taken for granted. While it is true that this shock over the 'enormity of the situation' was not, as Jonas' critics point out, accompanied by specific reflection on the plurality of technology, disparity of agents, diversity of cultures and complexity of societal conditions, this diagnosis can nevertheless be granted a certain degree of plausibility.

7 This is a translation from the foreword of the original German publication (1979) of the *Imperative of Responsibility* that was not translated and included in the English version (Jonas 1984, 7); the translation of the forword was done by L. Ferry 1995, 76–7, and was slightly modified by myself. In the English version of the *Imperative*, Jonas writes that 'an ever-deeper penetration of nature' is taking place: '[T]he other side of the triumphal advance has begun to show its face, disturbing the euphoria of success with threats that are as novel as its welcomed fruits. [...] The net total of these threats is the overtaxing of nature, environmental and (perhaps) human as well' (Jonas 1984, ix).

The Analysis: Tracing the Roots Back to the Concepts of Ethics and the Metaphysical

Apparently, we are incapable of taking appropriate action in the face of such 'threats'.[8] Jonas characterizes the untrodden ground of collective technological practice that we have entered with high technology as an 'ethical vacuum' (Jonas 1984, 23) and a 'no man's land for ethics'.[9] Conventional, well established concepts of ethics need to be supplemented. (1) Previously, all dealing with nature in the form of craftsmanship (*techne*) was considered 'ethically neutral' in so far as nature could be assumed to be largely independent of man's actions. (2) Only man's interactions with other humans were of ethical significance. (3) Man himself, as the prerequisite for ethical action, could be assumed to be a constant. (4) Global dimensions of space and time were not taken into account; conventional ethics was about 'the here and now' (Jonas 1984, 5) and confined to the 'proximate range of action': 'The short arm of human power did not call for a long arm of predictive knowledge' (Jonas 1984, 6). The critical assessment presented by Jonas is not restricted to any particular, well-established concept of ethics. It applies equally to Kantianism, utilitarianism, contractualism, forms of virtue ethics and ethics of compassion, and today also to discourse ethics. As Jonas is saying, however, he does not seek to replace other concepts of ethics, but to supplement and expand them.[10]

For Jonas, the ethical vacuum is not at all surprising – however, it is caused by an inadequate underlying metaphysics. He identifies deficits in the metaphysical fundament of contemporary society, by which is meant the set of implicit understandings about man, nature and science. If it is correct to say that even secular late-modern societies are influenced by a metaphysical fundament and ontological background – and therefore we have indeed not entered a 'post-metaphysical age'[11] – this prompts the question of whether it is necessary to revise the metaphysics,

8 Ethics has to prove itself not only within the context of theory, but also within the context of practice and action. According to Jonas, the context of justification that defines the twentieth-century tradition of ethics is – though necessary – (far) too limited. From a different perspective, E. Tugendhat has argued that philosophers have broadly neglected to consider and reflect on the different types of justification that different concepts of ethics provide (Tugendhat 1993).

9 The latter is my translation from the foreword of the original German publication (Jonas 1979, 7).

10 Jonas does not regard his approach as a contradiction of well-established ethics. Jonas takes from Kant a certain deontological background, from utilitarianism the consequentialism and focus on the results of actions, and from Aristotle some virtues. Therefore, the critique that Jonas aims to provide a 'new ethics', as levelled by Hastedt 1994 and others, is not very sound.

11 Habermas 1992. The fact that metaphysics is populating late-modern societies and spreading ubiquitously can be shown with regard to the field of 'neurophilosophy' and its approach to 'naturalizing the mind'. Analytical philosophy does not seem to be as 'analytical' as it claims with regard to its foundation and underlying convictions.

rationalities and underlying convictions governing such understandings about nature, man and science. Fundamental crises make it necessary, Jonas writes, to 'push the necessary rethinking beyond the doctrine of action, that is, ethics, into the doctrine of being, that is, metaphysics, in which all ethics must be grounded' (Jonas 1984, 8; see also Jonas 2009, 126):[12] '[W]hether and why mankind should exist' is ultimately a 'metaphysical question' (Jonas 1987, 48; my translation). Thus, 'metaphysics must underpin ethics' (Jonas 1984, x).

Metaphysics is not to be understood as a contingent positing or as a dogma immune to revision.[13] On the contrary, in light of the tradition of philosophy since the ancient Greeks, metaphysics 'has always been a business of reason' (Jonas 1984, 45).[14] Therefore, the question is not *whether* we have (or want) a metaphysics, but *which* one can and *should* it be. Jonas seeks to engender through rational thinking a metaphysics that is adequate to the recent threat to the survival of mankind – in brief, he advocates a (pragmatic) *shaping of metaphysics*. Recently, in line with Jonas, Jean-Pierre Dupuy has also spoken of the 'need for an adequate metaphysics'. Dupuy has in focus the 'foundations of a metaphysics adapted to the temporality of catastrophes' (Dupuy 2005, 96).[15]

How relevant is the metaphysical? Metaphysics is always around us. The natural and engineering sciences cannot avoid metaphysical thinking in their approach to nature and in their methodology. 'If the picture that the natural sciences portray of nature', Jonas says, 'were the last word on the condition of the world, the latter would be a value-neutral mechanical gear [...]. If this picture is an adequate description of reality, there is indeed no reason why we should worry about the coming millennium' (Jonas 1993, 44; my translation). According to Jonas, 'nature' here is constituted and understood in a reductionist's way as an external, self-referential, positivistic and law-following matter of fact having no relation at all to man. Max Weber, speaking in the same vein as Jonas, famously coined the phrase 'disenchantment of the world', while Horkheimer and Adorno identified a 'reification' and 'objectification' of nature (Horkheimer and Adorno 2002).[16] The

12 In his philosophical biology, Jonas argues that 'through the continuity of mind with organism and of organism with nature, ethics becomes part of the philosophy of nature' (Jonas 2001, 282).

13 On the relevance of ontology and metaphysics in Jonas' work, see, e.g.: Hösle 1994.

14 Making metaphysics explicit is the best starting point for rational argumentation and critique. Jonas argues: '[T]he worldly philosopher struggling for an ethics must first of all hypothetically allow the possibility of a rational metaphysics, despite Kant's contrary verdict, if the rational is not preemptively determined by the standards of positive science'. (ibid., 45)

15 See also an explicit and elaborated reference to Jonas in Dupuy 2007 (www.europa.eu.int/comm/health/ph_risk/documents/ev_20040301_en.pdf) and Dupuy 2009 (http://occasion.stanford.edu/node/28) (accessed 21 Nov. 2013).

16 Most interestingly, Habermas (2002, 86) has shown that the Critical Theory (of the Frankfurt School) and Jonas' philosophy have a common denominator. According to

disenchantment induces a devaluation and a 'dispersal and involution of value whose upshot for us is total confusion' (Baudrillard 2003, 10).[17] Jonas opposes the value-neutralization of nature – and insists 'that natural science may not tell the whole story about Nature' (Jonas 1984, 8). Hence, he is advocating an *approach thesis* and suggests that we should reflect on (and potentially revise) the metaphysical assumptions that underlie the one or the other approach. This thesis is entirely in accord with Goethe: 'The conclusions of men are very different according to the mode in which they approach a science or branch of knowledge; from which side, through which door they enter' (see Goethe 1840, x/vii).[18]

The approach argument transposes ethical considerations to the earlier stages of the process of knowledge production – for instance, to phases of understanding, insight and cognition – in other words, to the motives and attitudes of scientific activity, and the constitution and construction of research programmes. In contrast, the existence and emergence of (ethical) problems have always been uncritically accepted as a matter of fact in the various branches of (traditional) concepts of ethics; in fact the underlying dynamics that induces the emergence of new problems has not been questioned or addressed.[19] This deficit – for example, ignoring fundamental questions about knowledge production and the (technoscientific) construction of issues – should be eliminated. '[W]e can [achieve this transposition to an earlier stage] only if, before considering the question that is seemingly always the most immediate one and always the most urgent one: *What shall we do?*, we ponder this: *How must we think?*' – these are not the words of Jonas, but of his academic teacher Martin Heidegger (Heidegger 1977, 40).

The Argumentation Framework: On Jonas' Horizon of Justification

The requirements to be met by ethical reasoning are, indeed, debatable. Jonas was criticized for not having presented an argumentational grounding for his future-

Habermas, Jonas starts his diagnosis by underlining that techno-scientific development is part of the destructive power of the dialectic of enlightenment, in which men's technical power to rule over nature brings mankind deeper into the internal dynamics and forces of nature: there is no escape from the roots (of mankind) in nature.

17 Cf. also with regard to the cultural history of the devaluation of nature induced by the ambivalent success of science and technology: Höffe 1993.

18 Cf. the works of Gernot Böhme – in a similar vein to Goethe und Jonas: Böhme 1999 and Altner et al. 2000.

19 Jonas argues in favor of a kind of pluralism: the scientific approach is *one* approach to nature. However, there are others – e.g., approaches based on the life-world and direct sense perception. Jonas does not accept that natural sciences continuously present the problems that have to be solved by ethics. Such an instrumentalist view of ethics is a shortcoming that does not reach the internal dynamics of sciences and technology; this would limit ethics to a mere repair instrument that always comes too late.

oriented ethics. However, this objection fails in so far as it is intended as a general one. Despite an obvious lack of argumentational stringency, Jonas does voice clear premises and definitive conclusions.[20] Let us first consider the four premises or theses.

First: Jonas' argumentation is based on a teleological approach that forms a central part of his philosophy of nature and philosophical anthropology – and complements his ethics (*purposiveness thesis*). Of seminal significance is his main natural philosophical work *The Phenomenon of Life*, 1966, in which he develops an integral-monistic philosophy of life, encompassing his philosophy of organism and philosophy of mind (Jonas 2001). Jonas invokes Aristotle, criticizes Descartes, opposes Kant, shows an affinity with Schelling and also with Scheler. He interprets the realm of living organism in Aristotelian fashion as an 'ascending scale', but without the evolutionary optimism of a Teilhard de Chardin. Mind, Jonas believes, is prefigured in organic existence from the beginning and manifests itself most prominently in man. 'The great contradictions which man discovers in himself—freedom and necessity, autonomy and dependence, self and world, relation and isolation, creativity and mortality—have their rudimentary traces in even the most primitive forms of life, *each* precariously balanced between being and not-being, and each endowed with an internal horizon of "transcendence"' (Jonas 2001, xxiii; see also Jonas 1996, 60). In the famous terms coined by Schelling, *matter is not primitive, it is productive.* It is this nature coming into being and growing that is central to Jonas' concept of nature.[21] From an *anthropomorphic* stance,[22] beginning with and descending from man as a *natural* being in which nature testifies to itself, Jonas discerns 'nature's purposive labor' (Jonas 1984, 82) and sees an 'immanence of purpose in nature' (Jonas 1984, 78) – although in a weak sense: purposes are manifest in nature in so far as organic life carries an *ontological* '"Yes" of life' in itself: an intention to continue living and, accordingly, a goal orientation, namely the preservation of being. Jonas goes further than Kant's *As-If* and, like Schelling, accuses the mechanists and reductionists of viewing nature *as if* no intrinsic ends and purposes existed. Nevertheless, demonstrating that ends are rooted in nature is *not* equivalent to saying that conscious intention or subjectivity is a necessary prerequisite of natural purposiveness.

Second: Jonas asserts a *'natural purpose as value' thesis* or, stronger, an *'end as good-in-itself' thesis*, namely that '[n]ature, by entertaining ends, or having aims [...] also posits values' (Jonas 1984, 79). Purposes as such, regardless of their material content, represent a value, without 'judgment upon the goodness of the goal itself' being passed (Jonas 1984, 79): the material content of an end or a

20 Cf. Hubig (1995, 154), who perceives a 'rational argumentation' in Jonas' ethics that shows a stringency not all that different from Kant's.

21 Jonas' philosophy of life encompasses aspects from Aristotle to Schelling to modern theories of self-organization.

22 We have to be careful and draw a line between Jonas' anthropomorphic interpretation of organism and life on the one hand and his anti-anthropocentric (and anti-dualist) approach in ethics on the other hand.

purpose may be good or bad; ends must initially be regarded as being *good* in their very existence. Jonas even goes as far as to determine a 'purposiveness as good-in-itself' (Jonas 1984, 80). He presupposes that there is such a thing as a good-in-itself and that this is not merely a contingent ascription. The good-in-itself is filled with material content – *not* with love, truth or justice, but with purpose. Purposes are posited not only in relative terms (subjective status), but more comprehensively; values 'as such' are embedded in purpose (objective status).

Third: The presence of a 'good-in-itself' says nothing about its actualization. It could be self-sufficient and stand on its own. Jonas, however – with his *'good-in-itself as a requisite' thesis* – links an immanent claim to the good, namely to convey the latter from potentiality into reality. '[T]he good or valuable', Jonas observes, 'when it is this of itself and not just by grace of someone's desiring, needing, or choosing, is by its very concept a thing whose being possible entails the demand for its being or becoming actual' (Jonas 1984, 79). It carries an 'ought' within itself.

Fourth: Even if purposes in nature are bound to an 'ought', this does not mean that man is able to perceive the 'ought' as a normative standard or as an ethical obligation and, taking it further, must always fulfil it. The relevant *fourth premise* for this question differs from the foregoing three. It goes beyond the alleged naturalism of which Jonas was accused. It can be called a '*capacity for freedom*' or 'capacity for responsibility' thesis. The notion of freedom here is a *terminus technicus* which deviates somewhat from everyday word usage. What Jonas means is the active self-preservation in nature, descending from humans (at the tip of the pyramid) down to the basic forms of organic existence.[23] Man, and in particular his freedom, can be regarded as 'the supreme outcome of nature's purposive labor' whereas nature is understood in an integral-monistic sense (Jonas 1984, 82). Jonas' argument is that the special type of freedom inherent in man brings with it an obligation: 'This blindly self-enacting "yes" gains obligating force in the seeing freedom of man' (Jonas 1984, 82). It is a duty of man to 'adopt the "yes" into his will and impose the "no" to not-being on his power' (Jonas 1984, 82). Recognizing this and acting accordingly is precisely what makes man human, what characterizes his human condition. Man has to extend his will into an obligation *in favour of* being, as an 'ought-to-be' (Jonas 1984, 46–7).

To summarize, four premises underlie Jonas' conclusion and his argument of 'responsibility for the future'. It can be formally expressed as follows: purposive existence + purpose-as-value + good-in-itself + capacity for responsibility => obligation. Natural purposiveness, Jonas concludes, has a '"claim" to realization', the willing of which man has the duty to adopt into his 'ought'; this is the 'obligating force of the ontological "Yes" upon man' (Jonas 1984, 82). Clearly,

23 This idea is close to the descending ontology of his teacher Martin Heidegger: what nature is, is not only revealed in atoms and is not present in particles but in the most complex structure, i.e., in humans.

the conclusion is correctly structured. However, one may question the premises or theses. Are these true and justifiable?

First: The question regarding the existence of purposes or ends and their (essential) quality has always accompanied philosophy of nature. Despite the devaluation of the Kantian *As-If* and the verdict of teleology in the natural sciences, an absence of purpose is hardly conceivable. Even modern biology cannot do without purposes, although it has officially substituted the word 'teleonomy' for any type of teleology relating to functions (cf. Köchy 2008). In physical cosmology, the teleologically orientated Anthropic Principle (cf. Carter 1974) explains the selection of initial and boundary conditions realized in the Big Bang. And the current advancements in physics (physics of complex systems, chaos theory, self-organization theories, etc.) have revived the question of a natural teleology and contributed to a modified, late-modern physics (see, e.g., Schmidt 2008). Purposes are, moreover, also articulated *in* the actions of humans, which can be viewed as part of nature, following Jonas or evolution theory. Wherever man appears, ends appear with (and in) him. In addition, teleological thinking is part of the current bioethical debate, namely in the purview of the potentiality concept: an embryo has the right to develop into a complete human being.[24] – Thus it will not be that easy to dismiss Jonas' natural purposiveness thesis.

Second and third: The 'natural purpose as value' thesis and 'good-in-itself as a requisite' thesis are more problematic. They entail a leap across the *is-ought* or *fact-value* divide. Jonas seems to transgress the Hume–Moore verdict and thereby to commit a categorical (naturalistic) fallacy. He, too, does not wish to circumvent this. However, he identifies a tautology in the interdiction, based on an 'ontological dogma': critique of metaphysics is itself based on metaphysics (Jonas 1984, 131).[25] It is assumed that 'the [concept] serving as the premise here (ultimately borrowed from the natural sciences) is the true and complete concept of being' (Jonas 1984, 44). The divide, according to Jonas, presupposes a concept of being (and of nature, body, matter) 'that has been suitably neutralized beforehand (as "value-free")', in which case 'the nonderivability of an "ought" from it follows tautologically' (Jonas 1984, 44). The so-called fallacy is then a meaningless proposition; it is not an argument.[26] The same holds for a *second*, related dogma pertaining to knowledge or truth. The customary 'denial of metaphysical truth presuppose[s] a definite concept of knowledge, for which it is

---

24 In addition, Jonas also argues that the rejection of teleology is not a result of science, but rather one of its initial postulates (cf. Jonas 2001).

25 The methodology of natural sciences, as present for instance in the guiding idea of Ockham's razor, is based on – mostly implicit – metaphysics, e.g. a specific pre-concept and prejudice with regard to what nature is (and could be). This holds in particular for empiricism, positivism and critical rationalism.

26 By referring to Jonas and others, A. Briggle speaks about 'the fallacious naturalistic fallacy' (Briggle 2010, 93/96f.).

indeed true', namely for classical natural scientific knowledge (Jonas 1984, 44). With this critique Jonas underpins his own premise that a good-in-itself at least might exist in natural purposes beyond any ascriptions.[27] Jonas recognizes that this is not a strong argument, but nevertheless a good point of departure equal to that of his critics.

Metaphysical elements, therefore, do not only underlie Jonas' ethics of responsibility, but ethical concepts in general. '[I]n every other ethic as well, in the most utilitarian, [...] most this-worldly', Jonas writes, 'a tacit metaphysics is imbedded' (Jonas 1984, 44). One can, for example, think of anthropological, action-theory or physical/material assumptions which often exhibit a systemic, all-embracing character: it would be rash to want to call them 'non-metaphysical'. Metaphysics and methodology cannot be totally separated. The objection to metaphysics is thus not one that applies to Jonas in particular, but to ethical conceptions in general. If it encompasses everything, it says nothing.

Such analytic clarification of this circular reasoning of his critics – namely, that the critics are not critical enough of themselves – establishes the same initial conditions for Jonas as well as for his critics. Jonas can even go further and offer proof that bridges between 'is' and 'ought' do in fact exist. He takes a quintessential situation which is paradigmatic for his concept of ethics: a newborn, the 'archetype of responsibility'. For Jonas, the care relationship between parent and child illustrates the very core of his ethic of responsibility: the *caring-for* structure, including a 'role of stewardship' (Jonas 1984, 8). The 'is' of a helpless newborn addresses an 'ought' to the world around it – that is, to take care of it; the newborn articulates an 'ought-to-be' and with that a moral obligation: 'Look and you know' (Jonas 1984, 131). Even before Jonas, William K. Frankena spoke in a similar (intuitionistic) way of a 'principle of beneficence' (cf. Frankena 1973).[28] And William James has claimed: 'Take any demand, however slight, which any creature, however weak, may make. Ought it not, for its own sole sake, to be satisfied? If not, prove why not' (James 2000, 249). In line with Jonas' approach, the direction of argumentation is here reversed: the non-moral is now liable to justification.

Jonas is well aware that one can evade a newborn's demands. One can choose a different approach and view the newborn in a different way: '[I]ts [= the newborn's] call can meet with deafness' (Jonas 1984, 131). Perception with the senses, inner relating, and participation in the life process of the newborn are necessary conditions for acknowledging a newborn's claims. There is no universal

27 In a programmatic way Jonas argues: 'A philosophy of nature is to bridge the alleged chasm between scientifically ascertainable "is" and morally binding "ought"' (Jonas 1984, x).

28 Frankena assumes that the principle of beneficence encompasses various elements, such as the principle of non-maleficence which states that: one ought not to inflict evil or harm; one ought to prevent evil or harm; one ought to remove evil or harm; one ought to do or promote good.

way; what matters is the mode of approach because the newborn could, for instance, also be viewed as a conglomeration of cells. When we speak of a 'newborn' we are thus referring to a 'being' that, in its existence as such, escapes the reductive approach of classical-modern natural sciences.

In spite of the emphasis on approach and the framing, Jonas' argument is decidedly anti-constructivist. It is not we who construct or constitute 'being': 'being' is granted to itself and to us. Consequently, the appellative function of 'being' is precisely not based on a mere ascription. A newborn is *not* merely a physical entity, but a something whose mere being addresses a claim to its environment and in doing so presents itself to its contemporaries as a newborn.

Fourth: This premise, that man is de facto capable of taking responsibility, is considered a standard in moral philosophy: *freedom* – in particular, choosing between alternatives – is widely taken for granted. In addition, it is a position that can also be grounded under dualistic and pluralistic as well as under neutral-monistic ontologies. The possibility of responsibility is an obvious necessity for any ethical model.

Practice, Action and Solution: Ethics Needs to Be Good for Something ...

The ethical approach as proposed by Jonas encompasses the diagnosis, the analysis of causes and the argumentation framework, but its core lies in *praxis*: in the contribution to the survival of man in the technological age. Ethics claims to be *good* for something. A formal argumentation is necessary, but not sufficient.[29] In what is here termed (the context of) practice, action and solution the underlying diagnosis now reappears: fulfillment of the requirement formulated in the diagnosis necessitates the priority of praxis. Ethics serves to improve praxis; it *is* praxis in the original sense. The (context of) practice of Jonas' ethics centres on both the non-reciprocity dimension and the caution (or precautionary) dimension.[30]

'Nonreciprocity of the duties to the future' (Jonas 1984, 38) constitutes the formal core of the condition for the possibility of responsibility: 'responsibility' becomes the central notion of Jonas' ethics.[31] Responsibility as such can only ensue where

29 For instance, discourse ethics (Apel, Habermas) focuses on rationality principles, e.g. on procedures of justification and argumentation. In contrast with, and in addition to, discourse ethics, Jonas aims to provide a material contribution to ethics and not simply formal elements. Later on, in fact, discourse ethicists like Apel perceived the deficit of such a formal approach and developed 'bridge principles' (cf. Apel 1988).

30 These two dimensions might play one role or another in other concepts of ethics – however, they are typically regarded as being of minor relevance. Once more, it should be stressed that Jonas does not aim to replace traditional concepts of ethics but to supplement and underpin them.

31 We do in fact find an emergence and spreading of the notion of 'responsibility', accompanied by a decreasing use of notions like 'duty' and 'obligation', cf. Sänger 1991, 9f.; Schwartländer 1974, 1577–8; Weischedel 1958 and Schulz 1972, 632–3.

an asymmetrical structure of power relationships is present: man today possesses power over future man – but the reverse is not the case. He decides and determines the conditions of existence for future humans. Likewise, humans hold power over animals, adults over children, those already born over those just conceived, fully conscious individuals over the brain-dead, humans over the natural environment.

Reciprocity, on the other hand – as found, for instance, in theories of justice – presupposes a symmetrical relationship between free and equal discourse participants: the duty of *one* is the counterpart to the right of *another* – and vice versa.[32] Ethics then belongs essentially just to the sphere of social interaction, communication and discourse among discursively empowered, autonomous subjects. It is assumed that every person is in principle capable of speaking for herself or himself in the sphere of discourse; how this is supposed to be possible for future generations, animals, people with dementia or embryos appears unclear. According to Jonas, this 'scheme [of reciprocity] fails for our purpose [of a global ethics for the future]. For only that has a claim that makes claims—for which it must first of all exist. [...] The nonexistent makes no demands and can therefore not suffer violation of its rights' (Jonas 1984, 38–9). The reference to 'contemporaneity and immediacy' is insufficient (Jonas 1984, 17). The key to an expanded and supplemented ethics, Jonas argues, is its relation to the future: it should also embrace the 'not-yet-existent' (Jonas 1984, 39).[33] Jonas' aim is to promote a change in the direction and in the practice of knowledge production, in the course of which scientists acquire an awareness of the ambivalence of their actions in light of their asymmetrical power. For Jonas, this applies to the professional responsibility of the natural scientist for peace, of the engineer for safety, or of the physician for the patient, and in general the responsibility for the human subject in the process of acquiring medical technical insights.[34] He rejects the molecular-genetic instrumentalization of the 'biological material' of life at its very beginning and end.

Non-reciprocity can be described as a responsibility-*for* (caring-*for* stewardship structure), rather than primarily as responsibility-*to* in the sense of justification vis-à-vis an external instance or institution. Accordingly, it would not do justice to Jonas' approach to comprehend 'responsibility' in formal terms as an n-dimensional relation.[35] This would void the notion of responsibility of 'material' content – that is, of ensuring the future generations of mankind.

32 For a comparison of discourse ethics and Jonas' responsibility ethics, see Kuhlmann 1994, 277–302 and the discussions in Ott 1993.

33 In general, Jonas has in mind the responsibility of politicians and citizens for the natural environment.

34 For instance, in 1991 the Association of German Engineers (VDI) released a new code of engineering ethics that takes non-reciprocity explicitly into account (VDI-Richtlinie 3780, 1991).

35 Examples that lay out such a formal structure include Lenk 1987.

Indeed, the non-reciprocity dimension provides a general structure of Jonas' ethics – no more. Where ethical practice is concerned, it needs to be methodologically underpinned and extended. In this respect, Jonas introduces a further dimension: the *caution* (or *tutiorist*) *dimension.* Interlaced with the precautionary principle, the caution dimension forms the methodological core of his catastrophe-prevention ethics. Although the caution dimension cannot be inferred, it is partly contained within the non-reciprocity dimension in so far as prudent action taken today refers (non-reciprocally) to something in the future and can therefore be characterized as responsibility. '[C]aution is [...] a command of responsibility' (Jonas 1984, 191), because '[n]ever must the existence or the essence of man as a whole be made a stake in the hazards of action' (Jonas 1984, 37). Adopting such a methodological framework, Jonas calls for a 'heuristics of fear' with 'prevalence of the bad over the good prognosis' (Jonas 1984, 26/31). The anti-utopian precautionary principle – with its recognition of an objective indeterminacy of real futures (cf. Dupuy 2007, 71–93) – constitutes a conservativism appreciating the 'responsibility for existence'. Man's biological and socio-cultural existence in the future should be ensured and made possible by laying emphasis on conservation and preservation.

The precautionary principle is not based on the non-reciprocity dimension alone. If the future were anticipatable, it would be superfluous in spite of non-reciprocity. But the future is largely a closed book even if certain prognostic possibilities are available; in light of the cumulative effects of technological and scientific progress, the future is only partly accessible. Intentional planning that presupposes the possibility of acting according to means-ends schemata is limited. An 'essential inadequacy' and 'uncertainty of prognostications' must be taken into consideration when enabling adequate societal decisions on future technologies (Jonas 1984, 31/28). Accordingly, such a 'knowledge of the possible' (and of the uncertain) entails that 'the prophecy of doom is to be given greater heed than the prophecy of bliss' (Jonas 1984, 29/31). Waiver of action will sometimes be necessary – wherein Jonas assumes an asymmetrical relationship between action and waiver of action, for instance in biotechnology.

Jonas combines both dimensions into a 'new imperative' supplementing Kant's formulation with a future-oriented, and hence non-reciprocal dimension: '"Act so that the effects of your action are compatible with the permanence of genuine human life"; or expressed negatively: "Act so that the effects of your action are not destructive of the future possibility of such life"' (Jonas 1984, 11).[36] These words articulate a twofold claim to survival *and* to life: the survival of man as a species *and* of human life in the socio-cultural context. In formal terms, Jonas is guided by Kant and takes into account the unconditional obligatory

36 This formulation has evoked an extended discussion of the issue of whether Jonas' ethics should be considered as a kind of deontological ethics (cf. Grunwald 1996, 196) or, on the contrary, as a consequentialist form of ethics (cf. Lenk and Ropohl 1987, 10/14). Here, I argue that Jonas tries to combine these two major approaches: the consequences are present in the approach.

quality of duty with its generalizability. But, unlike Kant, Jonas fills his imperative with material content referring to man's future ability to survive – and in this a 'sense of morality' must come to the rescue. Moreover, Jonas' imperative, unlike Kant's, possesses little internally logical stringency. Jonas himself concedes that 'no rational [i.e. logical] contradiction is involved in the violation of this kind of imperative' (Jonas 1984, 11).

The imperative of responsibility might sound anthropocentric at first.[37] It is addressed to man as the acting subject. Further, it does not seem to refer to nature in general, but to man in particular: Jonas postulates a 'permanence of genuine *human* life'. Yet a classification of the imperative as anthropocentric would miss Jonas' intention, as would a holistic one. Jonas seeks to circumvent (outer) ascriptions of this kind by arguing for the common denominator of philosophy of nature, anthropology and ethics. He sees man from an anthropological perspective as part of nature conceived of in an (anthropomorphic) *integral monistic* sense: man participates in the natural process of life in its entirety. This process also encompasses the socio-cultural context and along with it man's freedom to act (as nature) within nature. It can therefore be said that man is the addressee of the imperative.

Contrary to the view held by some of his critics, the imperative and the two dimensions of Jonas' ethics – the non-reciprocity and the caution dimension – have not been without impact. They have even found their way into the wording of legislation, for instance (1) the non-reciprocity dimension in the German Embryo Protection Act 1990 and the German and Swiss Animal Protection Act ('animal as living creature', 'dignity of the creature') and (2) the caution dimension in the *Precautionary Principle* and *Risk Analysis* in the context of *Technology Assessment* methodologies (cf. Bender 1988; Liebert and Schmidt 2010; Grunwald 2002). Some years ago, Jean-Pierre Dupuy also evoked the precautionary principle as a methodologically-metaphysically well-founded framework of a new ontology of time for the assessment of nanotechnology; Dupuy speaks of the necessity of 'enlightened doomsaying' (Dupuy 2005, 81f.). The NGO ETC Group (Action Group on Erosion, Technology and Concentration), citing Jonas, is demanding a moratorium for nanotechnology. Most recently, Jonas' approach has been extended and applied to accelerated development in synthetic biology (cf. Schmidt 2012b).

Jonas has also influenced political programmes, such as the UN Commission for Environment and Development (UN General Assembly 1987). The Commission that propagated the notion of *sustainable development* was significantly inspired by Jonas.[38] In its report 'sustainable development' is defined as 'a development that meets the needs of the present, without compromising the ability of future generations

---

37 For instance if one compares Jonas' future-oriented ethics with other concepts, such as those of Schweitzer 1984.

38 This has been underlined explicitly by the German commission member Volker Hauff.

to meet their own needs' (UN General Assembly 1987, 55).[39] Jonas' imperative of responsibility is identical in content even down to the wording[40] – also in the analysis of a recent situation of a 'threatened future' (UN General Assembly 1987, 39). In order to foster sustainability as a political leitmotif and a sociocultural guideline, Jonas saw a need for 'a new science [...] which [would] have to deal with an enormous complexity of interdependencies', an interdisciplinary, integral 'environmental science', which he restated in his book *Technology, Medicine and Ethics* in the 1980s.[41] Present-day sustainability research, socio-ecological research, science and technology studies and Technology Assessment can be regarded as concepts of such 'new sciences' of which Jonas spoke. Looking back, it is clear that since Jonas' day certain changes have taken place in the sciences – without ethically responsible research and development having become mainstream. Moreover, Jonas has in mind a different type of natural science including more participatory and aesthetic elements; this position has certainly remained current. And indeed, such a type has actually emerged: late-modern physics (Schmidt 2008).

Considering the above, it therefore seems unwarranted to maintain that Jonas' ethics of responsibility is irrelevant for praxis and problem-solving.

Summary: On the Way to Underpinning Science and Technology Assessment ...

Hans Jonas' engaged public philosophy initially begins with a shock in the face of the present-day 'threat': 'Modern technology, informed by an ever-deeper penetration of nature and propelled by the forces of market and politics, has enhanced human power beyond anything known or even dreamed of before. It is the power over matter, over life on earth, and over man himself' (Jonas 1984, ix). The ambivalence of technological success 'has begun to show its face' – questioning the Baconian (science and technology) project of the modern age in general and, accordingly, challenging ethics (and any disciplinarily limited philosophy). According to Jonas and his future-oriented, anti-visionary thinking, despair does not offer a way out. Instead, a different framing, perception and understanding of nature – including a different awareness and attitude – is required in order to change man's manner of acting in (and interacting with) nature.

Jonas not only deserves historical credit for putting pressing issues of the life-world, induced by the massive advancement of modern technology, on the agenda

39 The report 'Our Common Future' is often called Brundtland report; Gro Harlem Brundtland chaired this famous UN commission.

40 In the German version of The Imperative of Responsibility this is even more obvious. Whereas in the German version Jonas uses the term 'Dauergebot', which is a cognate term with 'sustainability' (Jonas 1979, 337), this term does not appear in the English book.

41 In this collection, the papers are published in German only: Jonas 1987, 11–12. See also: Jonas 1984, 189–99.

of (disciplinary academic) philosophy and effectively influencing public debates (cf. Schmidt 2007; Winston and Edelbach 2009). In addition, along with a few woolly and awkwardly worded statements, he delivers a plausible argumentation of 'future-oriented responsibility': grounded in a diagnosis of the current state of affairs and in an analysis of the causes of the failure of ethics and with focus on practice, action and solution. Arguably, his grounding is the weakest part, as Jonas himself concedes: 'I know that this is no proof and compels no one to agreement' (Jonas 1996, 182). 'Logically', in the narrower, that is, formal analytical sense, an ultimate grounding is lacking (Jonas 1984, 11). On the other hand, Jonas finds the formal rationality of analytical or transcendental-pragmatic ethics – with their programmes of justification – not only foreign to his way of thinking but also inadequate and inefficient, because it is a certain rationality too closely interwoven with the present crisis: it has even contributed to causing the crisis. Consequently, ethics should go beyond an intra-philosophical context of justification and extend – quite classically – to praxis.

Fundamental issues require fundamental analyses, as Jonas points out. For Jonas, the social-ecological crisis is not a surface-phenomenon that one could master solely with modified rules (because these come to nothing!) – it is a deeper-seated problem located at the metaphysical foundations of contemporary culture. As a consequence, reflection on and a revision of the underlying concepts of framing and understanding nature, including the metaphysical notions, will become inevitable. This is because ethics relates to 'philosophy of nature' (often called 'metaphysics' by Jonas); 'metaphysics must underpin ethics' (Jonas 1984, x). In fact, ethics forms a major part of what Jonas considers 'philosophy of nature' – in distinction to 'natural philosophy': 'A philosophy of nature is to bridge the alleged chasm between scientifically ascertainable "is" and morally binding "ought"' (Jonas 1984, x). Most concepts of ethics (as well as those of the sciences) barely acknowledge the underlying metaphysical elements. They are blind to metaphysics – even if they themselves inherently incorporate a substantial portion of metaphysical assumptions. Jonas considers such concepts of ethics to be not only uncritical of themselves, but also tame and ineffective, and purely cosmetic compensation. They come into play far too late and in a too tentative way. These concepts, he argues, overlook the fact that the alleged 'post-metaphysical age' is riddled with (and based on) various types of metaphysics.

The question is not whether we have or want a metaphysics but which one can and should it be. From this perspective, Jonas can even be read (in the vein of the scholars of the Frankfurt School) as a critical theoretician who – beyond his metaphysically based criticism, for instance his criticism of the criticism of the so-called naturalistic fallacy – is seeking to engender through sound reasoning an enlightened and rationally justified metaphysics which is adequate to the crisis (Dupuy 2005; Schmidt 2000a): Jonas' position could be characterized – in the style of the famous work *Shaping Technology, Building Society* by Wiebe E. Bijker and John Law – as *shaping concepts of nature ('shaping metaphysics'), underpinning ethics, building society* (cf. Bijker and Law 1994). A political and practical 'philosophy of nature' in which metaphysics, anthropology, ethics and politics are conceptualized as a converging domain in a critical, discursive fashion is gradually emerging (Schmidt 2000a). That a (rational and pragmatic) shaping of metaphysics – as foundational for an ethics for an anticipative shaping of science and technology – hardly correlates with our late-modern self-stylization will be apparent. Jonas has, nevertheless, probably hit a nerve, reaching much further than most intra-philosophical debates and providing the key to a critical and productive analysis of contemporary technoscientific society.

Jonas' focus on culturally significant underlying convictions, guiding metaphysics, implicit concepts of nature and attitudes is therefore not outmoded for those living today. They influence perceptions, decisions and actions – and hence societal *practices*. And they also influence the early stages of technoscientific developments. Once such developments are so far advanced that a specific praxis has established itself and only minor path decisions remain, Jonas' ethics could come to nothing. Jonas thus rejects any compensatory and cosmetic ethics of technology and also Technology Assessment (TA) – but not a Prospective Science and Technology Assessment (Liebert and Schmidt 2010) that acknowledges the 'responsibility for the future' argument and brings philosophy of nature, ethics and anthropology together.

References

Altner, Günter, ed. 1986. *Die Welt als offenes System*. Frankfurt: Fischer.

Altner, Günter, Gernot Böhme and Heinrich Ott, eds. 2000. *Natur erkennen und anerkennen. Über ethikrelevante Wissenszugänge zur Natur.* Zug: Graue Edition.

Apel, Karl-Otto. 1988. *Diskurs und Verantwortung. Das Problem des Übergangs zur postkonventionellen Moral.* Frankfurt: Suhrkamp.

Baudrillard, Jean. 2003. *The Transparency of Evil: Essays on Extreme Phenomena.* London and New York: Verso.

Beck, Ulrich. 1986. *Risikogesellschaft. Auf dem Weg in eine andere Moderne.* Frankfurt: Suhrkamp.

———. 1988. *Gegengifte. Die organisierte Unverantwortlichkeit.* Frankfurt: Suhrkamp.

Bender, Wolfgang. 1988. *Ethische Urteilsbildung.* Stuttgart: Kohlhammer.

Bijker, Wiebe, and John Law, eds. 1994. *Shaping Technology/Building Society. Studies in Sociotechnical Change.* Cambridge, MA: MIT.

Böhler, Dietrich, ed. 1994. *Ethik für die Zukunft. Im Diskurs mit Hans Jonas*. Munich: C.H. Beck.

Böhler, Dietrich, Michael Bongardt, Holger Burkhart, Christian Wiese and Walther Ch. Zimmerli, eds. 2009 ff. *Kritische Hans Jonas Werksausgabe.* Freiburg: Rombach.

Böhme, Gernot. 1999. *Bios – Ethos. Über ethikrelevantes Naturwissen.* Bremen: Manholt.

Briggle, Adam. 2010. *A Rich Bioethics: Public Policy, Biotechnology, and the Kass Council.* Notre Dame: University of Notre Dame Press.

Carter, Brandon. 1974. 'Large Number Coincidence and the Anthropic Principle in Cosmology'. In *Confrontation of Cosmological Theories with Observational Data*, edited by Malcolm S. Longair, 291–8. Dordrecht: Springer.

Dupuy, Jean-Pierre. 2005. 'Aufgeklärte Unheilsprophezeiungen. Von der Ungewissheit zur Unbestimmbarkeit technischer Folgen'. In *Die Unbestimmtheitssignatur der Technik. Eine neue Deutung der technisierten Welt*, edited by Gerhard Gamm and Andreas Hetzel, 81–102. Bielefeld: Transcript.

———. 2007. 'Complexity and Uncertainty: A Prudential Approach to Nanotechnology'. In *Nanoethics: The Ethical and Social Implications of Nanotechnology*, edited by Fritz Allhoff, Patrick Lin, James Moor and John Weckert, 119–32. Hoboken: Wiley.

———. 2009. 'The Precautionary Principle and Enlightened Doomsaying: Rational Choice before the Apocalyse'. *Occasion: Interdisciplinary Studies in the Humanities* 1 (October 15, 2009; http://occasion.stanford.edu/node/28, accessed Nov 8, 2012).

Ferry, Luc. 1995. *The New Ecological Order.* Chicago: University of Chicago Press.

Frankena, William K. 1973. *Ethics*. Englewood Cliffs: Prentice Hall.

Frodeman, Robert, Julie Thompson Klein and Carl Mitcham, eds. 2010. *The Oxford Handbook of Interdisciplinarity*, Oxford: Oxford University Press.

Goethe, Johann Wolfgang von. 1840. *Theory of Colors.* London: John Murray.

Grunwald, Armin. 1996. 'Ethik der Technik. Systematisierung und Kritik vorliegender Entwürfe'. *Ethik und Sozialwissenschaften* 7(2/3): 191–281.

———. 2002. *Technikfolgenabschätzung. Eine Einführung*. Berlin: Edition Sigma.

Habermas, Jürgen. 1992. *Postmetaphysical Thinking: Philosophical Essays*. Cambridge, MA: MIT.

———. 2002. *Die Zukunft der menschlichen Natur. Auf dem Weg zu einer liberalen Eugenik?* Frankfurt: Suhrkamp.

Harris, Charles E., Michael S. Pritchard and Michael J. Rabins. 2005. *Engineering Ethics. Concepts and Cases.* Belmont: Wadsworth.

Hartung, Gerald, Kristian Köchy, Jan C. Schmidt and Georg Hofmeister, eds. 2013: *Naturphilosophie als Grundlage der Naturethik. Zur Aktualität von Hans Jonas*. Freiburg: Alber.

Hastedt, Heiner. 1994. *Aufklärung und Technik.* Frankfurt: Suhrkamp.

Heidegger, Martin. 1977. *The Question Concerning Technology and Other Essays*, translated by William Lovitt. New York and London: Garland.

Hirsch Hadorn, Gertrude. 2000. *Umwelt, Natur und Moral. Eine Kritik an Hans Jonas, Vittorio Hösle und Georg Picht*. Freiburg: Alber.

Höffe, Otfried. 1993. *Moral als Preis der Moderne. Ein Versuch über Wissenschaft, Technik und Umwelt.* Frankfurt: Suhrkamp.

Horkheimer, Max and Theodor W. Adorno. 2002. *Dialectic of Enlightenment* [1944], translated by Edmund Jephcott. London and New York: Standford University Press.

Hösle, Vittorio. 1994. 'Ontologie und Ethik bei Hans Jonas'. In *Ethik für die Zukunft*, edited by Dietrich Böhler, 105–25. Munich: C.H. Beck.

Hubig, Christoph. 1995. *Technik- und Wissenschaftsethik. Ein Leitfaden.* Berlin: Springer.

James, William. 2000. *Pragmatism and Other Writings.* New York: Penguin.

Jonas, Hans. 1979. *Das Prinzip Verantwortung: Versuch einer Ethik für die technologische Zivilisation.* Frankfurt: Insel Verlag.

———. 1984. *The Imperative of Responsibility: In Search of an Ethics for the Technological Age* [1979]. Chicago and London: University of Chicago Press.

———. 1987. *Technik, Medizin und Ethik.* Frankfurt: Suhrkamp.

———. 1993. *Dem bösen Ende näher. Gespräche über das Verhältnis des Menschen zur Natur.* Frankfurt: Suhrkamp.

———. 1996. *Mortality and Morality: A Search for the Good after Auschwitz,* edited by Lawrence Vogel. Evanston: Northwestern University Press.

———. 2001. *The Phenomenon of Life: Towards a Philosophical Biology* [1966]. Evanston: Northwestern University Press.

———. 2009. 'Technology and Responsibility: Reflections on the New Task of Ethics'. In *Society, Ethics and Technology,* edited by Morton E. Winston and Ralph D. Edelbach. Belmont: Wadsworth.

Köchy, Kristian. 2008. *Biophilosophie. Zur Einführung.* Hamburg: Junius.

Krebs, Angelika, ed. 1997. *Naturethik.* Frankfurt: Suhrkamp.

———. 1999. *Ethics of Nature.* New York and Berlin: Gruyter.

Kuhlmann, Wolfgang. 1994. 'Prinzip Verantwortung versus Diskursethik'. In *Ethik für die Zukunft,* edited by Dietrich Böhler, 277–302. Munich: C.H. Beck.

Lenk, Hans. 1987. 'Über Verantwortungsbegriffe und das Verantwortungsproblem in der Technik'. In *Technik und Ethik,* edited by Hans Lenk and Günter Ropohl, 112–48. Stuttgart: Reclam.

Lenk, Hans and Günter Ropohl. 1987. *Technik und Ethik.* Stuttgart: Reclam.

Levy, David J. 2002. *Hans Jonas: The Integrity of Thinking.* Columbia: University of Missouri Press.

Liebert, Wolfgang and Jan C. Schmidt. 2010. 'Towards a Prospective Technology Assessment: Challenges for Technology Assessment in the Age of Technoscience'. *Poiesis & Practice* 7(1–2): 99–116.

Luhmann, Niklas. 1992. *Soziologie des Risikos.* Berlin: Walter de Gruyter.

———. 2006. *Beobachtungen der Moderne.* Wiesbaden: VS.

Meyer-Abich, Klaus Michael. 1984. *Wege zum Frieden mit der Natur.* Munich: Carl Hanser.

Müller, Wolfgang E., ed. 2003. *Hans Jonas – von der Gnosisforschung zur Verantwortungsethik.* Basel: Kohlhammer.

Norton, Bryan. 2005. *Sustainability: A Philosophy of Adaptive Ecosystem Management.* Chicago: University of Chicago Press.

Ott, Konrad. 1993. Ökologie und Ethik. Tübingen: Attempto.

Passmore, John. 1974. *Man's Responsibility for Nature.* London: Duckworth.

Picht, Georg. 1969. 'Der Begriff der Verantwortung'. In *Wahrheit, Vernunft, Verantwortung. Philosophische Studien,* edited by Georg Picht, 318–71. Stuttgart: Klett-Cotta.

Sänger, Monika, ed. 1991. *Verantwortung*. Stuttgart: Reclam.
Schäfer, Lothar. 1993. 'Bacon's Project: Should It Be Given Up?' In *Man and World* 26(3): 303–17.
———. 1999. *Das Bacon-Projekt*. Frankfurt: Suhrkamp.
Schmidt, Jan C. 2000a. 'Ethische Perspektiven einer politischen Naturphilosophie'. In *Natur erkennen und anerkennen. Über ethikrelevante Wissenszugänge zur Natur*, edited by Günter Altner, Gernot Böhme and Heinrich Ott, 73–100. Zug: Graue Edition.
———. 2000b. 'Welche Natur wollen wir? Zur Standortbestimmung des Menschen in der Natur.' *Scheidewege* 30: 214–32.
———. 2007. 'Die Aktualität der Ethik von Hans Jonas. Eine Kritik der Kritik des Prinzips Verantwortung'. *Deutsche Zeitschrift für Philosophie* 55(4): 545–69.
———. 2008. *Instabilität in Natur und Wissenschaft. Eine Wissenschaftsphilosophie der nachmodernen Physik*. Berlin: Walter de Gruyter.
———. 2011. 'The Renaissance of Francis Bacon: On Bacon's Account of Recent Nanotechnosciences'. *Nanoethics* 5(1): 29–41.
———. 2012a. 'Das Argument "Zukunftsverantwortung". Versuch einer analytischen Rekonstruktion der naturphilosophischen Natur- und Technikethik von Hans Jonas'. In *Naturphilosophie als Grundlage der Naturethik. Zur Aktualität von Hans Jonas*, edited by Gerald Hartung, Kristian Köchy, Jan C. Schmidt and Georg Hofmeister, 155–85. Freiburg: Karl Alber.
———. 2012b. 'Selbstorganisation als Kern der Synthetischen Biologie. Ein Beitrag zur Prospektiven Technikfolgenabschätzung'. *Technikfolgenabschätzung – Theorie und Praxis* 3: 29–36.
Schulz, Walter. 1972. *Philosophie in der veränderten Welt*. Pfullingen: Klett-Cotta.
Schwartländer, Johannes. 1974. 'Verantwortung.' In *Handbuch philosophischer Grundbegriffe*, edited by Herman Krings, Hans M. Baumgartner and Christoph Wild, 1577–88. Munich: Kösel.
Schweitzer, Albert. 1966. *The Teaching of Reverence for Life*. London: Henry Holt.
———. 1991. *Die Ehrfurcht vor dem Leben*. Munich: C.H. Beck.
Tugendhat, Ernst. 1993. *Vorlesungen über Ethik*. Frankfurt: Suhrkamp.
UN General Assembly/World Commission on Environment and Development. 1987. *Our Common Future*, [Brundtland Report]. A/RES/42/187. New York.
Weischedel, Wilhelm. 1958. *Das Wesen der Verantwortung*. Frankfurt: V. Klostermann.
Wendnagel, Johannes. 1990. *Ethische Neubesinnung als Ausweg aus der Weltkrise? Ein Gespräch mit dem 'Prinzip Verantwortung' von Hans Jonas*. Würzburg: Königshausen & Neumann.
Wetz, Franz. 1994. *Hans Jonas zur Einführung*. Hamburg: Junius.
Winston, Morton E., and Ralph D. Edelbach, eds. 2009. *Society, Ethics and Technology*. Belmont: Wadsworth.
Wolters, Gereon. 1997. 'Orientierungswissen als Humanressource', In *Humankapital und Wissen. Grundlagen einer nachhaltigen Entwicklung*, edited by Günter Clar, Julia Doré and Hans Mohr, 33–51. Berlin: Springer.

Chapter 10
Ethics and Responsibility in a Technological Age[1]

David J. Levy

This book began with the bold claim that the philosophy of Hans Jonas provides a perspective on the present position and future prospects of mankind that is, in its power and wisdom, unequalled in the work of any of his contemporaries; in succeeding chapters I have shown the way in which his reflections proceed rationally in offering a scientifically informed account of the nature of man's being in the world that recognizes, at once, the material and biological foundations of that being and the unique features that set it apart from all other forms of life. In this chapter, we come to what is, in terms of its general significance, his masterwork, *The Imperative of Responsibility: In Search of an Ethics for the Technological Age* (1984). Jonas was, as I have indicated, a master of the essay form, and the bulk of his writing consists of essays, some relatively brief and others extended, but each, as Leon Kass observes, 'a self-contained little gem – hard, compact, offering many facets of the complex issues discussed'. His concentration on the essay form is partly a matter of taste and partly a function of the circumstances of his life. Because of the disruption of his academic career brought about by his exile from Germany, and the fact that, in contrast to other intellectual exiles, he responded by taking up the profession of arms, he was already in his forties when he took up his first academic post. Such a life leaves room enough for reflective thought – indeed, in Jonas' estimation, required it – but it is not conducive to the production of lengthy systematic treatises requiring ready access to the materials of research. Thus it is hardly surprising that only the first of his major works, the study of Gnosis, and the last, *The Imperative of Responsibility*, take the form of monographs.

As I have indicated in my discussion of *The Phenomenon of Life*, this matters less in Jonas' case than it would in that of other thinkers, for his thought is characterized by an enviable capacity to systematically cross the boundaries of individual essays and apparently discrete areas of inquiry. This is why his work evinces a quality of integrity in the dual sense that not only is it profoundly moral in seeking to respond, rightly and rationally, to the troubles of his age, but also that

---

1 Reprinted from *Hans Jonas: The Integrity of Thinking* by David J. Levy, by permission of the University of Missouri Press.

it integrates the diversity of his concerns in a single, unified philosophical project that is both inclusive and coherent. The path that begins with the comparative study of ancient and modern forms of nihilism culminates in the formulation of an ethics for a technological age. The writings are many and varied; the project that guides them is intelligibly one. In its beginning is its end.

We may speak of the intrinsic purposefulness of Jonas' work, its innate teleology; and this is especially apt in characterizing the philosophy of a thinker who, more than any other, restores to the account of nature that feature of teleological organization that vanished from the worldview of natural science with the end of Aristotelian physics and biology in the seventeenth century. I hope that I have said enough about Jonas' philosophical biology, his theory of the organism, to indicate that this retrieval of an understanding of the teleological dimension of organic being requires no sacrifice of the cognitive advances that mark the superiority of modern to ancient science.

Modern science was not wrong to reject the ancient view that every being was purposefully determined to seek its proper place in an innately ordered cosmos. Where it failed was in not recognizing that measurable processes, blind and purposeless in themselves, could nevertheless be structurally organized into forms that secured, if not their permanent endurance, then at least lasting survival as living beings. Such forms required no element of conscious creative design, as the Deists still assumed, nor their individual possession of an innate purposive essence, such as Aristotle supposed. The phenomenon of metabolism, in which foreign material is absorbed into the identity of the animate body, is enough to ensure that even in a world governed only, as Jacques Monod suggests in the title of his famous book, by *Chance and Necessity*, the element of teleology does not entirely disappear. Purposefulness is not a feature of human life alone; it is a common property of animate being that quite unconsciously seeks to survive in living form. And while the Darwinian theory of natural selection, in which only the fittest survive, allowed this ontologically unprecedented property of animate being to be explained without reference to conscious design by providing an account of the mechanism by which novel and more highly differentiated forms of organism, including man, could evolve, it also thereby reestablished the continuity of living forms that the dualism of Descartes had separated into the ontologically unrelated realms of mind and matter – realms that were, for Descartes himself and his immediate successors, mysteriously and uniquely conjoined in the miracle of man. By the same token, the account of evolutionary continuity in the history of life not only permits but even requires us to seek to identify the ways in which the features of each emergent species can be ontologically prefigured, as potential yet to be achieved, in the properties of its ancestors. The origin of life remains itself unexplained and, in Darwinian terms alone, inexplicable, but, once existent, the natural history of life is pregnant with the possibilities of man.

To articulate this is the grand design of Jonas' work. It is the link that binds, in a single chain of argument, the theory of ethics to the philosophy of life. More than this, it is possible to conceive the sum of Jonas' philosophy as a single, uniquely articulate response to the imperative of survival already primitively embodied in the dynamic process of metabolism. There is no element of nature mysticism in this idea. It is based on the observation that the same orientation to self – preservation in living form that governs metabolic activity also explains why one particular twentieth-century thinker should seek, through the processes of mental activity, philosophical reflection and response, to think his way out of the mortal threat to his own continuing existence posed by the challenge of life-destroying nihilism. In so far as that nihilism was embodied physically in the armies of Nazi Germany, that challenge would have to be met by recourse to equal and, as fortune would have it, superior physical force. But inasmuch as the ideology of Nazism was itself conditioned by a climate of ideas that permitted its emergence, and even made it appear, to Heidegger at least, to provide a life-enhancing purposeful solution to the survival requirements of his race – a means by which the German people, but not Jonas, could secure their historical existence in the face of the challenge of global technology – the challenge could only be met by answering the Heideggerian account of existence with one at once more rational and more humanly inclusive. This is what Jonas sought to accomplish and, in my view, succeeded in doing.

Hans-Georg Gadamer, perhaps the most perceptive because most sympathetic critic of Heidegger's work, speaks of Heidegger's 'one way', his single governing path of reflection that guides his life's work in an unbroken sustained attempt to think the question of Being in ever new ways, but always with the intent of seeking to answer the enigmatic challenge of history to his own being. The guiding questions of his thought, late as well as early, are, to use Heidegger's own terms, anchored in the concernful appropriation of whatever possibilities are still available in the historical situation as he perceives it to be. Unfortunately, after the disastrous miscarriage of National Socialism, which proved to be not what Heidegger had first taken it to be, the only form of appropriation turns out to be resigned attendance upon the unforeseeable but hoped-for dispensations of the history of Being to deliver us from the forgetfulness into which we have been cast, potentially fatally, by the realization of metaphysics in the objectified form of the age of world technology. In a quite different way, Jonas, starting from the same premise, pursues, no less implacably, an alternative, single, responsive path that parallels and answers Heidegger's own.

In order to get the full measure of the significance I attach to *The Imperative of Responsibility* and, with it, the basis of my claim, exaggerated as it may seem, for the unequalled importance of Jonas' philosophical work, greater than that of Wittgenstein and more salutary than that of Heidegger, the twin peaks of the contemporary philosophical universe, it is necessary to make a few preliminary clarifying remarks before turning to an examination of the argument of the book. For Jonas is, in comparison with either Wittgenstein or Heidegger, a relatively unknown thinker, especially in Britain and America, and when a commentator makes so bold a claim for such a figure, it will inevitably raise the suspicion that he is endeavoring to build up a cult, a philosophical sect, around the ideas of someone who happens to be his favorite thinker with all the parochial eccentricity which that implies.

I, for one, have no wish to add to the number of such sects, of which there are already quite enough on the intellectual scene, each with its body of hagiographic literature, its more or less academically respectable journal, its regular gatherings at which the faithful may meet to exchange ideas, and now its websites, too. What Jonas says is too important to become the property of such a group, however admirable its intentions. He needs not to be memorialized but to be introduced to a wider public in order that his work, especially in ethics, can enter into general circulation where it will, when appreciated and understood, serve to counterbalance both the academic confinement of philosophy, which is the regrettable legacy of Wittgenstein, and its deviation into forms of antiscientific irrationalism, which is the major legacy of Heidegger. Only further examination and popularization of the argument of *The Imperative of Responsibility* will allow this to occur and permit us to see him as something more than yet another relatively minor figure in the intellectual firmament, a mere name in the history of twentieth-century thought. But for that to happen I must clarify further what I mean in saying both that Jonas provides an alternative, parallel and yet opposed path of reflection to that of Heidegger and why the provision of such a path should be so necessary.

And here it is reference to Heidegger, rather than to Wittgenstein or any other supposed master thinker, that is crucial, not only because of the influence that Heidegger has on so many areas of our culture, informing the spirit of a deeply unspiritual age, but because there is a real, identifiable sense in Leo Strauss's claim that 'Only a great thinker could help in our intellectual plight', and that our current misfortune is that 'the only great thinker in our time is Heidegger'.

Note that Strauss says 'great thinker', not 'great philosopher'; for as a philosopher in a strict sense, Wittgenstein, perhaps Husserl, and maybe others too have as much if not more title to the term *great* as does Heidegger; but their work, in contrast to Heidegger's, has a more narrow cultural reference and import. It serves, in Wittgenstein's case, to cleanse the language of confusions and, in Husserl's, to direct our attention to the ultimate derivation of scientific theories from the data of immediate perception of what he calls the 'life-world', *Lebenswelt* – the world as it appears in the uneducated form of natural experience that we share by virtue of our birth of human stock. In neither case, however, does such a work, however estimable and necessary it may be, provide us, as Heidegger's does, with a worldview that encompasses not only our common experience of everyday existence but a powerful understanding of the impact that the expanding influence of global technology has on the quality of that experience and the prospects for that existence. I do not know if Jonas is, in Strauss's sense, a great thinker proportionate to Heidegger – only time will tell. What I do think is that his work provides an equivalent but more rational worldview of just these dimensions.

In *The Imperative of Responsibility*, we find just the measure of these dimensions. First published in Germany in 1979 as *Das Prinzip Verantwortung*, it received an acclaim and achieved a circulation unmatched when, five years later, it appeared in English translation. This, to some extent, was the result of the popularity and prestige that Jonas then enjoyed as a lecturer to foundations and conferences that brought together academics, businessmen, and political leaders in a distinctively if not uniquely German way. The existence of such institutions and events provided a more fertile ground for the book's acceptance than was the case in English-speaking lands, while also ensuring that it reached a wider audience than that of interested university teachers. Then again, the style of philosophy it exemplified, so much broader in scope than the analytical mode fashionable in Britain and hardly less so in the United States, resonated more naturally in continental Europe and ensured that in its pages Jonas's fellow philosophers could recognize a masterly example of their craft and not a trespassing beyond professional boundaries by one who should know better.

In Germany in particular, the subtitle of the book, *In Search of an Ethics for the Technological Age*, seemed to answer a question broached philosophically by Heidegger in 1962 in a widely discussed work translated into English as *The Question Concerning Technology* (1977); in its invocation of the theme of ethics, it promised a perspective on the matter that was notably absent from Heidegger's own discussion of the issue in terms of the fatality of the history of Being – a discussion that in any terms other than Heidegger's own seemed almost exclusively metaphysical and devoid of ethical content. This too contributed to the book's success not simply in Germany, where it sold more than two hundred thousand copies, but, notably, in Italy, where it was awarded the 1992 Premio Nonino for the best book translated into Italian that year.

It would be wrong to say that Jonas' new work passed unnoticed in Britain, but certainly, in comparison with its reception in continental Europe, it seems to have caused little stir even among those ecologically oriented circles to whom it might have been expected to have a special interest and appeal. Nor did the fact that its translation, by Jonas himself in collaboration with David Herr, resulted in an exceptionally eloquent work of English prose seem to make much difference to its British circulation when first it appeared. Perhaps today, when concerns induced by fears of various forms of technological innovation, if not of ethics, are more prevalent in the public mind, the situation may be changing. If so, the time may be ripe for a proper appreciation of a philosophical voice that can bring a much-needed balance to debates in which there is too much confusion and mutual incomprehension between the well-funded but widely distrusted proponents of technological innovation and a public greedy for the material benefits such innovations may bring but dangerously ignorant of the science that underlies them and understandably fearful of where the increasing pace and uncertain direction of change may lead.

Nothing could be more damaging to our prospects than the domination of popular debate by an ill-informed distrust of science as such and an equivalent ignorance among scientists of the genuine ethical concerns that their work inevitably involves when carried over into technological developments that may alter radically the quality and nature of our existence in areas as diverse as reproductive technology and the genetic modification of foods. Unfortunately, despite an abundance of government-funded advisory bodies charged with the sometimes conflicting tasks of providing legislators with expert guidance on matters in which they have little competence and with informing the public of the implications of emergent technologies, a state of confusion seems to prevail among politicians and public alike. Never, perhaps, has there been more need for the balanced voice that only a scientifically literate and ethically sensitive philosophy can provide. It is this that we presently lack and that Jonas can preeminently provide.

Despite the years that have elapsed since its publication, *The Imperative of Responsibility* provides, even today, a framework for debate in which the considerations of ethics, the implications of science, and the interests of a suspicious public can each be given due consideration; it does so because, better than any other work I know, it articulates a clear understanding of just what is novel and what is unchanged about the choices we face in consequence of an ongoing technological revolution of unprecedented speed and scope. The power of modern technology has decisively changed the dimensional range of possible human actions, extending the consequences of our decisions spatially, temporally, and even ontologically into regions that previously lay beyond human interference or control, Consequently, many of our traditional ethical responses, concerned as they were with regulating the proper conduct of people toward one another and with the short-term results of their actions, are quite unable to cope, practically or theoretically, with activities that have an unprecedented causal reach. Responsibility is the correlate of power, and such is our transformative power not only over other men but over the nature on which our survival depends, including our own genetically determined nature as beings capable of exercising ethical choice, that all previous systems of moral belief seem inadequate. This is not because they were necessarily wrong but because they were not designed to cope with the current and prospective scope of human agency.

As John Herz put it at the time of the book's publication, 'Traditional ethics has always dealt with individual action within a given space (family, tribe, nation) and a given period (the present, or at most the immediate future); it took the existence of surrounding nature and that of indefinite numbers of succeeding generations for granted. Now everything is changed. An ethics of responsibility must give priority to the maintenance of the possibility of life on earth; it is an ethics of common survival.' This requires not abandonment of well-tried forms of ethical reasoning and judgment but the radical revision of our convictions in ways that will take account of the technologically conditioned extension of human agency. Such a reformation can only be effective if undertaken in a spirit of rational appreciation of the intrinsic risks of the course on which we are set. It has become common to appeal to what is called the 'precautionary principle' in trying to decide whether or not we should pursue a particular, currently available line of scientific research and seek out its practical applications. Jonas puts matters rather more strongly than that, proposing that we be guided by what, strikingly, he calls a 'heuristics of fear'.

By this Jonas means that in our pursuit of technological innovation we should educate ourselves to imagine always what may be the worst consequences of what we do; he bases this apparently unbalanced recommendation, formulated in polemical opposition to what the explicitly utopian Marxist theorist, Ernst Bloch, called the 'principle of hope', on the recognition that now, no more than ever before, can we hope to foresee the full consequences of what we do, and that, given the unprecedented causal reach of our innovations, we must be aware of the fact that the consequences of our actions are such that the very possibility of human survival may be put at risk. I cannot emphasize too strongly that, contrary to what the apparently apocalyptic overtones of his formulation may suggest, Jonas is anything but an apocalyptic prophet preaching an antiscientific prophecy of despondency and doom. Toward the end of *The Imperative of Responsibility*, he has a passage in which he justifies the bias of his formulation by observing that such a bias is necessary in view of the 'heuristics of hope which has hitherto lighted mankind's path' in his pursuit of technological innovation.

He concedes the charge of one-sided emphasis in what he says but denies that this embodies a 'bias against technology as such, let alone against science'. The 'technological imperative is nowhere questioned' in what he says,

> as it is indeed unquestioned in its anthropological primacy and integral to the human condition. But it needs no advocates in the Western world of the twentieth century: intoxication has taken its place. As things are with us, the technological drive takes care of itself – no less through the pressure of its self-created necessities than through the lure of its promises, the short-term rewards of each step and not least through its feedback-coupling with the progress of science. There are times when the drive needs moral encouragement.

But 'ours is not one of them. In the headlong rush, the perils of excess become uppermost. This necessitates an ethical emphasis which, we hope, is as temporary as the condition it has to counteract. But,' he adds,

> there is also a timeless precedence of 'thou shall *not*' over 'thou shalt' in ethics. Warning off from evil has always been more urgent than and peremptory than the positive 'thou shalt' with its disputable concepts of moral perfection. To keep free from guilt comes first in moral duties, the more so when the temptations to guilt become more powerful. Our particular version of this emphasis is in answer to the particular, epochal, perhaps passing phase of civilization and its particular, overpowering temptations. In thus paying tribute to the present state of things, our one-sidedness follows the ancient ethical council of Aristotle that, in the pursuit of virtue as the 'mean' between the two extremes of excess and deficiency, one should fight that fault more which one is more prone to and therefore more likely to commit, and rather lean over in the opposite direction, toward the side less favoured by inclination and circumstances. (Jonas 1984, 203–4).

It is in the Aristotelian perspective of seeing merit in the pursuit of the golden mean that we should understand the primacy that Jonas accords in his ethics to 'the heuristics of fear' in an age intoxicated with the dynamism of a largely self-propelling process of technological advance. Such a position, far from representing an anthropological fantasy, reminiscent of the 'back to nature' school of Rousseau or, more recently, Ludwig Klages and many but not all of our current Greens, rests upon Jonas' recognition of the intrinsically technological character of man's being in the world. The slogan 'back to nature' is only a slogan, not least because the only nature that man has ever been able to inhabit is nature as changed and modified by culture; and culture, even in its most primitive stone age forms, has always made use of and depended on technology, as evidenced by the ubiquitous presence of hand axes among ancient remains uncovered from our prehistoric past by archaeologists.

This means that even the term *technological age*, though apt enough for Jonas' purpose, must be treated with due caution. The technological modification of nonhuman nature is, from the beginning, inscribed in the human form of being in the world. *Homo sapiens* is, by the same token, and at least as originally, *Homo faber*, the use of technology, matter rationally fashioned to a given purpose, is what primordially sets humanity apart from other forms of animal life. For while other animals must adapt to their environment or perish, we survive by adapting the environment to our requirements, whether through the first use of furs and fire to protect us from the cold or in our centrally heated and air-conditioned dwellings from which all impact of the natural climate has been excluded. In this sense, the idea that ours is a distinctively technological age is, while heuristically useful, a somewhat simplistic misconception of a stage in what is a natively human form of being. All ages in which men have existed have been, to some degree, technological; it is in the degree to which technological modification of nature is possible and not such modification per se, that ours is unique. Technology alone is what makes the continuation of human life possible; and technology becomes questionable only when its development ceases to serve that end. We have now reached this point and must thus cope with its problems. And it is this, Jonas argues, that fundamentally alters the relationship between technology and ethics – what we can and what we ought to do – even though both are innately human dimensions that pertain *ab origine* to our specific form of life.

Furthermore, even the intrinsic dynamism of technological change that is such a feature of our present state is, in itself, nothing new. While extremely slow in the early stages of human history, it has tended to increase exponentially over time but is not, any more than the use of technology itself, a unique feature of contemporary man. Rather, what is altered today is neither our dependence on technology nor the changing forms it takes, still less the requirement that we judge how and when any given technology should be used. The crucial change of which we must take account lies elsewhere – in the change in the balance between man and the nature brought about by the cumulative effects of past technological advance. The result of this is described by Jonas in a memorable passage in which he characterizes the position we have now achieved and which deserves to be cited at some length as indicative of his understanding of the position in which appeal to the heuristics of fear becomes a justifiable and even necessary part of an ethical stance oriented to our future survival.

> [Today] the boundary between 'city' and 'nature' has been obliterated: the city of men, once an enclave in the nonhuman world, spreads over the whole of terrestrial nature and usurps its place. The difference between the artificial and the natural has vanished, the natural is swallowed up in the sphere of the artificial, and at the same time the total artifact (the works of man that have become 'the world' and as such envelops their makers) generates a 'nature' of its own, that is, a necessity with which human freedom has to cope in an entirely new sense. Once it could be said *Fiat justitia, pereat mundus*, 'Let justice be done, and may the whole world perish' – where 'world,' of course, meant the renewable enclave within the imperishable whole. Not even rhetorically can the like be said anymore when the perishing of the whole through the doings of man – be they just or unjust – has become a real possibility. Issues never legislated come into the purview of the laws which the total city must give itself so that there will be a world for the generations of man to come (Jonas 1984, 10).

From this it follows that the field of ethics, once confined to the ordering of relationships between men, must be extended to man's dealings with nature as providing the now fragile foundation for his own continued being as a moral agent capable of making decisions.

This, as Jonas notes, adds a new spatial and a new temporal dimension to Kant's moral teaching, whose categorical imperative tells us that we ought to treat other human beings as we would ourselves be treated. As Kant formulates it, the categorical imperative is adequately contained in the injunction: 'Act so that you can will that the maxim of your action be made the principle of a universal law.' But in the changed circumstances of today's world, this must now be reformulated, more inclusively, as: 'Act so that the effects of your action are compatible with the permanence of genuine human life', or, alternatively, 'in your present choices include the future wholeness of Man among the objects of your will' (Jonas 1984, 11). The required extension of the spatial dimension lies in its inclusion within the scope of the moral law of the material conditions, the integrity of nature, which alone permits the endurance in being of moral beings, men. The concomitant extension of the temporal dimension is the novel inclusion within the moral calculation of reference to the future effects of action and thereby 'the continuance of human agency in times to come' (Jonas 1984, 12).

Thus, while Kant's injunction is essentially private and addressed primarily to the individual in his dealings with other individuals – an ethic of private citizenship – Jonas' reformulation is necessarily collective and political. It is addressed to statesmen, and it requires attention to questions of public policy in which the fate of nature and so of future moral agents can be decided. Here, once again, we note the characteristic combination of innovation and retrieval in Jonas' thought; for, in extending Kant's categorical imperative as he does, Jonas retrieves the political dimension that was, in Aristotle, inseparable from ethics. At the same time, and again in keeping with the Aristotelian tenor of his thought, consideration of moral rectitude is reinserted within a general philosophy of nature of which human nature is an integral part.

This is what I mean when I say that while Jonas' ethical theory is Kantian in form, embodying as it does a reformulation of the categorical imperative that enjoins us to treat human beings as ends to be valued in themselves, it is Aristotelian in content insofar as responsibility toward our fellow men is conceived to be inseparable from our responsibility for stewardship of nature on whose endurance the continuing survival of human, moral agents recognizably depends. In an age of global technology that potentially threatens to undermine the humanly supporting order of nature, only such a recovery of the broader ethical perspective of Aristotelian thought, and of classical thought in general, can be considered adequate to meeting the needs of the time.

Lawrence Vogel, the editor of Jonas' posthumous volume of theological essays, *Mortality and Morality* (1996), calls his overall introductory essay to the collection 'Hans Jonas' Exodus', and in it he describes Jonas' philosophy as offering 'one of the most systematic and challenging rejoinders to the legacy of Heidegger in particular, and to the spirit of the twentieth century as a whole' (Jonas 1996, 4). The title and the characterization are both apt. 'Exodus' invokes not only Jonas' exile from Germany but also his philosophical passage from the nihilistic assumptions of post-Nietzschean German existentialism, exemplified in the teachings of Heidegger, to a philosophical position based on a rational metaphysical account of the phenomenon of life, in whose intrinsic structure he seeks to found a no less rational ethics of responsibility. This ontologically grounded ethics endeavors to show that our sense of what is right and wrong is not a matter of subjective personal preference but an objective property disclosed to reason as inherent in the structure of Being. We do not posit values by an act of will or choice; we discover them as present in the facts of life of which we are an evolutionary product but one in whom, uniquely, the intrinsic rationality and goodness of Being, its worthiness to survive, is disclosed to consciousness.

Jonas' thinking encompasses a theology, to which we will turn in our next chapter, but it is essential to his position that we should recognize that these properties of goodness and rationality are not a function of faith in a supernatural God, envisaged as the author of creation, but are knowable to reason alone. Jonas describes theology as 'a luxury of reason', meaning that belief in a beneficent but not, as we shall see, omnipotent deity is compatible with what we know of the structure of the world, and our nature and place within it, but is not required in order to perceive the world as inherently both reasonable and good. The objective validity of an ethics of responsibility is not a teaching of revelation but, according to Jonas, a rational apprehension of the way the world is; and, as Vogel puts it, a 'rational metaphysics must be able to ground an imperative of responsibility without recourse to faith' (Jonas 1996, 6).

In this sense, Jonas is a philosophical naturalist though emphatically not a materialist; and thus a thinker more akin to Aristotle than to any of his contemporaries. No more is he an historical idealist in the Hegelian mold, for there is in his philosophy no sense that the process of world history can be understood as a logical or dialectical unfolding of a governing principle culminating in the ever more rational being of man. The process that Jonas describes in *The Phenomenon of Life* is a process of ever increasing differentiation of life forms but one which is governed by contingency alone. It is apprehensible to reason but is not itself a rational process embodying an overall purpose or a rationally intelligible developmental idea. Reason is a contingent feature of man alone, and man is a contingent product of the intelligible but purposeless history of life. The history of life is intelligible as a succession of developmental events, but each of these events is the result of a mutation that is, so far as we can apprehend, a product only of chance. What is intelligible in this process is why some of these events should have produced enduring results in the form of beings capable of survival. What is unintelligible is why any of these events should first have occurred. This is why we must say, apparently paradoxically, that though the history of life is intelligible in terms of evolution, there is no overall intelligibility to an evolutionary process which, while engendering purpose, is not itself inherently purposeful. If, nevertheless, we attribute an overall purpose to this process, that attribution can only be a function not of empirical knowledge but of religious faith that our knowledge of reality may allow but does not logically require. This is why Jonas is so insistent in his separation of the realm of knowledge, including that unfashionable form of knowledge that we call metaphysics, from the realm of faith.

Where he differs from most other contemporary philosophers is not only that he regards metaphysics as a form of knowledge that is independent of faith, a function of rational reflection on the empirically available evidence of nature, but that he sees it as the necessary foundation for an ethics of responsibility capable of guiding us through the dilemmas of our time. One has only to consider what this implies in order to recognize how unusual it must seem in the context of our current postmodernist climate of ideas and how far it seems to fly in the face of the spirit of the age. For if there are any two beliefs that the various divergent forms of postmodernist thought can be said dogmatically to share, they are, first, that metaphysics is obsolete and, second, that ethical choice is a matter of personal preference alone. Both are beliefs that Jonas would lead us to reject. Small wonder then that even a commentator as sympathetic as Lawrence Vogel should 'worry that a pluralistic culture cannot bear the burden of such a substantive metaphysics', and that 'if our future depends on citizens agreeing with Jonas' speculations, then I fear we are not up to the task' (Jonas 1996, 6). And yet, if Jonas is right, the price we will pay for rejecting his view is, at best, continuing intellectual and moral confusion and, at worst, our extinction as a species. Indeed, given the extent of the powers that technology has put at our disposal and the ease with which they can be employed, the second seems a rather more likely outcome than the first.

At this point we can see how serious a business Jonas takes philosophy to be. A metaphysical philosophy is always a more serious business than one that is metaphysically empty; and a metaphysics that is as devoid of providential reassurance as that of Jonas is perhaps as serious as anyone can conceive. Nor, as we shall see in the next chapter, is there anything in Jonas' theology to which we could look for alternative assurance or consolation, for his is a theology that takes seriously the idea that if God created man, as Jonas believed he did, he created him as a free being endowed with powers that permit him to choose not only his own fate but that of the earth in which he has been set. What man does with his entrusted world is left to him alone, and though Jonas believes in a certain sophisticated, but not sophistical, sense in the immortality of the human soul, about which he writes movingly and persuasively in his essay 'Immortality and the Modern Temper' (Jonas 1996, 115–30), there is nothing even in his religious convictions that leads him to suppose that the story of earthly life necessarily ends in success. Quite the reverse, for it is in the nature of life, and not simply of human life, that every evolutionary advance is attained at the cost of increasing risk of individual and collective group extinction.

In the case of man, possession of theoretical and practical reason results in the achievement of a life form quite capable of bringing to an end its own and every other form of life. Equally, however, the same faculties that can bring about universal destruction are, when turned reflectively toward understanding the conditions of survival and well-being, capable of ensuring indefinite if not eternal existence. But this requires of man the exercise of rational choice in an ethics of responsibility and prudential care that encompasses not only human life but the integrity of the nature on which his own depends. The metaphysics that shows this is devoid of appeal to either providence or progress. It is rational but makes no claim to be complete; it begins, modestly enough, with a single, apparently metaphysically innocent, sentence in which Jonas states the grounding principle of his ethics, proceeding deductively from there. The sentence runs: 'Man is the only being known to us who can assume responsibility.' On which Jonas observes that: 'We immediately recognize this "can" as more than a simply empirical fact. We recognize it as a distinguishing and decisive feature of human existence. Thus, we have in this fact a basic principle of philosophical anthropology, i.e. of the ontology of the being "Man", and with it already a principle of metaphysics but only of the metaphysics of man' (Jonas 1996, 106). Yet from this modest beginning, the rest of metaphysics and, with it, ethics may be said to follow.

Here, in brief, is how the metaphysical deduction proceeds:

> We intuitively recognize in this ontological distinction of man – his capacity for responsibility – not only its *essentiality* but also a *value*. The appearance of this value in the world does not simply add another value to the already value – rich landscape of *being* but surpasses all that has gone before with something that generically transcends it. This represents a qualitative intensification of the valuableness of *Being as a whole*, the ultimate object of our responsibility. Thereby, however, the capacity for responsibility as such besides the fact that it obligates us to exercise it from – case to case – becomes *its own object* in that having it obligates us to perpetuate *its presence in the world*. This presence is inexorably linked to the existence of creatures having that capacity. Therefore,

> the capacity for responsibility per se obligates its respective bearers to make existence possible for future bearers. In order to prevent responsibility from disappearing from the world – so speaks its immanent commandment – there ought to be human beings in the future. (Jonas 1996, 106)

This is, however, only a first step, for what is required in order that the phenomenon of responsibility be sustained is not only the future presence of human beings as such but humans who have not just the ontological capacity for responsibility but also the 'psychological openness' to perceive its obligation, and this is 'an historically acquired vulnerable possession that can be lost collectively, even if calculative reasoning and power arising from it survive with the biological subjects' (Jonas 1996, 106). This introduces a cultural dimension to the argument, for as Aldous Huxley describes it in *Brave New World*, and B.F. Skinner in *Beyond Freedom and Dignity*, it is possible to conceive of human beings from whom awareness of such an obligation has been removed. In the case of Skinner at least, this may even be regarded as an advantage, and so, even though persuasive, the argument for the persistence of a disposition to act responsibly remains at least debatable – an object of evaluative judgment; and this is why, though persuasive, the argument that Jonas advances falls something short of being a conclusive proof. And here we must, I think, refer back from the argument for human responsibility as such, to Jonas' account of the intrinsic orientation of life to its own preservation in being already primitively foreshadowed or prefigured in the process of metabolism that is a universal feature of animate being. This, I would suggest, demonstrates more potently than anything else the continuity between the philosophy of the organism and Jonas' ontologically grounded ethics, and so the integral unity and rational coherence of his thought.

In an essay on biological engineering, collected in his 1974 anthology of philosophical essays (Jonas 1980, 141–67), Jonas explicitly engages with the ethical problems entailed with the extension of human technological agency into a field, human cloning, that was when the essay was written, only a possibility dimly foreseen. It is impossible to read that essay today without being struck by the prophetic clarity with which he perceived the issues that such an undertaking would raise and by the emotive yet rational force and discriminating intelligence with which he warns against its pursuit. Rather than trying to summarize his argument, which is as scientifically informed as it is persuasive but would require a chapter in itself, I shall end this chapter on ethics and technology by citing the final paragraphs of what he has to say in a passage that exemplifies, more topically than anything other, Jonas' contribution to the continuing claims of philosophical reason to be heard in the age of science:

> We have been moving for some stretch now at the very boundaries of things human and of possible discourse about them. A spectral sense of unreality must have communicated itself to the reader, which I share. Yet he would be wrong to regard the discourse therefore as otiose. The danger is that we may be gliding

into fateful beginnings unawares, innocently as it were by the thin end of the wedge, namely pure science. I have tried, in discussing these borderline cases, to suppress the metaphysical shudder I feel at the idea of a man-made homunculus. To let it out now with an archaic word, the production of human freaks would be an abomination; let alone the unspeakable thought of human–animal hybrids which, quite consistently, has not failed to enter the lists. Steering clear of metaphysics and categories of the sacred, which this topic makes it not easy to do, I resort at the end, and with reference to the whole field of biological control, to the plainest of moral reflections: Deeds with no accountability are wrong when done to others. The moral dilemma in all human-biological manipulation, other than negative [...] is this: that the potential accusation of the offspring against his makers will find no respondent still answerable for the deed, and no possible redress. Here is a field for crimes with complete impunity to the perpetrator. This alone should call forth the utmost scrupulousness and sensitivity in applying the rising powers of biological control on man. And though much more is involved, the simple ethics of the case are enough to rule out the direct tampering with human genotypes. from the very beginning of the road – that is, impalatable as it sounds to modern ears, at the fountainhead of experimental research. (Jonas 1980, 166–7)

References

Huxley, Aldous. 1998. *Brave New World.* Hamburg: Rowohlt.

Jonas, Hans. 1963. *The Phenomenon of Life: Towards a Philosophical Biology.* New York: Harper and Row.

———. 1980. *Philosophical Essays: From Ancient Creed to Technological Man.* Chicago: University of Chicago Press.

———. 1984. *The Imperative of Responsibility: In Search of an Ethics for the Technological World.* Chicago and London: The University of Chicago Press.

———. 1996. *Mortality and Morality: A Search for the Good after Auschwitz,* edited by Lawrence Vogel. Evanston: Northwestern University Press.

Monod, Jacques. 1970. *Chance and Necessity.* London: Penguin.

Skinner, Burrhus F. 1971. *Beyond Freedom and Dignity.* New York: Knopf.

Chapter 11

Refined Marxism and Moral Enhancement

John-Stewart Gordon

Introduction

Hans Jonas' book *The Imperative of Responsibility* (1979) is a true classic, a highly thought-provoking contribution to literature on the great dangers of technological development and its negative impact on modern civilization. Without any doubt, it is still a very relevant work on the ever-increasing pursuit of modern technology at the expense of nature written by one of the leading German-Jewish philosophers of the twentieth century. His influential ideas and the problem he was concerned with are still significant today, even though admittedly his voice has become weaker. One main reason why scholars are less attracted to his approach to 'the ethics of the future' is certainly his rather 'archaic' and most eloquent but complex language which reminds the reader of Hegel and Heidegger and poses some difficulties for those who are not used to this particular style of writing. The declining interest in reading authors with this style of writing has been accelerated by virtue of the growing interest in analytical philosophy, with its rather clear and precise writing style, at the end of the last century. This is unfortunate since a close reading of Jonas reveals his great expertise, his deep intuitive understanding of the nature of the civilization-changing problems, and his unrivalled far-sightedness concerning the dangers and consequences of modern technology for human and non-human nature alike. This makes his valuable contribution as relevant today as it was in his time.

Whether Jonas' profound understanding of the serious problems facing civilization is equally matched by the cogency of his approach to saving humanity from destruction might be questioned. For example, in his excellent and sympathetic article 'Moral Responsibility for the Preservation of Humankind' (1983), Walter A. Weisskopf rightly claims that 'we believe that Jonas is "emotionally right" but "rationally wrong"' (Weisskopf 1983, 99). The prime example is Jonas' derivation of the claim that 'humankind should be' and must be preserved. In a nutshell, Jonas argues that there should rather be something and not nothing (Jonas 1979, 90), and additionally he claims that purpose is a universal feature in nature, which implies value that, in turn, implies goodness. Furthermore, if human beings have the capability to be responsible for their actions, then they have the duty to be responsible. This line of reasoning poses a difficult problem if one does not, for example, believe in the goodness of creation. If one believes in a *benevolent* God, then the problem is solved (religious justification). If one attempts to provide a non-religious justification, then the problem cannot be solved by adhering to empirical sciences (e.g. Weisskopf 1983, 101–5). Here, one might sympathetically acknowledge the fact that Jonas might not provide a strong (analytical) justification, but simply poses the not unconvincing intuitive axiom – based on his general view of nature – that humanity should be rather than not be. According to Jonas, non-human life and inorganic nature have no positive value as such.

In his readable article 'Die Aktualität der Ethik von Hans Jonas. Eine Kritik der Kritik des Prinzips Verantwortung' (2007), Jan Schmidt correctly claims that Jonas does not want to exchange other ethical theories with his own approach, but attempts to refine modern ethics by adding the important notion of responsibility to the debate (Schmidt 2007, 11). Jonas famously proposes to 'act so that the effects of your action are compatible with the permanence of genuine human life'. One might rightly assume that there is hardly any reasonable person who would argue against this convincing moral principle. However, on further reflection, one might indeed question some of the important claims Jonas makes for the justification of his ethical approach that culminates in his moral principle, which, in turn, jeopardizes the overall cogency of his main argument to substantiate his principle of responsibility.

After these rather general considerations, this chapter mainly deals with Jonas' critique of Marxism[1] and the vital question of whether moral enhancement could preserve the existence of humanity against the background of the ever-increasing technological development and its severe dangers for humankind. The first section provides a general overview of the initial dangerous situation described by Jonas, paying particular attention to the main structure of the principle of responsibility. After providing a table highlighting the main differences between capitalism and Marxism in the second section, the counter-arguments against Marxism are examined in more detail. The third section offers a possible solution to the important question of who should rule the state by focusing on the controversial issue of moral enhancement as the main key to avoiding human destruction. The last section offers some concluding remarks.

Initial Situation

Technological Development and Its Negative Consequences

Modern civilization strives for the ideals of progress and liberation through the means of science, technology and industrialization at the expense of non-human

1 According to Jonas, the notion of 'Marxism' concerns every socio-economic and political system that is not capitalist. He does not define the terms in any detail but simply adheres to the common-sense usage. However, one must acknowledge the fact that Marx's ideas do not really apply to contemporary communist and socialist systems, with their mixture of command and free market economies, as Weisskopf has correctly claimed (Weisskopf 1983, 112).

nature. The Baconian ideal of material progress, of which Jonas claims Marxism is the *executor* (Jonas 1979, 256), encourages the harvesting of nature in order to gain empirical knowledge, which is necessary to deal with the social and economic problems of modern civilization. 'Knowledge is Power!' is the credo of the Baconian ideal. Technological development and scientific progress are the prerequisites of Marxism in order to gain material abundance and to provide all people with the means to live according to their needs in an equal and fair way. Without doubt, there are great dangers in using a risky technology with unpredictable negative consequences that recklessly exploits non-human nature as *the* means to provide the right socio-economic and political environment for the Marxist's eschatological fulfilment of the so-called 'new human being'. Some of the important issues with which modern civilization is concerned raise the following lines of reasoning:

- Population explosion and prolongation of human life – global food and drink shortages – new technologies/chemical methods – erosion of the soil and poisoning of inland and coastal waters – contaminating the food chain.
- Deficient human beings – behaviour control and genetic manipulation – danger of misuse and irrevocably altering the DNA.
- Scarcity of non-renewable energy – mining of deeper-lying sources – destroying nature.
- Nuclear power – nuclear waste – danger of contaminating nature in cases of accidents – misuse of nuclear power (i.e. atomic bomb) – endangering the existence of humanity and non-human nature.
- Deforestation – detrimental climatic effects – global warming – sea-level changes – flooding.

Jonas' general idea is that human beings might not be able to deal with the spirits that they have summoned once they unleash a technology they cannot master, bringing irreversible problems for human and non-human nature. In this context, he had already stated in his thought-provoking article 'Responsibility Today: The Ethics of an Endangered Future' (1976) that 'the prophecy of doom is to be given greater heed than the prophecy of bliss' (Jonas 1976, 89). One understands that Jonas proposes to modify the role of Marxism as the 'bringer of consumption' to that of 'preventer of disaster' (Jonas 1976, 86). This refined Marxism, as Jonas correctly states, would abandon the utopian goal – the ultimate material abundance of a classless communist society in which every person lives according to his or her needs – by restraining its exploitative and reckless use of modern technology regarding nature; 'for one can live without the supreme good but not with the supreme evil' (Jonas 1976, 92). By 'supreme evil' Jonas does not necessarily mean, for example, the danger of using the atomic bomb, but rather the inherent danger of the technology as such (Jonas 1976, 94–5). Under certain circumstances, he has (almost) no problems using nuclear power via *nuclear fusion* to provide humanity with energy, if it does not jeopardize the biological existence of human and non-human nature (Jonas 1979, 337).

Anthropocentrism and Human Nature

One might consider that Jonas' future ethics is anthropocentric by nature because he claims that the human responsibility to preserve 'the future of humanity' is the *first* duty without explicitly mentioning nature. However, he further argues that the future of humanity contains 'the future of nature' as an *independent* metaphysical responsibility in itself (Jonas 1979, 245), which means that he adheres to a non-anthropocentric view. He clearly states:

> Die Verengung auf den Menschen allein und als von aller übrigen Natur verschieden kann nur Verengung, ja Entmenschung des Menschen selbst bedeuten, die Verkümmerung seines Wesens auch im Glücksfall biologischer Erhaltung – widerspricht also ihrem vorgeblichen, eben von der Würde seines Wesens beglaubigten Ziel. Im wahrhaft menschlichen Blickpunkt bleibt der Natur ihre Eigenwürde, die der Willkür unserer Macht entgegensteht. (Jonas 1979, 245–6)[2]

Thus, nature has its own dignity, but the beginning of the same section calls such a view into question when Jonas argues that the future of nature is part of the future of humanity; '*nachdem* der Mensch nicht nur sich selbst, sondern der ganzen Biosphäre gefährlich geworden ist' (Jonas 1979, 245, emphasis is mine).[3] This formulation rather suggests that *only after* humanity has gained the power to jeopardize not only its own existence but also that of non-human nature is nature attributed an independent moral status. But this is counter-intuitive, since the independent moral status of nature would then depend on the power of humankind to jeopardize nature. This point, however, is substantiated by the fact that in existential cases where one must choose between humanity and nature, humanity must always come first by virtue of its higher dignity (Jonas 1979, 246). Even though Jonas' point of view is reasonable at first sight, it poses some difficulties concerning his initial statement that both humankind and non-human nature have an independent moral status by claiming that his future ethics is non-anthropocentric by nature. For example, if both have an inherent worth – that is, dignity – then it is difficult to see why humankind should always come first and what it means to claim that the value of dignity comes in degrees. One might usually assume – and maybe rightly so – that one has either dignity or no dignity at all, but it does not come in degrees. Furthermore, it is not clear why preserving humanity must always be

2 'Such narrowness in the name of man, which is ready to sacrifice the rest of nature to his purported needs, can only result in the dehumanization of man, the atrophy of his essence even in the lucky case of biological survival. It therefore contradicts its professed goal, the very preservation of himself as sanctioned by the dignity of his essence. In the truly human aspect, nature retains her dignity, which confronts the arbitrariness of our might' (Jonas 1985, 136–7).

3 '[…] since man has become dangerous not only to himself but to the whole biosphere' (Jonas 1985, 136).

preferred over the existence of non-human nature in existential cases, at least from a 'neutral' point of view that is non-anthropocentric by nature.

In addition, one might argue that if human beings are good by nature, then this offers a perfectly good reason to prefer humankind to non-human nature, *if* the latter has only a neutral or less high value. As we have seen above, Jonas argues that nature has a lower value than humanity, which gives him a good reason to prefer humankind to non-human nature. However, Jonas does not claim that 'the nature' of human beings is good (or bad); he states that 'the nature' of human beings is the inherent *capability* to become good or bad (Jonas 1979, 385). Of course, one might argue that 'the nature of human beings' is different from 'humankind' as such and hence there is no real problem but a pseudo problem. This can be reasonably questioned since both notions are tantamount and only differ in their grammatical form. But, what remains? It seems that Jonas wholeheartedly believes that his position should be characterized as non-anthropocentric, but his main line of reasoning and vague formulations rather show that his viewpoint can be equally described as anthropocentric. I do not want to press this point any further but simply make the reader aware of this difficulty in the context of Jonas' future ethics.

The Notion of Responsibility – A Very Brief Overview

The notion of responsibility has two main parts: the first part is the aspect of non-reciprocity, the second part is the aspect of caution. Both parts are necessary for Jonas' future ethics. The first part is related to the notion of responsibility itself, in which the asymmetry of power is of utmost importance since it creates the responsibility for the weak – either fellow human beings or non-human nature – by establishing an ethical situation (e.g. Schmidt 2007, 10–15). The foundation of responsibility is exemplified by the parent–infant analogy as the prime example of being in charge of someone else (e.g. Jonas 1979, 234–42; Weisskopf 1983, 110–11).[4] For now, it is important to characterize briefly the notion of responsibility in more detail by quoting Jonas' own words:

4 For centuries, political philosophy held that there is a reasonable analogy between the responsibility of parents for their children and the responsibility of statesmen for their citizens. In contemporary political philosophy, however, scholars commonly tend to debunk this idea because the analogy suggests that citizens are unable to participate in political affairs and determine the process of political decision-making. The former view that there is no enlightened citizenship and that people would, in general, be better off if they are governed (e.g. political paternalism) rather than partake in mob rule, i.e. based on individual autonomy, has vanished into thin air due to the modern process of democratization. Jonas, however, still believes in this essential analogy that lies at the heart of his approach when he derives his principle of responsibility 'from evolution and from the innate love of parents for their offspring' (Weisskopf 1983, 107). He claims that parents are fully responsible for their children to nurture them and provide them with a proper education for their future lives, while the statesmen must protect the future of humankind which is their responsibility (Jonas 1979, 184–98).

> Verantwortung ist die als Pflicht anerkannte *Sorge* um ein anderes Sein, die bei der Bedrohung seiner Verletzlichkeit zur 'Besorgnis' wird. Als Potential aber steckt die Furcht schon in der ursprünglichen Frage, mit der man sich jede aktive Verantwortung beginnend vorstellen kann: was wird *ihm* zustoßen, wenn *ich* mich seiner *nicht* annehme? Je dunkler die Antwort, desto heller gezeichnet die Verantwortung. (Jonas 1979, 391)

The second part, the aspect of caution, contains two methodological points; first, the general principle of caution, which always gives precedence to the bad and not the good prognosis (Jonas 1979, 70–75) and, secondly, the important heuristic of fear, which teaches us that we need the sense of menace regarding the idea of man so that by acknowledging the terror we can be assured of the true idea of man (Jonas 1979, 63–4; here 63). Both methodological points of the aspect of caution of the notion of responsibility can be seen as a conservative point of view against the background of the state of not knowing. In this context, the possible dangers of the ever-increasing technological development and its possible negative consequences clash with the conservative stance and, thereby, make us more cautious about technology, science and industrialization.

According to Jonas, the notion of responsibility – brought to the fore by his ethical imperative of responsibility – attempts to secure two crucial points: first, the biological existence of humanity and, secondly, the social-cultural heritage of humankind. Whether this is best put into practice by a capitalist or Marxist socio-economic and political system will be discussed in the next section.

The Baconian Ideal and the Theory of Power

The unrivalled and unforeseeable success of the Baconian ideal to exploit nature recklessly in order to meet the many needs of a growing world population has become a universal threat for the existence of humanity. Jonas mentions two main sources of the inherent dynamic of the success of modern civilization. The first point is economic success, and the second concerns biological success (Jonas 1979, 251). The economic success is responsible for the increasing per capita production of goods that brings general abundance for humanity at the expense of the finite resources of nature. This situation is severely exacerbated by the biological success – that is, the population explosion that calls for the harvesting of even more natural resources and thus calamitously adds fuel to the fire (Jonas 1979, 251–3).

However, this process, according to Jonas, could be stopped by a 'purified' humanity that is no longer interested in consumption but rather in attempting to avoid the disaster. In his 'theory' of the three powers Jonas briefly describes this dynamic process (Jonas 1979, 253–5):

- **The First Power:** Unrestricted power over the seemingly infinite resources of nature, leads to:

- **The Second Power:** Humanity has lost its power and control over nature and therefore is headed for its own destruction. As Jonas states: 'Die Macht ist selbstmächtig geworden, während ihre Verheißung in Drohung umgeschlagen ist, ihre Heilsperspektive in Apokalyptik' (Jonas 1979, 253).[5]
- **The Third Power:** The regaining of the power of humanity over the second non-human controlled power should be accomplished by a 'purified' society. This new society might be a refined Marxist non-utopian system (see below).

In fact, Jonas' theory of power logically follows from his basic assumptions about the Baconian ideal and humanity's relation to nature; in this sense, it is a reasonable way to frame the point in question. The next section examines whether Marxism is able to execute the third power and regain control over the 'selbstmächtig gewordene Macht'.

Marxism – A Viable Solution?

It is idiomatic to say that one is unable to put the genie back in the bottle; that is, humankind's loss of power over the ever-increasing modern technology and its possible universal dangers. Whether Marxism will become the master of the 'unleashed spirits' and eventually resolve the problem of a future universal disaster –that is, whether Marxism is better equipped to preserve humankind than its rival, capitalism – will be analysed in this section. Jonas thoroughly examines this vital issue in the excellent last two chapters of his book.

As has been mentioned before, Jonas believes that Marxism – compared with capitalism – is the real executor of the Baconian ideal (the idea of progress) by virtue of its more rigorous exploitation of nature in order to provide the necessary means for the new human being to live a life of material abundance and leisure (Marxist utopia). In short, without the fruits of industrialization and modern technology there is no equality and fairness of income distribution in the Marxist society (Jonas 1979, 258). Initially, Jonas discusses Marxism sympathetically as a viable solution (Jonas 1979, 256–70), if it is able to give up the utopian ideal of being the 'bringer of consumption' rather than the 'preventer of disaster' (Jonas 1979, 86). However, he then rejects the idea of Marxism altogether (Jonas 1979, 271–86) and eventually comes to the conclusion that only a non-utopian ethics of responsibility will save humanity from universal disaster. The following subsections examine his general line of reasoning.

5 'The power has become self-acting, while its promise has turned into threat, its prospect of salvation into apocalypse' (Jonas 1985, 141).

Table 11.1 Jonas' comparison of capitalism and Marxism

Areas	Political systems		Jonas' comments
	Capitalism	Marxism	
Economy (260–62)	Private and corporate industry	Needs-based industry and bureaucracy	Production for use is more rational than production for profit; central planning to satisfy collective needs might avoid the waste of the competitive market and extravagant consumerism.
Governmental power (262–3)	Capitalist-liberal democracies	Communist tyranny of a well-informed and benevolent elite	Lowering the standards of living, austerity and other unpopular hardships might be better realized by an autocratic socialist model.
Moral attitude and standard of living (263–5)	Moral pluralism, individuality, hedonism, lowering the standard of living are problematic and might not be enforceable	Ascetic moralism, lowering the standard of living might be more easily enforceable	Long-lasting austerities are easier to endure by the identification of the public with the government, as is the case in Marxism. Whether the global class struggle can be resolved by Marxism remains to be seen. Time will tell whether, in practice, Marxist national states will be (more) free from collective egoisms than their capitalist counterparts.
Politics and truth (265–7)	Less enthusiasm	Great enthusiasm for the Marxist utopia	It is unclear whether one should adopt Plato's 'noble lie' in order to mislead the public about the true goals of a refined Marxism that no longer adheres to the utopian ideal because no one knows how the public will react and whether it can face the truth. Capitalism has no force comparable with the enthusiasm of the public in Marxism.

Areas	**Political systems**		**Jonas' comments**
	Capitalism	**Marxism**	
Equality and relinquishment (267–9)	Distrust of elites in democracies in cases of austerity on account of the probably uneven distribution of burdens	'Real' equality through classless society and tolerable distrust of the 'privileged' members of the party in cases of austerity	There is no real classless Marxist society because there are still privileged members of the party, who must show integrity to avoid distrust. A democracy based on periodic re-election is unable to face the great unpopular austerities that must be endured in order to save humanity from a universal disaster. A temporary benevolent tyranny is recommended.
Result	Put simply, the usefulness of the utopian ideal – but only in its appearance and not proposing the eschatological Marxist 'truth' – and its inherent principle of equality can be viewed as viable means, in contrast to capitalism, of successfully resolving the great dangers facing humankind.		

Source: Jonas 1979.

Jonas' Meta-critique of Marxism

Whether Marxism has a better chance of being put into practice is the vital question of Jonas' evaluation of the 'abstract chances' (Jonas 1979, 271–86). He raises four important objections and offers some vital reasons why one should not rely on Marxism to deal with the difficult problems and thus to avoid universal disaster. His four objections are as follows:

1. The possibility of collective profit-seeking at the expense of other countries cannot be ruled out (Jonas 1979, 271–3).
2. World communism is no guarantee for achieving the ultimate goals as long as there is no radical redistribution of resources on a global level (Jonas 1979, 273–4).
3. The Marxist quasi-religious desire for modern technology and its power to overcome all problems can be called into question (Jonas 1979, 275–7).
4. The utopian ideal of a classless society of the 'new' human beings seems unrealistic (Jonas 1979, 278–9). The objections are dealt with in order.

The Profit Motive and the Maximizing Incentive

Individually speaking, the profit motive of the new human being has vanished in Marxism; however, there is no good reason – according to Jonas – to assume that there will be no collective profit-seeking at the expense of other non-Marxist countries. With regard to economy, the maximizing incentive is tantamount to the capitalist profit motive and hence Marxist society will exploit nature in order to offer each person the possibility to live according to his or her needs. The friendly coexistence of Marxist countries with non-Marxist countries might be jeopardized by patriotism, collective egoisms and national power politics. Furthermore, inner and external reasons may lead to a more rigorous exploitation of nature by Marxist countries aimed at accomplishing industrial development that can compete with non-Marxist countries.

Undoubtedly, Jonas' line of reasoning is powerful and convincing; in practice, the dynamics of the Cold War between Marxist and non-Marxist countries has been evident, as well as the negative effects (including the many proxy wars during the decades after World War II). One might object that this has only been so because it was not the 'real' Marxism. The new human being, arguably, would not jeopardize humanity and non-human nature by wrong decisions and power politics. This claim, however, can be questioned by depicting a situation that will never become reality, since *ideal* conditions will never come into practice by virtue of their *ideal* character. History has already shown that the many attempts to establish Marxism failed miserably. Protagonists might still argue that the success of Marxism exclusively depends on material abundance and the new human beings, which have not yet come into existence. Therefore, there was no 'real' chance of establishing the ideal Marxist society in the past. It remains to be seen, then, whether the high Marxist ideals will ever give rise to a truly Marxist society; what works in theory might not be applicable in practice.

World Communism is No Real Guarantee Against Regional Economic Egoism
The idea that it is necessary to establish world communism in order to accomplish the Marxist ideals is confronted by two problems, according to Jonas. First, world communism can be reached only after a global war, which is in itself an absurd proposition by virtue of its inevitably disastrous outcome. Second, if it were possible to establish a Marxist world state by friendly means, for some parts of the world it would be a foreign domination. In turn, that would cause several problems such as regional freedom movements; for example, in cases where affluent societies must forgo material abundance or less affluent societies are unable to become more affluent. The result would be an unstable Marxist world state. In addition, Jonas convincingly questions the idea that a federation of sovereign Marxist nation states is better suited to avoiding conflicts of 'life advantages', since there has hitherto been no nation state showing the necessary 'collective altruism'. In this context, Jonas seems correct to claim the following:

> Das heißt, erfolgreicher (nämlich friedlicher) Weltsozialismus ist an wirtschaftliche Expansion gebunden, ohne welche eine Behebung der Not ganzer Weltteile nicht möglich ist, es sei denn durch radikale internationale Neuverteilung schon bestehenden Reichtums (und die, wie gesagt, müßte durch jenes Gewaltmittel erzwungen werden, nach welchem nicht viel mehr zu verteilen wäre). (Jonas 1979, 274)[6]

Today – as it was for Jonas – it seems indeed inconceivable that the establishment of a Marxist world state will be reached by peaceful means unless there is a win-win situation for every nation state on the global level. This would, however, require an almost universal material abundance, which is impossible to provide given the finite non-renewable resources of nature against the background of the population explosion. This is why Jonas seems right when he claims that Marxism could deal with future problems if and only if it becomes not the bringer of consumption but the preventer of disaster.

The Cult of Technology
Jonas observes an almost (fanatical) religious belief in Marxism in the omnipotence of modern technology to accomplish the good. The technological impulse is inherently Marxist and comes in combination with an extreme anthropocentrism, in which nature is only the means to accomplish the material abundance for the new human beings. Even the problem of food supply related to population explosion can be dealt with by Marxist controlled sciences and technology. There

6 'In other words, successful (namely, peaceful) world socialism is tied to economic *expansion*, without which the destitution of vast regions of the earth cannot be alleviated – unless it be through a radical international redistribution of existing wealth (and this, as noted, would require that use of force which would not leave much to distribute)' (Jonas 1985, 153–4).

is no limit. Scarcity is due to either insufficient technology – which is ultimately the fault of the class system – or malicious manipulation of the market. The danger according to Jonas lies in obfuscating the truth ideologically.

Without doubt, a more modest view of the technological possibilities that are available in order to deal with current and future problems is appropriate. The very idea that technology will solve all problems by proposing that there exists, in principle, no limit is dangerous if one completely relies on this claim as the only means to material abundance and thus a precondition of a Marxist classless society. Nature is no 'golden ass' but provides humanity and non-human nature with *limited* resources that need to be shared equally in a just way. Even if one sympathetically assumes – as I do – that most problems can be solved by modern technology, several vital (unresolvable) problems will necessarily remain. The decisive remaining question is *how* to deal with these unresolvable problems, such as the problem of population explosion, in addition to the future possibility of prolonged human life – it is difficult to conceive that our earth is able to deal with, for example, 20 (or more) billion people, which is part of a not-so-far-distant future.

The Utopian Ideal

Marxist theory not only proposes that the external conditions are responsible for the development of humanity and a new society, but also maintains that *only after* one has accomplished material abundance will morality come to the fore – that is, 'first food, then morals'. Jonas rightly complains that Marxists do not offer any information about this new state, except that everything will be better than now. They simply claim that it is so completely different from the current state of affairs that one cannot say anything meaningful about it, and this is obviously not enough (see also Jonas 1979, 280–86, 309–10).

This reminds one of Wittgenstein's saying that 'what can be said at all, can be said clearly, and what we cannot talk about we must pass over in silence'. The underlying idea that the 'real' human being does not yet exist and will only come into existence within the Marxist classless society – namely, when the current history of humanity as 'the antecedent' of the real history of humanity is past – seems to be wishful thinking. Whether this new human being, however, *should* come into existence by other means such as genetic moral enhancement will be discussed in the third section. If there is a real opportunity to create human beings according to the Marxist ideals, which would help to prevent universal disaster, should one, then, welcome such a future?

Additional Claims against the Marxist Solution

In addition to the four main objections, Jonas substantiates his main line of reasoning by making two minor but equally important claims (Jonas 1979, 280–86). First, by referring to Nietzsche's idea of the 'Übermensch' – Nietzsche's version of the *new* human being – Jonas points out that he is equally silent about how to create and foster this new human being (despite some occasional but vague remarks about breeding). Nietzsche does not provide any important details about the true nature of this most advanced human being, despite the fact that he will possess an unmatched rigour and courage making him unprecedented. Jonas rightly mentions that the so-called 'unmatched rigorousness and courageousness' is an improvement of *previous* conditions, so that the term 'unprecedented' is out of place (Jonas 1979, 280–81).[7] In Jonas' own words: 'Kurz, der "Übermensch" war immer schon da, wie auch der "Mensch", und der zukünftige wird zwar anders sein als jeder vorher, aber das war der bisherige jeweils auch' (Jonas 1979, 281).[8] This important issue will be further discussed below by responding to the question of how – in more moderate terms – an enhanced human being will save himself and non-human life from destruction (see below). It is not necessary to depict the new human being as a mortal 'human God'. Rather, it is sufficient to see him or her as a *morally* enhanced human being that is, for example, less aggressive and more attentive towards his or her fellow human beings, animals and nature. If this can be done, then much has been accomplished.

The second point concerns the idea of the classless Marxist society as the precondition of the *good* human being. The main idea is that the human being is good by nature and that circumstances – class society and class conflicts – undermine the true potential of the human being, so that he or she cannot develop as he or she is supposed to develop by nature. The *good* human being is the product of the classless Marxist society (Jonas 1979, 281–2). As we have already noted, Jonas questions the idea of a *unique* nature of human beings; human beings are neither good nor bad by nature but simply have the ability to become good or bad individuals (Jonas 1979, 385). However, the vital question is what Marxists mean by 'good'

7 The particular problem – the inability to provide more valuable information about the *new* human being who has never before existed – follows from the more general problem that the human mind cannot comprehend something that is completely different from what the human being knows. That is, completely new information will always be framed in old patterns depending on our brain and particular sense perception so that human beings can deal with the information more easily. For example, if our highly advanced modern technology of space travel, e.g. the Mars mission or the Moon landing, were shown to some 'normal' people of the Middle Ages, they would be unable to process this information properly. It would be quite reasonable to expect that people of the Middle Ages would either believe that this is pure nonsense, or some terrible force against God. Alternatively, if shown the rocket and spaceship, they may describe this unknown visual information in familiar but very opaque patterns since they would lack adequate words to describe these objects properly. And if this is not enough, then show a rocket and spaceship to people from the Stone Age. That means, if one believes that the *new* human being is completely different from the current human being, then it follows that the depiction of this new human being is necessarily opaque and framed in a way that is familiar to us. Here, the important question is: 'How can the completely unknown be described?'

8 'In short, "the superman" has of old been with us, just as "man" was; and although future superman will surely be different from all his predecessors, so was each of them in his time' (Jonas 1985, 158).

in this context. According to Jonas, there are two possibilities; goodness either refers to human character and behaviour (moral goodness), or, to the productivity of trans-economical values and their distinctive quality (cultural goodness). That is to say, Jonas does not believe in the superiority of the cultural goodness of the classless Marxist society (Jonas 1979, 282–4), nor is he convinced by the Marxist claim of the moral superiority of the new Marxist human being to become a truly virtuous and non-violent person. Human beings, according to Jonas, can be led into temptation; they are not angels. This is precisely the reason why even the 'classless' Socialist societies in the twentieth century maintained a sophisticated police and investigative apparatus (Jonas 1979, 284–5). If the fairy tale of the good human being had been true, there would have been no reason to establish such an apparatus in the first place, unless one additionally claimed that the circumstances were still inadequate to provide the almost infinite abundance for the new human being. The underlying Marxist idea is not (only) to avoid poverty, but to strive for ultimate wealth and to house the true human beings. Jonas claims that this Marxist utopian ideal is not only something we cannot afford, but it is also a false ideal to follow (Jonas 1979, 286).

Jonas' initial assessment is certainly correct given the state of technology at his time, but one might pose the question whether an attempt to realize a less utopian version of moderate Marxist ideas is still within our reach and should be put into practice. For example, it seems possible that human beings can be morally enhanced within the next one to two decades, so that they become, for example, less aggressive and more attentive as well as less egoistic and more social. The next section examines this line of reasoning in more detail and offers a fresh approach to avoiding universal disaster and creating a non-utopian world in which the idea of responsibility is (still) right at the heart of a refined future ethics that is compatible with moderate Marxism.

Avoiding the Universal Disaster by Moral Enhancement

Jonas raises two important objections against the utopian ideal of Marxism (Jonas 1979, 326). The first critique concerns the supposed success story of the (empirical) sciences; the drive of modern technology towards a world of complete abundance in which all human beings can live according to their needs. Jonas rightly claims that it is technologically *impossible* to gain abundance *if* the population is too big (Jonas 1979, 339). However, the goal to reach abundance might still be realizable if one reduces the population so that the 'chosen people' will be able to live according to their needs at the expense of fellow members of the global society who are killed. To put this so-called 'Insel der Seligen' into practice would be outrageous, according to Jonas (Jonas 1979, 340; see 'Island of the Blessed', Jonas 1985, 192).

Jonas' second critique concerns the anthropologic-philosophical idea of the new human being and the problem of leisure for the Marxist society (Jonas 1979, 343–7).

True freedom for human beings – according to Marxism – will be accomplished through industrialization. If all *necessary* work is eventually done by machines, that, in turn, would lead to superior productivity. Global abundance would then be possible. The Marxist thinker Ernst Bloch emphatically embraces this idea but, unlike Marx, Bloch claims that this Golden Age leads to *the* fundamental 'problem of leisure'. Human beings must engage in pure non-necessary work; that is, they must perform an activity that is meaningful in order to avoid an existence that is unworthy of a human being. Jonas critically examines Bloch's approach to dealing with the problem of leisure in great detail and eventually rejects his solution of the 'Steckenpferd als Beruf' (Jonas 1979, 348–75).[9]

Who Should Rule?

The most important question of Jonas' book is the following: 'Wenn, wie wir glauben, nur eine Elite ethisch und intellektuell die von uns angczeigte Zukunftsverantwortung übernehmen kann – wie wird eine solche Elite erzeugt und wie mit der Macht ausgestattet, sie auszuüben?' (Jonas 1979, 262).[10] In order to save humankind from universal disaster, Jonas believes – as we have already seen – that this can best be accomplished by adhering to a temporary Marxist tyranny of a well-informed and benevolent elite. According to Jonas, people in capitalist-liberal democracies are less likely to accept the lowering of their living standards, and to endure austerities and other hardships during this long and difficult transition period. The strong identification of the public with the government by virtue of its promise to provide 'real' equality together with the great enthusiasm of the people for the utopian ideal are the biggest advantages of Marxism (and, at the same time, its greatest weakness). The utopian ideal of Marxism as 'the bringer of consumption' must be abandoned so that it becomes 'the preventer of disaster' (Jonas 1979, 86). For Jonas, this *refined* Marxism is most difficult 'to advertise' because it lacks the essential Marxist components. Hence, it should probably be kept as a state secret in order to avoid a public outcry since one does not know how people will react. In this context, Jonas refers to Plato and the institution of the so-called 'noble lie'. That is, sometimes it is very useful and even necessary for the government to lie about the facts because the truth might be intolerable and even dangerous for the survival of the state. In other words, Jonas eventually rejects a refined Marxist society for reasons we have already discussed above.

It might still be the case, however, that Jonas' decision is premature and that a more refined Marxist global society is able to face the manifold problems such as racism and aggressive behaviour (see Douglas 2008). Global problems need

9 Here, we do not have to discuss in detail Jonas' analysis since it would lead us away from the main line of reasoning.

10 'If, as we believe, only an elite can assume, ethically and intellectually, the kind of responsibility for the future which we have postulated – how is such an elite generated and recruited, and how is it invested with the power for its exercise?' (Jonas 1985, 147).

a global solution. The main problem is that it seems unimaginable to enforce globally burdensome measures to save humanity from universal disaster unless, for example, there is a powerful regime that is capable of doing what is necessary. Before we examine the methods of accomplishing this goal, it is important to discuss further some of the most burdensome measures that must be introduced to protect the future of humankind.

Burdensome Measures

- **Global society:** Separate nation states are unable to face the universal disaster on their own; it needs a concerted action *enforced* and *supervised* by a centralized super regime – that is a global regime – to put the burdensome measures into practice.
- **Redistribution of resources from developed affluent societies to developing parts of the world to end poverty:** This will certainly lower the living standards of many people in the world but, at the same time, help billions of otherwise extremely poor people in developing and developed societies alike.
- **Global introduction of a needs-based industry:** Avoiding the waste of the competitive market and extravagant consumerism to satisfy collective and more frugal needs. No profit at the expense of the poor.
- **Taking steps to slow down overpopulation:** Overpopulation is the ultimate threat for the survival of humankind given the shortages of energy, food and water. A strict global one-child policy must be introduced for the transition period (as already implemented in China).
- **Regulating food and water supply:** The squandering of food and water, particularly in affluent societies, must be stopped by appropriate measures. The technology of extracting drinkable water from sea water must be further developed.
- **Solving the energy problem:** Appropriate steps must be taken to find new and clean ways of power generation and to perfect the technological development of water and solar energy.
- **Protecting non-human nature:** The exploitation of the earth, for example the clearing of the rain forest in the Amazon and the massive emissions of carbon dioxide, must be stopped (or reduced to a reasonable amount) to save the planet and its inhabitants.
- **Modern technology:** The development of technology is key to the survival of humankind, even though it involves dangers as well (nuclear power stations, weapons of mass destructions, etc.). However, to develop carefully new technologies to solve some of the contemporary problems seems to be a necessary step.
- **Weapons:** Weapons of mass destruction such as atomic bombs must be reduced and eventually destroyed.

Certainly, the abovementioned measures are burdensome, but they are necessary to save humanity from universal disaster. It might well be the case that there are other equally important burdensome measures that have not been listed here. However, this list is a promising start. It is not argued that there are no other ways to save humanity and non-human nature, but I do think that this proposal is a reasonable way of securing the *long-term existence of humanity*. Burdensome measures require extraordinary methods of enforcement. One might object that it is unrealistic to put the measures into practice because they are too demanding. Nevertheless, one should keep in mind that there is a point of no return, where 'humanity' must either decide whether to live as before and eventually perish, or to take the chance to fight against universal disaster by adopting appropriate but burdensome measures. The following list describes some important methods that will facilitate the transition period in a responsible and sustainable way.

Methods

- **Transitional agreement to install a global regime with enough power to enforce all burdensome measures:** A growing fondness of liberties and freedoms must be (partially) sacrificed in order to guarantee that the measures will be successfully enforced in a reasonable time. After the transition period, which will certainly last for several years if not decades, the global community will be asked either to vote in support of the global regime or to replace it with a different political system. The power relation between the global regime and the former autonomous nation states is more or less comparable with the states of the USA and the federal government.
- **Moral enhancement:** To deal with the rather aggressive nature of human beings and to enhance pro-social behaviour as well as to facilitate moral action, it seems obvious that all human beings should be morally enhanced once the appropriate technology is available. This new type of morally enhanced human being is the best means to prevent universal disaster (see below).
- **Intelligent artificial life forms:** Recent technological development concerning intelligent artificial life forms suggests that within the next two to three decades – for the first time in human history – it might be possible for intelligent robots to do most of the necessary work with minimum human supervision.

Whether it is really possible to stop the negative consequences of modern technology cannot be foreseen with certainty. It might even be possible that moral enhancement alone is sufficient for preventing universal disaster. It seems reasonable to assume, however, that morally enhanced human beings would act quite differently – that is, *in a more responsible way* – in comparison with non-enhanced human beings, on a variety of occasions without undermining their own moral agency. The following section will examine this point in more detail.

Refined Marxism and the New (Morally Enhanced) Human Being – The Last Chance?

Since the 1970s Jonas repeatedly and convincingly claims, humanity has been faced with universal disaster by virtue of the great dangers of the technological development and its negative consequences for modern civilization. For the first time in history, human beings have reached such a high level of technological development that they are able to destroy the whole world through, for example, the misuse of weapons of mass destruction in (world) wars, terrorism and severe accidents of global dimensions, such as the explosion of nuclear power stations either caused by human error or nature itself (e.g. Fukushima, Japan, in 2011). Furthermore, modern humanity has caused severe global and civilization-changing problems, such as climate change (i.e. global warming), new artificially produced viruses and bacteria (e.g. danger of bioterrorism) and overfishing, as well as water and food shortages. Humankind is also responsible for an unrivalled quantity of poverty in the world – mainly in the developing countries. But even within the most highly developed countries poverty has become a serious problem, which is augmented by the exploitative nature of private and corporate industry – that is, the free market – in addition to an almost unrestricted form of egoism in capitalist societies. The global financial crisis caused by so-called approved banks in recent years – which almost catapulted humanity back to the Stone Age – is a good example of the greed of many of the people who are in charge either of the financial system or politics. This is why Jonas can reasonably claim that humanity is on the verge of universal disaster.

Many prominent scholars, such as the famous physicist Stephen Hawking and the influential scientist Martin Rees, share Jonas' view concerning the great danger for both humanity and non-human nature due to (the negative consequences of) modern technology and the rather aggressive nature of human beings. For example, Hawking, characteristically, claims:

> There's a sick joke that the reason we haven't been visited by aliens is that when a civilisation reaches our state of development, it becomes unstable and destroys itself [...] The long-term survival of the human race will be safe only if we spread out into space, and then to other stars. This won't happen for at least 100 years so we have to be very careful. Perhaps, we must hope that genetic engineering will make us wise and less aggressive. (Hawking 2006)

In addition, Rees quite distinctly claims that 'the odds are no better than fifty-fifty that our present civilisation on the Earth will survive to the end of the present century' (Rees 2003, 8). Both recent statements confirm Jonas' warning. Many important contemporary scholars in ethics and moral philosophy working on the topic of moral and cognitive enhancement – even though they do not directly refer to Jonas – believe that humanity is, indeed, on the verge of universal disaster. They hold the view that human beings must (or should) be morally or cognitively enhanced in order to keep up with technological development (Douglas 2008, 2011; Fenton 2010; Harris 2011, 2012a, 2012b; Persson and Savulescu 2008, 2010, 2011). As a result, (moral) enhancement – that is, the *new* human being – is seen as *the ultimate weapon* against universal disaster.

Jonas rejects this idea because he wholeheartedly believes that we should not engage in altering the nature of human beings (Jonas 1979, 392; Jonas 1987). Whether Jonas would also take side with the particular arguments brought to the fore by some prominent opponents of moral enhancement such as Fukuyama (2002), Kass (2002), Habermas (2003), Annas (2005) and Jotterand (2011) cannot be examined in this chapter. It is correct to assume, however, that the opponents in general adopt a precautionary approach as well; they are against the use of biotechnology to modify human nature in order to save humanity from its destruction. They believe that the risks of irreversibly altering human nature by genetic means are too high because, first, one cannot revoke the process if something went wrong and, second, researchers are not yet capable of performing this intervention safely. This general line of reasoning is independent of other possible arguments against moral and cognitive enhancement; for example, altering human nature is against God and nature itself, it is against human rights, it undermines human dignity as well as free will, it subverts moral agency and it wrongfully modifies human nature (which is seen as a fixed set of biological traits).

Before I say something about my own view in support of moral enhancement to save humanity from destruction in the context of the previous discussion, I want to add a table on the methods of moral and cognitive enhancement and discuss briefly some possible goals of enhancement. Both are important parts in understanding and appreciating the debate on moral enhancement more properly.

Moral and Cognitive Enhancement

Table 11.2 Methods of moral and cognitive enhancement

Enhancement	Means of enhancement	
	Biomedical	Non-biomedical (i.e. traditional)
Cognitive	Pharmaceutical means (e.g. drugs), genetic means (genetic therapy), breeding by using biotechnology Harris 2011, 2012a, 2012b The use of drugs to enhance cognitively a human being is possible.	Education, socialization, parental and peer group guidance, social and personal example, role-modelling, ethical reflexion, transmission of knowledge and skills, breeding by choosing a supposedly intelligent partner

continued ...

Enhancement	Means of enhancement	
	Biomedical	**Non-biomedical (i.e. traditional)**
Non-cognitive (i.e. moral)	Pharmaceutical means (e.g. the drug citalopram affects the neurotransmitter serotonin, which enhances the pro-social behaviour in patients, Crockett et al. 2010), genetic means (genetic therapy), breeding by using biotechnology	Stimulus avoidance, increasing personal costs to oneself, breeding by choosing a supposed moral partner
	Douglas 2008, Faust 2009, Persson and Savulescu 2008, 2010, 2011	
	It is currently impossible to enhance morally human beings (long-term) via emotion modulation (only in a very limited sense) or by genetic therapy.	

The above classification helps to understand the rather complex nature of moral and cognitive enhancement. For example, there is a lively and highly important contemporary debate between Douglas, Persson and Savulescu, on the one side, and Harris, on the other, regarding the vital issue of whether human beings should be enhanced cognitively (Harris) or morally (Douglas, Persson and Savulescu). Harris is, in general, concerned with the possibility that a direct (emotional) moral enhancement could undermine free will since human beings are then unable to decide to act immorally because the emotions are modified directly without appealing to cognition (he prefers to enhance cognition so that an enhanced rationality together with education improve moral behaviour). This is an important objection that should be taken seriously. However, Harris's objection is based on the tacit assumption that human beings *have* free will. This is, in turn, a highly contested claim among scholars in the contemporary debate on the existence of free will and hence moral agency. In other words, it might well be the case that human beings have *no* free will, which would, therefore, undermine Harris's objection in the first place. The opponents, however, could still claim that emotional moral enhancement is yet another way of adding a further valuable *determinant* in order to influence moral behaviour in a deterministic or semi-deterministic setting.

Furthermore, Jotterand (2011) forcefully claims that moral enhancement cannot make human beings more virtuous by neural manipulation, but only by the reflective exercise of moral agency (Jotterand favours a virtue ethical approach). He has been criticized by Schaefer (2011) and Dees (2011). Schaefer, referring to Douglas (2008) and Persson and Savulescu (2008), points out that the *reasonableness* of enhancement depends on the particular *goal* of moral enhancement (see below). For example, it could be the case that moral enhancement does not make people more virtuous (Jotterand), but that it only leads to better consequences (e.g. Persson and Savulescu). Dees, instead, claims – among other things – that Jotterand fails to prove that altering moral emotions (necessarily) implies that human beings have no moral agency at all. On the other hand, he acknowledges Jotterand's point of view that one can evaluate modified moral emotions – which putatively lead to an improvement in morality – only if there is a reliable moral measuring standard in the first place.

The following classification of the appropriate goal(s) of moral enhancement and the dangers that could be avoided should deepen our understanding of whether the project of moral enhancement is worth while and should be put into practice.

The Goals of Moral Enhancement

The following (incomplete) list of the main goal(s) of moral enhancement[11] may influence the evaluation of moral enhancement itself because some of the supposed goals could be better accomplished than other more demanding ones:

- Moral enhancement should make people more virtuous (e.g. virtue ethics).
- Moral enhancement should make people more disposed to act rightly (e.g. deontology).
- Moral enhancement should improve the moral motivations in human beings.
- Moral enhancement should lead to the best consequences of human action (e.g. consequentialism).

Contrary to what Harris claims, I believe that moral enhancement does not undermine moral agency or free will if people still have the opportunity to act against their better knowledge (see also Douglas 2008, 2011). Faust (2009) provided a convincing case; his thought-experiment MoralKinder+ showed that moral enhancement would not *determine* but (positively) *influence* our decisions (Faust 2009, 404). It is my belief that the following moral defects – which lead to social evils – could be prevented or reduced by making moral enhancement a global requirement:

- racism and anti-Semitism
- organized criminality, e.g. human trafficking, forced prostitution, corruption
- terrorism, e.g. religious and political fanaticism
- greed for profit and money, corruption
- enviousness
- criminal acts
- aggressive nature of human beings.

If moral enhancement leads, in general, to pro-social behaviour as well as moral action, and if it is possible to calm down successfully the aggressive nature of

11 See, for example, Schaefer 2011, 10–11.

human beings without undermining moral agency, then it is a moral requirement to develop further such biotechnological means to prevent moral defects that lead to social evils. It would be *irresponsible* not to enhance morally human beings against the background of the tremendous dangers of misusing modern technology for egoistical goals, for example religious and political terrorism.

Hans Jonas and global responsibility – the case for moral enhancement

One might think that my proposal is radically different from Jonas' approach to responsibility, but this would be a mistake. It does seem that Jonas only fears the dangers of modern sciences and technology (Jonas 1976, 94–5), on the one hand, and that I am rather concerned with eliminating the aggressiveness of human nature by promoting the development of biotechnology in order to accomplish pro-social behaviour and eventually moral action, on the other hand. However, one must acknowledge the fact that, even according to Jonas – though he might have been unaware of this – the problem is not the supposed dangerousness of modern sciences and technology; the real danger – even for Jonas – lies in *deficient* human nature. Humanity is able to *misuse* the products of modern technology and, therefore, act in an irresponsible way. For example, no one would blame the knife for being stabbed into another person's body. It is not the tool but the user who is responsible for misusing the tool. If humanity could be made more responsible by moral enhancement, then both human beings and non-human nature would greatly profit because many social and natural defects would be prevented.

A further objection could be that the above proposal is too demanding and against Jonas' general line of reasoning regarding the burdensome measures and methods of implementation needed to save humanity from its destruction. First, the proposal is demanding but severe global problems need far-reaching global solutions; even Jonas suggests – for the transition period – to adopt a communist tyranny of a well-informed and benevolent elite to implement more effectively the unpopular measures, for example lowering the standards of living, austerities and other hardships. Whether it is also possible simply to enhance humanity morally without taking further steps of reorganizing the global political structure remains to be seen. Second, it is correct that Jonas rejects the idea of enhancement to alter the nature of human beings. But, as we have seen, the real danger – also according to Jonas – is the *misuse* of modern technology. In my view, Jonas' own account would have prompted him to use biotechnology to calm down aggressive human nature once there was a safe and successful way of achieving the goal(s) of moral enhancement. As Persson and Savulescu have repeatedly claimed, the great dangers of modern technology and its misuse must be absorbed by moral enhancement. This is global responsibility at its best.

Conclusions

A refined Marxism could save humanity and non-human nature from universal disaster. The morally enhanced 'new' human being will be less aggressive and act in a more responsible way than humans hitherto. Jonas' reservations concerning the modification of the nature of human beings should be taken seriously, at least as long as modern technology is unable to enhance morally human beings in a safe way. Additionally, in the long term, artificial intelligent life forms will be able to do almost all *necessary* work so that the new human being will be able to live a life of leisure. Nature is able to fulfil the needs of all morally enhanced human beings on certain conditions, such as proper regulation to avoid overpopulation, adequate water and food supply, as well as enough energy to cover all necessary consumption. However, nature is unable to do the same for human beings who are greedy for profit and money. The general idea is that most morally enhanced human beings will be in accord with other fellow members and non-human nature – that is, animals, plants and non-organic life – since their behaviour is *influenced* – but not determined – to act in a more moral and responsible way. It has not been argued that *all* morally enhanced human beings will *always* act morally, rather that a huge number of human beings will, it is hoped, act in a more moral way than before their enhancement. Against this background, there is no doubt that Jonas' imperative of responsibility 'to act so that the effects of one's actions are compatible with the permanence of genuine human life' will not be ignored but become the maxim for morally enhanced human beings.

References

Annas, George J. 2005. *American Bioethics: Crossing Human Rights and Health Law Boundaries.* New York: Oxford University Press.

Crockett, Molly J., Luke Clark, Marc D. Hauser and Trevor W. Robbins. 2010. 'Serotonin Selectively Influences Moral Judgment and Behavior through Effects on Harm Aversion'. *Proceedings of the National Academy of Sciences* 107(40): 17433–8.

Dees, Richard H. 2010. 'Moral Philosophy and Moral Enhancements'. *AJOB Neuroscience* 2(4): 12–13.

Douglas, Thomas. 2008. 'Moral Enhancement'. *Journal of Applied Philosophy* 25(3): 228–45.

———. 2011. 'Moral Enhancement via Direct Emotion Modulation: A Reply to John Harris'. *Bioethics.* doi: 10.1111/j.1467-8519.2011.01919.x.

Faust, Halley S. 2009. 'Kindness, Not Compassion, in Healthcare'. *Cambridge Quarterly of Healthcare Ethics* 18(3): 287–99.

Fenton, Elizabeth. 2010. 'The Perils of Failing to Enhance: A Response to Persson and Savulescu.' *Journal of Medical Ethics* 36(3): 148–51.

Fukuyama, Francis. 2002. *Our Posthuman Future: Consequences of the Biotechnology Revolution.* New York: Farrar Straus & Giroux.

Habermas, Jürgen. 2003. *The Future of Human Nature.* Cambridge: Polity Press.

Harris, John. 2011. 'Moral Enhancement and Freedom'. *Bioethics* 25(2): 102–11.

———. 2012a. '"Ethics Is for Bad Guys!" Putting the "Moral" into Moral Enhancement'. *Bioethics*. doi: 10.1111/j.1467-8519.2011.01946.x.

———. 2012b. 'Moral Progress and Moral Enhancement'. *Bioethics.* doi: 10.1111/j.1467-8519.2012.01965.x.

Hawking, Stephen. 2006. 'News 3'. *The Guardian* (London) 8 March 2006.

Jonas, Hans. 1976. 'Responsibility Today: The Ethics of an Endangered Future'. *Social Research* 43(1): 77–97.

———. 1979. *Das Prinzip Verantwortung: Versuch einer Ethik für die technologische Zivilisation.* Frankfurt am Main: Insel Verlag.

———. 1985. *The Imperative of Responsibility: In Search of an Ethics for the Technological Age*. Chicago: University of Chicago Press.

———. 1987. *Technik, Medizin und Ethik: Zur Praxis des Prinzips Verantwortung*, 7th edn. Frankfurt am Main: Suhrkamp.

Jotterand, Fabrice. 2011. '"Virtue Engineering" and Moral Agency: Will Post-Humans Still Need the Virtues?' *AJOB Neuroscience* 2(4): 3–9.

Kass, Leon R. 2002. *Life, Liberty and the Defense of Dignity: The Challenge for Bioethics.* San Francisco: Encounter Books.

Persson, Ingmar, and Julian Savulescu. 2008. 'The Perils of Cognitive Enhancement and the Urgent Imperative to Enhance the Moral Character of Humanity'. *Journal of Applied Philosophy* 25(3): 162–77.

———. 2010. 'Moral Transhumanism'. *Journal of Medicine and Philosophy* 35(6): 656–69.

———. 2011. 'Getting Moral Enhancement Right: The Desirability of Moral Bioenhancement'. *Bioethics.* 10.1111/j.1467-8519.2011.01907.x.

Rees, Martin J. 2003. *Our Final Century: A Scientist's Warning.* Oxford: Heinemann.

Schaefer, Owen. 2011. 'What Is the Goal of Moral Engineering?' *AJOB Neuroscience* 2(4): 10–11.

Schmidt, Jan C. 2007. 'Die Aktualität der Ethik von Hans Jonas. Eine Kritik der Kritik des Prinzips Verantwortung'. *Deutsche Zeitschrift für* Philosophie 55(4): 545–69.

Weisskopf, Walter A. 1983. 'Moral Responsibility for the Preservation of Humankind.' *Social Research* 50(1): 98–125.

Bibliography of Hans Jonas' Works

1958. *The Gnostic Religion: The Message of the Alien God and the Beginnings of Christianity*. Boston: Beacon Press.

1966. *The Phenomenon of Life: Towards a Philosophical Biology*. Chicago: The University of Chicago Press.

1969. *Ethical Aspects of Experimentation with Human Subjects*. Boston: American Academy of Arts and Sciences.

1971. 'Change and Permanence: On the Possibility of Understanding History'. In *Die Interpretation in der Altertumswissenschaft*, edited by Wolfgang Schmid, 26–54. Bonn: Bouvier Verlag.

1974. *Philosophical Essays: From Ancient Creed to Technological Man*. Chicago and London: Chicago University Press.

1976. 'On the Power or Impotence of Subjectivity'. In *Philosophical Dimensions of the Neuro-Medical Sciences*, edited by Stuart F. Spicker und H. Tristam Engelhardt, 143–61. Dordrecht: Kluwer.

1978. *On Faith, Reason and Responsibility: Six Essays*. San Francisco: Harper and Row.

1984. *The Imperative of Responsibility: In Search of an Ethics for the Technological World.* Chicago and London: The University of Chicago Press.

1996. *Mortality and Morality: A Search for the Good after Auschwitz*. Evanston: Northwestern University Press.

2010 ff. *Kritische Gesamtausgabe der Werke von Hans Jonas*, edited by Dietrich Böhler, Michael Bongardt, Holger Burckhardt, Christian Wiese and Walther Ch. Zimmerli. Freiburg, Berlin and Vienna: Rombach.

Index

References to footnotes consist of the page number followed by the letter 'n' followed by the number of the footnote, e.g. 84n18 refers to note no. 18 on page 84. References to tables are shown in **bold**.

abundance, and Marxism 29, 31, 32, 33, 34–5, 37, 198
Adorno, Theodor W. 153, 155
ageing
  authenticity (gratitude vs creativity) 55–6
  bioconservatism and ethics of gratitude 63–4, 70
    Daniel Callahan 57, 63, 67–9
    Hans Jonas 57, 63, 64–6
    Leon Kass 57, 61, 63, 66–7, 68, 69
  human lifespan extension issue 56–8
  mortality/ageing as a gift 58–9
  posthumanist stance 59–62, 69–70
  posthumanists and consequentialist debate 62–3
  see also health; medicine; prolongation of life; teleological naturalism and medical practice
ageism 62, 68, 70
agency
  human agency 176, 179
  hyperagency 55, 66–7
alarmism 21, 75, 149, 150
  see also enlightened catastrophism; prophecy
ambiguity 28–9, 37–8, 40
analytical philosophy 1, 154n11, 175, 185
anguish, vs fear 84
animals
  Animal Protection Act (Switzerland) 164
  and Jonas' ethics 3–4
  as moral objects 96
Annas, George J. 203
Anthropic Principle 159
anthropocentrism
  and animals 96
  and Jonas' ethics 3, 9, 10, 151, 157n22, 164, 188–9
  and Marxism 195
anthropology
  anthropological error of utopia 37, 39
  Christian anthropology 107
  and discourse of rationality 95, 97
  and Jonas' concept of God 122
  and Jonas' ethics 3, 148, 149, 150, 164
  philosophical anthropology 157, 182
anthropomorphism 39, 157
Apel, Karl-Otto 45, 47, 49, 93, 97, 161n29
apocalyptic perspective 12–15, 20–21, 23, 148, 152, 177
  see also destruction; risk moderation; universal disaster
Arendt, Hannah 64
Aristotle
  Aristotelian–Christian ethics 44
  Aristotelian physics and biology 172
  causae finales 130
  chorus' fright 80
  golden mean 177
  and Jonas' *Organism and Freedom* 157
  nature (physis) vs *techne* 153
  nature's intrinsic goals 129
  neo-Aristotelian teleological naturalism 131, 132, 136
  political dimension of ethics 179–80
  rationality 95
  virtues 154n10
Aronson, Ronald 55
artificial, vs natural 153, 179
artificial intelligence 201, 207

asymmetry of power 3, 162, 163, 189
atheism 115, 123
atom bomb 20–21
  see also nuclear weapons
Augustine, Saint 107, 109–10, 121, 123
Auschwitz 44n6, 120, 121
  see also Nazism
authenticity 55–6, 57, 62, 70, 118
autonomy 43–4, 95, 139, 157, 189n4

'back to nature' school 178
Bacon, Francis
  vs Aristotle 153
  Baconian project 12–13, 147, 150, 151, 152, 165
  Baconian project and Jonas' theory of power 190–191
  Baconian project and Marxism 15, 29, 31, 34, 187, 191
  nature and causality 130
bad/evil
  and heuristics of fear 3, 16, 80–81
  imagined and distant 82n14
  supreme evil 18–19, 187
  theodicy 40, 46, 64, 121
  see also good/goodness
Bailey, Ronald 60–61, 62
Baudrillard, Jean 156
Bayertz, Kurt 43
Beck, Ulrich 149
Bellini, Giovanni, *Madonna* 37
Big Bang 159
Bijker, Wiebe 166
bioconservatism 57, 61, 63–9, 70
biodiversity, decline of 2–3
bioethics, potentiality concept 159
biology
  Aristotelian biology 172
  biological functioning 136–7, 139, 140–141
  biological individuality concept 141
  biological roots of responsibility 27–9
  philosophical biology 115–17, 120
  synthetic biology 164
  teleonomy 159
  see also human organism
biotechnology
  dangers of 1, 2, 65
  and extension of healthspan 60–61, 62
  hyperagentic tendency of 67
  and modernization of ageing 67
  and moral enhancement 203, **203–4**, 206
  and mortality 69
  and posthumanism 57
  see also genetic engineering; human cloning; tissue regeneration
Bloch, Ernst 29, 35–6, 37, 38, 153, 177, 199
Böhler, Dietrich 46n7, 47–8, 48n11, 49, 131n5
Böhme, Gernot 152n6
Bonaldi, Claudio 110n11
Bongardt, Michael 5
Boorse, Christopher 136–7, 138, 139, 140–141, 142
Bostrom, Nick 57, 60, 62, 63
Brave New World (Aldous Huxley) 183
Briggle, Adam 159n26
Brundtland Commission/Report (1987) 150, 164–5
Buber, Martin 50, 107
Bultmann, Rudolf 107, 120
Burckhart, Holger 4, 5
Buyx, Alena M. 135

Callahan, Daniel 57, 63, 67–9
Campbell, Joseph 24
Čapek, Karel, *The Makropulos Case* 65
capitalism
  Jonas' critique of 12, 14–15, 31–5, 36, 38, **192–3**, 199
  see also Marxism; Marxism and moral enhancement
Caplan, Arthur 60, 62–3
Cassandra's paradox 74–6
  see also alarmism; prophecy
Castoriadis, Cornelius 83n16
catastrophism, *see* enlightened catastrophism
caution dimension 17, 19, 161, 163, 164, 189, 190
  see also precautionary principle
Chernobyl nuclear accident 2, 73
children, *see* one-child policy; parent-child relationship

Christ, *see* Jesus Christ
Christianity
  Aristotelian/Judeo–Christian ethics 44
  Augustinian theology 107, 109–10, 121, 123
  Christian anthropology 107
  Christian charity 50
  Christian theology 106, 107, 114
  Christian theology and Jonas 106, 107–10, 121, 180, 182
  and Gnosticism 113
  Pauline theology 107–8, 110, 114, 121, 123
  and teleological naturalism 129–30
  Ten Commandments 25
  see also Gnosticism; God; Jesus Christ; religion; speculative theology
classless society 15, 33, 34, 35–6, 38, 187, 194, 197–8
  see also communism; Marxism; socialism
climate change 2, 4, 73n2, 146, 150, 187, 202
cloning, *see* human cloning
co-responsibility 42n2, 44–50
cognitive enhancement **203**, 204
  see also Marxism and moral enhancement
communicative competence 96, 99, 100
communism 14, 29, 32, 33, 34, 35
  see also classless society; Marxism; socialism
communitarianism 56
community 28, 44, 45, 94, 98, 138, 201
compassion, ethics of 154
consequentialistic ethics 51, 163n36, 205
constructivism 150, 161
contractualism 154
cosmology, Anthropic Principle 159
cosmos 44, 111, 113, 115, 118, 122, 172
creativity
  authenticity as 62, 70
  vs gratitude 55–6, 70
critical rationalism 159n25

Darwinism 172
  see also evolution
de Grey, Aubrey 60, 61, 62, 64, 67n3
death
  death drive 39
  and health 66, 67–8
  and Heidegger 114
  premature death 64, 65, 66, 68, 142
  tolerable death concept 68
  see also immortality; mortality
'Death' (Thomas Nagel) 61–2
deconstructivism 150
Deepwater Horizon oil spill (2010) 3, 148
Dees, Richard H. 204, 205
democracy
  capitalist democracy 33, **192–3**, 199
  and heuristics of fear 48
  and participation 99
demythologization 107, 120
deontological ethics 4, 50, 96, 154n10, 163n36, 205
Descartes, René 19, 118, 157, 172
destruction
  and principle of existence 10
  self-destruction 39, 40
  and technology 9, 11, 13, 25, 31
  see also apocalyptic perspective; universal disaster
dialogical-discursive ethics, *see* discourse-ethics
disability
  and biotechnology 2
  see also inclusion and disability
discourse-ethics
  co-responsibility and Jonas' theory 45–9
  co-responsibility in dialogical-discursive future ethics 49–50
  inclusion and disability 93–4, 97–8
  and Jonas' ethics 154
  moral courage vs fatalism 50–51
  rationality principles 161n29
  responsibility and practical philosophy/ethics 41–5
discourse universe 45, 47
disengagement theory 68
Douglas, Thomas 204
dualism
  Cartesian 118, 172
  Gnostic 77, 111–12, 114–15, 116, 122, 123

see also fact and value
Dupuy, Jean-Pierre 82n14, 152n6, 155, 164

ecology
ecological ethics 50n15
laws of 10, 13, 29
see also environmental science
economy
and apocalyptic perspective 12–13, 14–15
see also capitalism; Marxism
education, inclusive vs integrated 94, 99
Eliade, Mircea 24
Embryo Protection Act (Germany, 1990) 164
emergency ethics 12, 131, 132n7, 147
empiricism 130, 134, 159n25, 186
energy problem 2, 29–30, 200
see also natural resources
enhancement technologies 56
enlightened catastrophism 82n14
see also alarmism; prophecy
Enlightenment, and moral norms 25
environmental science 165
Epicurus 61
Eranos group 24
Erikson, Erik 70
essence, *see* human essence
ethics
and anthropology 3, 148, 149, 150, 164
bioethics 159
Christian ethics 44
consequentialistic ethics 51, 163n36, 205
deontological ethics 4, 50, 96, 154n10, 163n36, 205
duty-based ethics 44
ecological ethics 50n15
emergency ethics 12, 131, 132n7, 147
ethical fear 81
ethics of compassion 154
ethics of happiness 96
ethics of the future 185
internet ethics 50n15
and metaphysics 148, 149, 154–6, 166–7, 181–3
political dimension of 179–80
and praxis 161
repair ethics 148
and technology 154, 176
in university science curricula 147
virtue ethics 154, 204, 205
see also discourse-ethics; ethics of responsibility (Hans Jonas); *Imperative of Responsibility, The* (Hans Jonas); Jonas' philosophy of nature and ethics
ethics of responsibility (Hans Jonas)
apocalyptic perspective 12–14, 20–21
common destiny of man and nature 9–12
Marxism and the apocalypse 14–15
ontological imperative 20–21
prophecy rule and heuristics of fear 15–18, 20, 21
unacceptable risks principle 18–20
see also discourse-ethics; Jonas, Hans
eupraxia 94, 97, 98
evil, *see* bad/evil
evolution 26, 115, 117, 141–2, 159, 172, 181
see also natural evolution
exclusion 94–5
see also inclusion and disability
existential analysis 107, 108, 109, 112, 113, 114, 123
existentialism 57, 62, 180
exploitation
of natural resources 1, 2, 4, 12–13, 200
of nature 31, 34, 191, 194

fact and value 25–7, 159
fairness, principle of 47
fatalism, dangers of 49, 50–51
fear
vs anguish 84
disinterested fear 79, 80
and guilt 74
principle of fear vs principle of hope 15, 33
rational fear 79–84
spiritual/ethical fear 81
see also heuristics of fear
Fedoryka, Kateryna 136
Feuerbach, Ludwig 122
Foucault, Michel 95

Frankena, William K. 160
Frankfurt School 155n16, 166
free will, and moral enhancement 204, 205
freedom
  and Augustine 121
  and Jonas 108–10, 114, 116, 121, 152, 158, 161, 182
  and Kant 41, 109
Freud, Sigmund, death instinct 39
Frodeman, Robert 149
Frogneux, Nathalie 5
Fukushima nuclear accident (2011) 2, 73, 148, 150, 202
Fukuyama, Francis 203
future
  ethics of the future 16, 185
  future generations 3, 63, 68–9, 70, 88–9, 152, 162, 165
  future of humanity vs nature 188–9
  imperceptible future 76
  responsibility for the future 158, 167
futurology 38, 82

Gadamer, Hans-Georg 173
Garvey, James 73n2
generativity 70
genetic engineering 57, 60, 150, 187, 202
  see also biotechnology; human cloning; tissue regeneration
genetic enhancement, dangers of 2
Germany
  Auschwitz 44n6, 120, 121
  Embryo Protection Act (1990) 164
  Nazism 105, 106, 173
Gewirth, Alan 132n7
Gilje, Nils 134
global warming 2, 4, 187, 202
  see also climate change
Gnosticism 77, 90, 106, 110–115, 116, 120, 121–2, 123
  see also Christianity; God; religion
God
  benevolent 185
  vs cosmos 111
  vs demiurge 113
  'God is dead' 24
  and Heidegger 114–15
  imago dei (God's image) 39, 40, 95
  and Jonas 106, 117–22, 151, 180, 182
  Judeo-Christian ethics 44
  and Kant 123
  'Let there be light' 26
  and nature 130
  and 'ontological proof' 20
  and Pascal's wager 77, 78
  see also Christianity; Gnosticism; Jesus Christ; religion
Goethe, Johann Wolfgang von 156
Goffman, Erwin 73, 75n3
good/goodness
  bonum humanum 38–9
  good for the sake of good 110
  goodness of creation/Being 26, 27, 28, 40, 64, 180, 185
  and heuristics of fear 3, 16, 80–81
  supreme good 18–19, 187
  see also bad/evil
Gordon, John-Stewart 5
gratitude
  and bioconservatism 63–9
  vs creativity 55–6, 70
Greens 178
Greisch, Jean 79n9
Gronke, Horst 47, 49
Grunwald, Armin 151
Guernica (Pablo Picasso) 42n2
guilt 37, 43, 44n6, 45, 51, 74, 177
Gulf of Mexico, *Deepwater Horizon* oil spill (2010) 3, 148
Gulliver's Travels (Jonathan Swift) 65

Habermas, Jürgen 97, 150, 152n6, 154n11, 155n16, 161n29, 203
happiness
  ethics of 96
  see also eupraxia
Harris, John 63, 65–6, 204, 205
Hastedt, Heiner 151, 154n10
Hauff, Volker 164n38
Hawking, Stephen 202
health
  and death 66, 67–8
  extension of healthspan 57, 60–63
  health as wholeness 66, 67, 68
  and medicine 133–9, 140, 142
  and overpopulation 2, 12–13

see also ageing; disability; medicine; prolongation of life; teleological naturalism and medical practice
Hegel, Georg Wilhelm Friedrich 1, 23n2, 180–181, 185
Heidegger, Martin
antiscientific irrationalism of 174
archaic language of 1, 23n2, 185
and Christianity 107
death 114
descending ontology 158n28
fear vs anguish 84
God 114–15
'having been thrown' 123
how to think vs what to do 156
indifferent world concept 116
and Jonas 80n10, 107, 108n6, 109, 114–15, 118, 120, 123
mortality 57
and Nazism 173
'ownedness' 110
and Paganism 115, 123
post-Nietzschean existentialism 180
'project to death' 118
Question Concerning Technology, The 175
'standing reserve' 56
Heilbroner, Robert 21n2
Herr, David 175
Herz, John 15, 176
heuristics of fear 3, 15–18, 20, 48, 74, 79n9, 80–83, 147, 163, 176–8, 190
see also fear
Hillman, Mayer 73n2
Hirsch Hadorn, Gertrude 151
Hobbes, Thomas 80, 130
Höffe, Otfried 44
Homo Ludens (Huizinga) 37
Homo sapiens vs Homo faber 153, 178
hope, principle of 15, 29, 33, 177
Horkheimer, Max 153, 155
Hubig, Christoph 149, 157n20
Huizinga, Johan, *Homo Ludens* 37
human agency 176, 179
human cloning 64–5, 183–4
see also biotechnology; genetic engineering; tissue regeneration
human essence
and ambiguity 28–9, 37–8, 40
and nature 9, 11–12, 188n2
and unacceptable risks principle 19–20, 163
and utopia 38
see also freedom; good/goodness; humanity/humankind
human nature, *see* human agency; human essence; human organism; humanity/humankind
human organism 133, 135, 136–7, 140–142
see also biology
humanity/humankind
and future of nature 188–9
hate against 30
'mankind is' imperative 19, 46
and moral enhancement 206
new human being 34, 187, 191, 194, 195–8, 203, 207
preservation of 3, 9, 23–4, 25, 27–8, 30–31, 40
purpose of evolution 117
and technical civilization 1–4, 25
see also human agency; human essence; self-preservation
Hume, David 130, 159
Husserl, Edmund 159, 174
Huxley, Aldous, *Brave New World* 183
hyperagency 55, 66–7

Illich, Ivan 85n20
immortality 60, 65–6, 67, 118–19, 123, 182
see also mortality
imperative
categorical 3, 20, 43, 97, 132n7, 179–80
ethical 93–4
hypothetical 20
'mankind is' imperative 19, 46
ontological 20–21
of responsibility 3, 77, 79, 150, 164, 165, 180, 190, 207
see also Imperative of Responsibility, The (Hans Jonas)
Imperative of Responsibility, The (Hans Jonas)
book's critiques 151
book's relevance 1, 185

and Cassandra's paradox 74
and discourse of rationality 97
English/German versions 1n1, 84n17, 153n7, 165n40
and fear 83–4
Levy's analysis
essay vs monograph 171
ethics and philosophy of life 172–3
ethics and technological age 175–9
Jonas vs Heidegger and Wittgenstein 173–4, 180
Jonas vs Kant and Aristotle 179–80
philosophical premises 180–184
reception of book 174–5
and Pascal's wager 76
and reflective modernity 149
and sustainable development 147, 150
and teleological naturalism 131, 132n7
and utopia 80n10
Weisskopf's review
assessment and overview 23–4, 39
biological roots of responsibility 27–9
dichotomy of fact and value 25–7
Marxism vs capitalism 31–4
Marxist utopia, critique of 29–31
utopia East and West 34–40
see also Jonas, Hans
inclusion and disability
ethical imperative issue 93–4
exclusion and discourse of rationality 94–5
inclusion vs integration 94
moral responsibility and disability 96
participation as a basic rights 97–100
inclusive education 94, 99
industrialization 1–2, 15, 25, 29
see also progress
infants, *see* parent-child relationship
integration
vs inclusion 94
integrated education 94, 99
internet ethics 50n15
intrinsic goals 129, 130, 131, 132n7, 133, 135, 140
Irrgang, B. 46
is/ought dichotomy 23, 25–6, 64, 130, 131, 132, 159, 160, 166
see also naturalistic fallacy

James, William 160
Japan, Fukushima nuclear accident (2011) 2, 73, 148, 150, 202
Jefferson, Thomas 58
Jesus Christ 108, 109, 113, 121
Jewish tradition, *see* Judaism
Jonas, Hans
archaic language 1, 23n2, 185
autobiographical details 80, 105, 107, 171
and Boorse 139
current relevance of 1–3, 185–6
and Heidegger 80n10, 107, 108n6, 109, 114–15, 118, 120, 123
and Kant 154, 154n10, 155n14, 157, 157n20, 163–4, 179–80
main theses
caution dimension 17, 19, 161, 163, 164, 189, 190
critique of capitalism 12, 14–15, 31–5, 36, 38, **192–3**
critique of Marxism 14–15, 29–36, 37, 38, 39, 186, 187, 191–8, **192–3**
freedom 108–10, 114, 116, 121, 152, 158, 161, 182
God 106, 117–22, 151, 180, 182
heuristics of fear 3, 15–18, 20, 48, 74, 79n9, 80–83, 147, 163, 176–8, 190
metaphysics 3, 9, 26–7, 122, 148, 149, 154–6, 159–60, 166–7, 181–3
mortality 57, 63, 64–6, 81–2
nature 3–4, 9–12, 39, 46, 152–3, 157–8
non-reciprocity 3, 161–3, 164, 189
overview of theses 3–4, 148–50
parent-child (newborn/infant) relationship 27–9, 31, 44, 74, 83, 88–9, 160–161, 189
power 190–191
rationality 39, 97, 166, 180–181, 182
religion 24, 26–7, 37–8, 39, 40, 85n20

science 24, 26–7, 39
technology 1, 17–18, 25, 29–30, 148, 186–7
works
'Ärztliche Kunst und menschliche Verantwortung' 132–3
'Concept of God after Auschwitz, The' 120, 121
Ethics for the Technological Age 131
'Gnosticism and Modern Nihilism' 114–15
'Immortality and the Modern Temper' 182
'Is God a Mathematician?' 131n4
'Medical Art and Human Responsibility' 129
Mortality and Morality 180
Organism and Freedom 157
Phenomenon of Life, The 83, 131, 138, 171, 181
'Responsibility Today: The Ethics of an Endangered Future' 4, 9–21, 187
Technology, Medicine and Ethics 165
see also ethics of responsibility (Hans Jonas); *Imperative of Responsibility, The* (Hans Jonas); Jonas' philosophy of nature and ethics; Jonas' philosophy of religion; Marxism and moral enhancement; risk moderation; teleological naturalism and medical practice
Jonas' philosophy of nature and ethics
concept of public philosophy 147
Jonas' approach 148–50
Jonas' critics 150–152
Jonas' diagnosis of current situation 152–3
Jonas on ethics and metaphysics 154–6
Jonas' theses 156–61
practice, action and solution 161–5
summary 165–7
see also Jonas, Hans
Jonas' philosophy of religion
background and Judaism 105–6
Bultmann and Heidegger's teaching 107
Christian theology
Augustine 107, 109–10, 121, 123
Paul 107–8, 110, 114, 121
Gnosticism 110–114, 121–2
Gnosticism and Heidegger 114–15
origin, God and the world 117–22
philosophical biology 115–17, 120
responsibility and religion 122–3
see also Jonas, Hans
Jotterand, Fabrice 203, 204, 205
Jouvenel, Bertrand de 35, 37
Judaism 105–6, 111, 113, 118–19, 120, 121, 123
Judeo-Christian ethics 44
Jung, Carl Georg 24

Kant, Immanuel
as-if 137, 139, 140, 157, 159
categorical imperative 20, 179–80
deontology 50
duty-based ethics 44
fact and value 25
freedom 41, 109
God and practical reason 123
good for the sake of good 110
and Jonas 154, 154n10, 155n14, 157, 157n20, 163–4, 179–80
and metaphysics 122
neo-Kantianism 132n7
rational beings 95
transcendentality 42n4
Kass, Leon 57, 61, 63, 66–7, 68, 69, 171, 203
Kemp, Peter 73n2
Kierkegaard, Søren 107, 109
Klages, Ludwig 178
'knowledge is power' 13, 187
Korsgaard, Christine 132n7, 141
Krebs, Angelika 151
Kuhlmann, Wolfgang 47

Law, John 166
Leibniz, Gottfried Wilhelm von 82
leisure society 35, 36–7, 199, 207
Lenk, Hans 162n35
Lévinas, Emmanuel 50, 105–6

Levy, David J. 5
  see also Imperative of Responsibility, The (Hans Jonas)
life-world 94, 100, 147, 149, 156, 165, 174

Madonna (Bellini) 37
Maio, Giovanni 135
Makropulos Case, The (Karel Čapek) 65
Malthus, Thomas Robert 10
mankind, *see* humanity/humankind
Marcion of Sinope 113
Marcuse, Herbert 36n3
Marxism
  and abundance 29, 31, 32, 33, 34–5, 37
  Jonas' critique of 14–15, 29–36, 37, 38, 39, 186, 187, 191–8, **192–3**
  see also capitalism; classless society; communism; hope, principle of; Marxism and moral enhancement; socialism
Marxism and moral enhancement
  Jonas' current relevance 185–6
  Jonas' ideas
    anthropocentrism and human nature 188–9
    Baconian ideal and theory of power 190–191
    notion of responsibility 189–90
    technology's negative consequences 186–7
  Jonas' rejection of Marxism 191–8
    comparison of capitalism and Marxism **192–3**
  moral enhancement
    avoiding disaster and political governance 199–200
    burdensome measures and methods 200–201
    moral and cognitive enhancement **203–4**, 204–5
    moral enhancement and Jonas' responsibility theory 206
    moral enhancement and refined Marxism 202–3, 207
    moral enhancement, goals of 205–6, 207
  see also Jonas, Hans
medicine
  and health 133–9, 140, 142
  and nature 134
  wish-fulfilling medicine 135, 136
  see also ageing; health; prolongation of life; teleological naturalism and medical practice
meliorism 14, 35, 85
metabolism 12–13, 45, 115, 116, 172, 173, 183
metaphysics
  and anthropocentrism 10
  and Jonas 3, 9, 26–7, 122, 148, 149, 154–6, 159–60, 166–7, 181–3
  and Kant 122
  and natural sciences 155, 156, 159
  post-metaphysical age 150, 154, 166
  rational metaphysics 155n14, 180
  see also ontology
Methuselah Project 67
Meyer-Abich, Klaus Michael 46n7
Mittelstraß, Jürgen 148
modernity
  and moral norms 25
  and nature 129–30
  reflective modernity 149
  see also postmodernism
Monod, Jacques 172
Moore, George E. 130, 159
moral enhancement, *see* Marxism and moral enhancement
moral obligations 25, 28, 38, 131, 132n7, 158
moral philosophy 16, 29
mortality
  and bioconservatism 63–4
  and biotechnology 69
  and cycle of generations 70
  as a gift 58–9, 63
  global decline in 2
  and Heidegger 57
  and Jonas 57, 63, 64–6, 81–2
  and Kass 63, 66–7
  and posthumanism 57
  and prolongation of life 31
  see also death; immortality

Nag Hammadi Library 111
Nagel, Thomas, 'Death' 61–2

nanotechnology 148, 164
natality concept 64–5
natural, vs artificial 153, 179
natural evolution 17, 87
    see also evolution
natural functioning 141
    see also teleological naturalism and medical practice
natural lifespan 57–9, 62–3, 65, 68
    see also health; medicine; prolongation of life; teleological naturalism and medical practice
natural philosophy 150, 164, 166
    see also philosophy of nature
natural resources
    exploitation of 1, 2, 4, 12–13, 200
    non-renewable 2, 4, 30, 187, 195
natural science
    abstinence of 26
    causality vs final cause 117
    limitations of 27, 29
    and metaphysics 155, 156, 159
    new type of 165
    and teleology 172
natural selection 142, 172
    see also evolution
naturalism, *see* Jonas' philosophy of nature and ethics; natural philosophy; philosophy of nature; teleological naturalism and medical practice
naturalistic fallacy 46, 59, 64, 123, 159, 166
    see also is/ought dichotomy
nature
    'back to nature' school 178
    exploitation of 31, 34, 191, 194
    and future of humanity 188–9
    and human essence 9, 11–12, 188n2
    integrity of 10, 179, 182
    intrinsic goals of 129, 130, 131, 132n7, 133, 135, 140
    and Jonas 3–4, 9–12, 39, 46, 152–3, 157–8
    and Marxism 196
    and material progress 31
    and medicine 134
    and modernity 129–30
    and moral enhancement 207
    natural vs artificial 153, 179
    non-human nature 185, 187–9, 194, 197, 200, 201, 202, 206, 207
    power over 10–11, 12–15, 29, 31, 34
    purposiveness of 157–60
    and responsibility as imputation 43
    and science 11, 12, 25, 130, 132
    and technology 148, 152–3, 165, 178
    see also biology; human organism; philosophy of nature; teleological naturalism and medical practice
Nazism 105, 106, 173
    see also Auschwitz
neurophilosophy 154n11
new human being 34, 187, 191, 194, 195–8, 203, 207
    see also humanity/humankind
newborns, *see* parent-child relationship
NGO ETC Group 164
Nietzsche, Friedrich 56, 74, 95, 122, 180, 196–7
nihilism 30, 114–15, 173, 180
nominalism 130
non-human nature 25, 178, 185, 187–9, 194, 197, 200, 201, 202, 206–7
    see also nature
non-reciprocity 3, 161–3, 164, 189
normativity 130, 131, 134, 138–9, 140–141, 142, 150
nuclear power 1, 2, 30, 187
    Chernobyl nuclear accident 2, 73
    Fukushima nuclear accident 2, 73, 148, 150, 202
nuclear weapons 20–21, 30, 200, 202
Nuland, Sherwin 58–9, 60, 63–4, 68, 70

Ockham's razor 130, 159n25
oil spills, *Deepwater Horizon* oil spill (2010) 3, 148
one-child policy 200
ontology 20–1, 23, 47, 107, 151, 155, 157, 158n23, 164, 182–3
    see also metaphysics
ought/is dichotomy, *see* is/ought dichotomy
overpopulation
    and abundance 198
    dangers of 1, 2, 12–13, 20–21, 187, 190
    and Marxism 196, 198

one-child policy 200
and posthumanism 63
and preservation of mankind 30–31
and surgical sterilization 139
see also ageing; health; medicine; prolongation of life

Paganism 115, 123
Parens, Eric 56, 62
parent-child relationship 27–9, 31, 44, 74, 83, 88–9, 160–161, 189
see also vulnerability
Parfit, Derek 66
participation 97–100
see also inclusion and disability
particularization 150
Pascal, Blaise 74, 76–9
Paul the Apostle 107–8, 110, 114, 121, 123
personal identity 66
Persson, Ingmar 204, 205, 206
phenomenology 131
philosophical anthropology 157, 182
philosophical biology 115–17, 120
philosophy
analytical philosophy 1, 154n11, 175, 185
critical rationalism 159n25
engaged philosophy 149, 165
existentialism 57, 62, 180
moral philosophy 16, 29
natural philosophy 150, 164, 166
neurophilosophy 154n11
nominalism 130
philosophy of life 115
political philosophy 189n4
of *praxis* 24
process philosophy 115
public philosophy 147
teleology 159, 172
Western philosophy and rationality 94–5
see also Jonas' philosophy of nature and ethics; Jonas' philosophy of religion; metaphysics; ontology; philosophy of nature; teleological naturalism and medical practice
philosophy of nature 3, 129, 136, 155n12, 157, 160n27, 166–7, 180
physics
Aristotelian physics 172
late-modern physics 159, 165
Picht, Georg 153
Plato 33, 95, **192**, 199
pluralism 156n19
pluralization 150
Polidowa, Sebastian 120n26
political philosophy 189n4
politics
political dimension of ethics 179–80
political governance 199–200
see also capitalism; democracy; Marxism; Marxism and moral enhancement; power
population explosion, *see* overpopulation
positivism 27, 39, 159n25
post-metaphysical age 150, 154, 166
see also metaphysics
posthumanism 57, 59–64, 65–6, 67n3, 68, 69–70
postmodernism 150, 181
see also modernity
potentiality 95, 158, 159
power
asymmetry of power 3, 162, 163, 189
centralized power and rationality 32–3
Jonas' theory of power 190–191
'knowledge is power' 13, 187
over nature 10–11, 12–15, 29, 31, 34
and responsibility 9, 28
see also nuclear power; politics
precautionary principle 3, 77, 147, 163, 164, 176
see also caution dimension
preservation
of humankind 3, 9, 23–4, 25, 27–8, 30–31, 40
self-preservation 10, 133, 134, 138, 141, 142
Prichard, Harold A. 138
Principle of Responsibility, The, see Imperative of Responsibility, The (Hans Jonas)
process philosophy 115
progress
Baconian ideal of 13, 29, 187
and nature 31

progressivism 14, 15
utopia of 39, 79
see also industrialization
prolongation of life 29, 30, 31, 56–8, 187
see also ageing; health; medicine; teleological naturalism and medical practice
prophecy
Cassandra's paradox 74–6
prophecy of doom vs prophecy of bliss 17, 21, 75, 163, 177, 187
see also alarmism; enlightened catastrophism
purposiveness 25, 26–7, 117, 157–60, 172, 185

rainforests, clearing of 1, 2, 200
rationality
and capitalism 12, 32
and centralized power 32–3
critical rationalism 159n25
and discourse-ethics 161n29
and exclusion 94–5
and Jonas 39, 97, 166, 180–181, 182
and moral status 98
and preservation of humanity 24
rational metaphysics 155n14, 180
and technology 38
and utopia 38
Rees, Martin 202
religion
and the death drive 39
and Jonas 24, 26–7, 37–8, 39, 40, 85n20
and moral obligations 25
and participation 99
and responsibility 122–3
In the United States 24
Western religion and anthropocentrism 10
see also Christianity; Gnosticism; God; Jesus Christ; Jonas' philosophy of religion; Judaism; speculative theology
repair ethics 148
reproduction 138, 139, 140, 141, 142
responsibility
co-responsibility 42n2, 44–50
imperative of 3, 77, 79, 150, 164, 165, 180, 190, 207
as imputation 43
'Medical Art and Human Responsibility' (Jonas) 129
and moral enhancement 189–90, 206
and non-reciprocity 161–3
ontological capacity for 182–3
possibility of 161
and power 9, 28
and practical philosophy/ethics 41–5
and religion 122–3
responsibility for existence/life 116, 163
responsibility for the future 158, 167
scientific responsibility 42n3, 49n12
see also ethics of responsibility (Hans Jonas); *Imperative of Responsibility, The* (Hans Jonas); moral obligations; parent-child relationship
Ricoeur, Paul 80
risk moderation
Jonas' current relevance 73–4
Jonas on unacceptable risks 18–20, 163
Jonas' theory
Cassandra's paradox 74–6
Pascal's wager 76–9
rational fear 79–84
risk internalization scale 84–8
vulnerability 86–7, 88–90
vs programmes of innovation 150
and *Technology Assessment* methodologies 164
Rousseau, Jean-Jacques 178

Salamander, Rachel 105
Sandel, Michael 55–6, 66
Savulescu, Julian 204, 205, 206
Schaefer, Owen 204
Schäfer, Lothar 150–151
Scheler, Max 131, 157
Schelling, Friedrich Wilhelm Joseph 157
Schmidt, Jan C. 5, 186
Scholem, Gerhardt 24
Schultz, Walter 153
Schweitzer, Albert 98, 164n37
science
and ethics in university curricula 147

and Jonas 24, 26–7, 39
and nature 11, 12, 25, 130, 132
and risk-taking 87–8
scientific responsibility 42n3, 49n12
see also ecology; environmental science; medicine; natural science; progress; technology
Scotus, Duns 130
Searle, John 96, 140
self-destruction 39, 40
see also destruction
self-preservation 10, 133, 134, 138, 141, 142
see also preservation
Sève, Bernard 75n3
Shaping Technology, Building Society (Bijker and Law) 166
Sikora, Jürgen 51n16
Skinner, B.F. 60, 183
Skirbekk, Gunnar 93, 96, 97, 99, 100, 134
socialism 14–15, 32, 33, 34, 35
see also classless society; communism; Marxism
Spaemann, Robert 46n7, 120n26
speculative theology 105, 120, 122
speech-act theory 96
Spinoza, Baruch 118
spirituality
and gratitude 55
spiritual fear 81
sterilization 135, 139
Stoicism 112–13, 129
Strauss, Leo 174
surgical sterilization 135, 139
sustainable development 147, 150, 164–5
Switzerland, Animal Protection Act 164
synthetic biology 164

Taminiaux, Jacques 75n3
technology
and capitalism 36
dangers of 1, 17–18, 25, 29–30, 148, 186–7
and destruction 9, 11, 13
and division of labor 35
enhancement technologies, 56
and ethics 154, 176
and Marxism 31–2, 34, 36, 194, 195–6
and nature 148, 152–3, 165, 178
new technologies 200
Question Concerning Technology, The (Heidegger) 175
and rationality 38
and risks 79, 87–8, 164
Shaping Technology, Building Society (Bijker and Law) 166
technical age 24, 161, 172, 178
technological civilization 13, 151
Technology Assessment methodologies 164, 165
see also apocalyptic perspective; artificial intelligence; biotechnology; progress; science
Teilhard de Chardin, Pierre 157
teleological naturalism and medical practice
nature and modernity 129–30
teleological naturalism
Jonas' theory 130–134, 140
and medical practice 133–9
summary and discussion 140–142
see also ageing; health; Jonas, Hans; medicine; prolongation of life
teleology 159, 172
teleonomy 159
Ten Commandments 25
Tennyson, Alfred 59
theodicy 40, 46, 64, 121
see also bad/evil
theology, *see* Christianity; speculative theology
threat
and denial 73
and fear 80–81
and inability to act 154
of nonbeing 39
see also apocalyptic perspective; destruction; heuristics of fear; technology; universal disaster
Thucydides 80
tissue regeneration 57, 60, 61
transcendence 38, 42n4, 106, 111, 114–15, 116
Tugendhat, Ernst 154n8

Ukraine, Chernobyl nuclear accident 2, 73

United States
  belief in leisure society 36
  form of capitalism 32, 34
  'liberalism' 35
  religion 24
  short-run material self-interest 23
  unionism 35
universal disaster 191, 194, 196, 198–203, 207
utilitarianism 96, 138, 154, 154n10
utopia
  anthropological error of 37, 39
  and biotechnology 65
  of both East and West 34–40
  and Ernst Bloch 37
  and heuristics of fear 3
  and Marxism 15, 29–31, 191, 194, 196–8
  and progress 39, 79
  and rationality 38

value and fact 25–7, 159
virtue ethics 154, 204, 205
Vogel, Lawrence 5, 180, 181
vulnerability 64, 73, 74, 83, 86–7, 88–90, 96, 153
  see also parent-child relationship

Weber, Max 23n2, 33, 155
Weisskopf, Walter A. 4, 185–6, 186n1
  see also Imperative of Responsibility, The (Hans Jonas)
Weizsäcker, Carl Friedrich von 153
Wendnagel, Johannes 151
Werner, Micha H. 5
Whitehead, Alfred North 115
Wilder, Billy 70
William of Ockham 130, 159n25
Williams, Bernard 65, 66
Wittgenstein, Ludwig 96, 173, 174, 196
Woody, Melvyn 69n4
World War I, Jonas' memories of 80
Wright, Larry 137

Zweig, Stefan 84n18

For Product Safety Concerns and Information please contact our EU representative GPSR@taylorandfrancis.com
Taylor & Francis Verlag GmbH, Kaufingerstraße 24, 80331 München, Germany

www.ingramcontent.com/pod-product-compliance
Ingram Content Group UK Ltd.
Pitfield, Milton Keynes, MK11 3LW, UK
UKHW011005180926
475701UK00004B/568
9780367600853